19th Workshop on Multiword Expressions (MWE 2023)

Dubrovnik, Croatia
6 May 2023

ISBN: 978-1-7138-7386-0

Printed from e-media with permission by:

Curran Associates, Inc.
57 Morehouse Lane
Red Hook, NY 12571

Some format issues inherent in the e-media version may also appear in this print version.

Association for Computational Linguistics
209 N. Eighth Street
Stroudsburg, Pennsylvania 18360

Phone: 1-570-476-8006
Fax: 1-570-476-0860

acl@aclweb.org

Additional copies of this publication are available from:

Curran Associates, Inc.
57 Morehouse Lane
Red Hook, NY 12571 USA
Phone: 845-758-0400
Fax: 845-758-2633
Email: curran@proceedings.com
Web: www.proceedings.com

MWE 2023

The 19th Workshop on Multiword Expressions (MWE 2023)

Proceedings of the Workshop

May 6, 2023

Introduction

The 19th Workshop on Multiword Expressions (MWE 2023), colocated with EACL 2023 in Dubrovnik, Croatia, will take place as a hybrid event (on-site and virtual) on May 6, 2023. MWE 2023 is organized and sponsored by the Special Interest Group on the Lexicon (SIGLEX) of the Association for Computational Linguistics (ACL).

Multiword expressions (MWEs) present an interesting research area due to the lexical, syntactic, semantic, pragmatic, and/or statistical idiosyncrasies they exhibit. Given their irregular nature, they pose complex problems in linguistic modeling (e.g. annotation), NLP tasks (e.g. parsing), and end-user applications (e.g. natural language understanding and MT). For the past two decades, modeling and processing MWEs for NLP has been the topic of the MWE workshop. Impressive progress has been made in the field, but our understanding of MWEs still requires much research considering their need and usefulness in NLP applications. This is also relevant to domain-specific NLP pipelines that need to tackle terminologies that often manifest as MWEs. For the 19th edition of the workshop, we identified the following topics on which contributions were particularly encouraged:

- MWE processing and identification in specialized languages and domains: Multiword terminology extraction from domain-specific corpora is of particular importance to various applications, such as MT, or for the identification and monitoring of neologisms and technical jargon. We expect approaches that deal with the processing of MWEs as well as the processing of terminology in specialized domains can benefit from each other.

- MWE processing to enhance end-user applications: MWEs have gained particular attention in end-user applications, including MT, simplification, language learning and assessment, social media mining, and abusive language detection. We believe that it is crucial to extend and deepen these first attempts to integrate and evaluate MWE technology in these and further end-user applications.

- MWE identification and interpretation in pre-trained language models: Most current MWE processing is limited to their identification and detection using pre-trained language models, but we still lack understanding about how MWEs are represented and dealt with therein, how to better model the compositionality of MWEs from semantics. Now that NLP has shifted towards end-to-end neural models like BERT, capable of solving complex tasks with little or no intermediary linguistic symbols, questions arise about the extent to which MWEs should be implicitly or explicitly modeled.

- MWE processing in low-resource languages: The PARSEME shared tasks, among others, have fostered significant progress in MWE identification, providing datasets that include low-resource languages, evaluation measures, and tools that now allow fully integrating MWE identification into end-user applications. A few efforts have recently explored methods for the automatic interpretation of MWEs, and their processing in low-resource languages. Resource creation and sharing should be pursued in parallel with the development of methods able to capitalize on small datasets.

Pursuing the tradition of MWE Section of SIGLEX to foster future synergies with other communities to address scientific challenges in the creation of resources, models and applications to deal with MWEs, and in accordance with one of our special topics in MWE 2023 on specialized languages and domains, we are organizing a special track on "MWEs in Clinical NLP" as part of the MWE 2023 Workshop, collaborating with the Clinical NLP Workshop (colocated with ACL 2023).

We received 21 submissions of original research papers (10 long and 11 short) and selected 14 of them (7 long and 7 short), with an overall acceptance rate of 66.67% for the archival submissions. 9 of the accepted papers will be presented orally and 5 will be presented as posters. Two of the 14 accepted papers will be presented in the Special Track on MWEs in Clinical NLP. In addition to the archival submissions, we also invited and accepted two non-archival submissions (published at other venues) for presentation (1 oral and 1 poster). The papers range from focus on (i) tasks such as identification or detection of MWEs, detection of idiomaticity, probing for idiomaticity, or measuring idiomaticity in the clinical domain, processing and comprehension of MWEs (experiments to measure human and computational processing), or comprehension of verbal MWEs; (ii) their evaluation through a survey of papers, e.g., on MWE identification focusing on their experimental designs; (iii) annotation or corpus development efforts, for example, annotations for lexical bundles used as discourse connectives, release of an annotated multilingual corpus of verbal MWEs and related recent developments of technical infrastructure for various languages, automatic generation of difficulty-graded vocabulary lists with MWEs graded based on their semantic compositionally, automated generation of pronunciation information for multiword terms in Wiktionary; (iv) methods to evaluate corpora, e.g., evaluating MWE lexicon formalisms based on observational adequacy; or (v) their applications, for example, studying effects of identifying MWEs on topic modeling, or development of a tool to enable complex queries over instances of verbal MWEs. The papers cover a large number of languages and a number of domains demonstrating the pervasiveness of MWEs and usefulness of research and synergistic efforts involving this area.

In addition to the oral and poster presentations of the accepted papers, the workshop features two keynote talks and a panel discussion with distinguished guests from the MWEs community and the Clinical NLP community. In the main session, Dr. Leo Wanner (ICREA and University Pompeu Fabra) will deliver a keynote talk titled 'Lexical collocations: Explored a lot, still a lot more to explore'. In the special track on MWEs in Clinical NLP, Dr. Asma Ben Abacha (Microsoft) and Dr. Goran Nenadic (University of Manchester) will deliver a keynote talk titled 'MWEs in ClinicalNLP and Healthcare Text Analytics'.

We are grateful to the keynote speakers and panelists for agreeing to share their experiences and insights, the members of the Program Committee for their thorough and timely reviews to help us select an excellent technical program, and all members of the organizing committee for the fruitful collaboration. Our thanks also go to the EACL 2023 organizers for their support, to SIGLEX for their endorsement, and to the Clinical NLP workshop organizers for their efforts and interest in collaborating with MWE 2023 to create synergies between the two communities. Finally, we thank all the authors for their valuable contributions to the workshop and to all the workshop participants for their interest in the event.

Archna Bhatia, Kilian Evang, Marcos Garcia, Voula Giouli, Lifeng Han, Shiva Taslimipoor

Organizing Committee

Program Chairs

Marcos Garcia, Universidade de Santiago de Compostela, Galiza (Spain)
Voula Giouli, Institute for Language and Speech Processing, ATHENA RC, Greece
Shiva Taslimipoor, The University of Cambridge, England
Lifeng Han, The University of Manchester, United Kingdom

Coordination and communication Chair

Voula Giouli, Institute for Language and Speech Processing, ATHENA RC, Greece

Publication Chair

Archna Bhatia, Institute for Human and Machine Cognition, USA

Publicity Chair

Kilian Evang, Heinrich Heine University, Germany

Program Committee

Program Committee Members

Iñaki Alegria, University of the Basque Country
Margarita Alonso-Ramos, Universidade da Coruña
Tim Baldwin, University of Melbourne
Verginica Barbu Mititelu, Romanian Academy
Chris Biemann, Universität Hamburg
Alexandra Birch, University of Edinburgh
Francis Bond, Palacký University
Claire Bonial, U.S. Army Research Laboratory
Tiberiu Boroș, Adobe
Jill Burstein, Educational Testing Service
Miriam Butt, Universität Konstanz
Marie Candito, Université Paris Cité
Fabienne Cap, Uppsala University
Marine Carpuat, University of Maryland
Helena Caseli, Federal University of Sao Carlos
Anastasia Christofidou, Academy of Athens
Ken Church, Baidu
Simon Clematide, University of Zürich
Matthieu Constant, Université de Lorraine
Paul Cook, University of New Brunswick
Silvio Cordeiro, Bloomin
Monika Czerepowicka, University of Warmia and Mazury
Béatrice Daille, Nantes University
Myriam de Lhonneux, University of Copenhagen
Koenraad Desmedt, University of Bergen
Mona Diab, George Washington University
Gaël Dias, University of Caen Basse-Normandie
Rafael Ehren, Heinrich Heine University Düsseldorf
Ismail El Maarouf, Adarga Ltd
Gülşen Eryiğit, Istanbul Technical University
Meghdad Farahmand, University of Geneva
Christiane Fellbaum, Princeton University
Joaquim Ferreira da Silva, New University of Lisbon
Teresa Flera, Uni Warsaw
Karën Fort, Sorbonne Université
Aggeliki Fotopoulou, Institute for Language and Speech Processing, ATHENA RC
Daniela Gierschek, Uni Luxembourg
Stefan Th. Gries, UC Santa Barbara & JLU Giessen
Bruno Guillaume, Université de Lorraine
Dhouha Hadjmed, University of Sfax
Chikara Hashimoto, Yahoo!Japan
Christopher Hidey, Columbia University
Rebecca Hwa, University of Pittsburgh
Uxoa Iñurrieta, University of the Basque Country
Laura Kallmeyer, Heinrich Heine University Düsseldorf
Diptesh Kanojia, Surrey Institute for People-Centred AI, University of Surrey

Elma Kerz, RWTH Aachen
Ekaterina Kochmar, University of Cambridge
Dimitrios Kokkinakis, University of Gothenburg
Ioannis Korkontzelos, Edge Hill University
Iztok Kosem, Jožef Stefan Institute
Cvetana Krstev, University of Belgrade
Tita Kyriakopoulou, University Paris-Est Marne-la-Vallee
Eric Laporte, Gustave Eiffel University
Qinyuan Li, Trinity College Dublin
Timm Lichte, University of Tübingen
Irina Lobzhanidze, Ilia State University
Teresa Lynn, Mohamed bin Zayed University of Artificial Intelligence
Gunn Inger Lyse Samdal, University of Bergen
Alfredo Maldonado, Trinity College Dublin
Stella Markantonatou, Institute for Language and Speech Processing, ATHENA RC
Yuji Matsumoto, RIKEN Center for Advanced Intelligence Project
John P. McCrae, National University of Ireland, Galway
Nurit Melnik, The Open University of Israel
Laura A. Michaelis, University of Colorado Boulder
Jelena Mitrović, University of Passau
Johanna Monti, "L'Orientale" University of Naples
Preslav Nakov, Qatar Computing Research Institute, HBKU
Stella Neumann, RWTH Aachen
Sanni Nimb, Det Denske Sprog- og Litteraturselskab
Malvina Nissim, University of Groningen
Joakim Nivre, Uppsala University
Diarmuid Ó Séaghdha, University of Cambridge
Jan Odijk, University of Utrecht
Petya Osenova, Bulgarian Academy of Sciences
Yagmur Ozturk, Grenoble Alpes University
Martha Palmer, University of Colorado Boulder
Pan Pan, School of Foreign Studies, South China Normal University
Haris Papageorgiou, Institute for Language and Speech Processing
Yannick Parmentier, University of Lorraine
Carla Parra Escartín, Iconic Translation Machines
Caroline Pasquer, University of Tours
Agnieszka Patejuk, University of Oxford and Institute of Computer Science, Polish Academy of Sciences
Marie-Sophie Pausé, Independent researcher
Pavel Pecina, Charles University
Ted Pedersen, University of Minnesota
Miriam R.L. Petruck, International Computer Science Institute
Scott Piao, Lancaster University
Maciej Piasecki, Wroclaw University of Technology
Prisca Piccirilli, Uni. Stuttgart
Alain Polguère, Université de Lorraine
Vinodkumar Prabhakaran, Google
Behrang QuasemiZadeh, University of Duesseldorf
Alexandre Rademaker, IBM Research Brazil and EMAp/FGV
Carlos Ramisch, Aix Marseille University
Sonia Ramotowska, Uni Amsterdam

Livy Real, americanas s.a.
Martin Riedl, University of Hamburg
Matīss Rikters, University of Tokyo
Victoria Rosén, University of Bergen
Mike Rosner, University of Malta
Fatiha Sadat, Université du Québec à Montréal
Manfred Sailer, Goethe-Universität Frankfurt am Main
Bahar Salehi, The University of Melbourne
Magali Sanches Duran, University of São Paulo
Federico Sangati, Independent researcher
Agata Savary, Université Paris-Saclay
Nathan Schneider, Georgetown University
Sabine Schulte im Walde, University of Stuttgart
Matthew Shardlow, Manchester Metropolitan University
Vered Shwartz, Allen AI
Kiril Simov, Bulgarian Academy of Sciences
Noah Smith, University of Washington
Gyri Smørdal Losnegaard, University of Bergen
Jan Šnajder, University of Zagreb
Ranka Stanković, University of Belgrade
Ivelina Stoyanova, Bulgarian Academy of Sciences
Pavel Straňák, Charles University
Stan Szpakowicz, University of Ottawa
Harish Tayyar Madabushi, University of Bath
Carole Tiberius, Dutch Language Institute
Beata Trawinski, Leibniz Institute for the German Language
Yulia Tsvetkov, Carnegie Mellon University
Zdeňka Urešová, Charles University
Ruben Urizar, University of the Basque Country
Ashwini Vaidya, Indian Institute of Technology
Lonneke van der Plas, University of Malta
Bertram Vidgen, Alan Turing Institute
Aline Villavicencio, University of Sheffield
Veronika Vincze, Hungarian Academy of Sciences
Martin Volk, University of Zürich
Zeerak Talat, Simon Fraser University
Jakub Waszczuk, University of Duesseldorf
Eric Wehrli, University of Geneva
Marion Weller-Di Marco, Ludwig Maximilian University of Munich
Seid Muhie Yimam, Universität Hamburg

Keynote Speakers

Leo Wanner, ICREA and Universitat Pompeu Fabra
Asma Ben Abacha, Microsoft
Goran Nenadic, University of Manchester

Keynote Talk: Lexical collocations: Explored a lot, still a lot more to explore

Leo Wanner
ICREA and Universitat Pompeu Fabra
2023-05-06 –

Abstract: Lexical collocations: Explored a lot, still a lot more to explore
Lexical collocations, i.e., idiosyncratic binary lexical item combinations, have been an active research topic already for a number of years. State-of-the-art neural network models report to detect and classify specific types of lexical collocations with high accuracy, which might suggest that the problem has been solved. However, a cross-type and cross-language analysis of the results of one of these models raises several relevant research questions. In the first part of my talk, I will present our recent work on the identification and classification of lexical collocations with respect to the fine-grained taxonomy of lexical functions (LFs) in English, French, Spanish and Japanese. Drawing on the outcome of this work, I will focus, in the second part of my talk, on the comparative analysis of the "LF profiles" of English and Japanese material. In particular, I will discuss (i) how the considered LFs are distributed in the given corpora; (ii) how rich the repertoires of the LF instances are in each of them; (iii) whether the contexts of the LF instances overlap; and (iv) to what extent the "profile" of an LF correlates with the accuracy of the recognition of its instances. To conclude, I will formulate the research questions that arise from this analysis.

Bio: Dr. Leo Wanner, ICREA and Universitat Pompeu Fabra
Leo Wanner is ICREA Research Professor at the Pompeu Fabra University in Barcelona, with 230+ peer reviewed publications and 10 edited volumes. He is Associate Editor of the Computational Intelligence and Frontiers in AI, Language and Computation journals and serves as regular reviewer for a number of high-profile conferences and journals on Computational Linguistics. Throughout his career, Leo worked on a number of topics in the field, including natural language generation and summarization, concept extraction, conversational agents, hate speech recognition, and, in particular, also lexical collocation identification and classification.

Keynote Talk: MWEs in ClinicalNLP and Healthcare Text Analytics

Asma Ben Abacha and Goran Nenadic
Microsoft and University of Manchester (respectively)
2023-05-06 –

Abstract: MWEs in ClinicalNLP and Healthcare Text Analytics
MWEs are a common phenomenon in the clinical domain: for example, diagnoses and clinical findings are often expressed using complex, compositional multi-word expressions that contain references to a disease, its anatomy, laterality, severity, temporality etc. This applies both to the 'formal' clinical language (e.g. in clinical letters, clinical terminologies) and spoken or written healthcare discussions (e.g. patient-doctor conversations, healthcare social media). Despite advances in language modelling, the extraction and disentangling of clinical MWEs are still challenging tasks. In this talk, we will first look at the structure of multi-word disease descriptions in clinical letters, and discuss the challenges in mapping such free-text mentions to standard clinical vocabularies. We will then discuss how MWE extraction could be evaluated using various automatic evaluation metrics. We will compare several evaluation methods and metrics, and explore the correlation between automatic metrics and manual judgments, in particular in the context of the summarization of doctor-patient conversations and generation of clinical notes.

Bio: Dr. Asma Ben Abacha (Microsoft) and Dr. Goran Nenadic (University of Manchester)
Asma Abacha is a Senior Scientist at Microsoft, with over 80 peer reviewed publications. Her research interests include Natural Language Processing, Machine Learning, Artificial Intelligence and their applications in medicine and healthcare.
Goran Nenadic is a Professor in the Department of Computer Science at University of Manchester and a Turing Fellow at the Alan Turing Institute, with more than 250 peer reviewed publications. His research interests include Natural Language Processing, text mining, and health informatics.

Table of Contents

Program

Saturday, May 6, 2023

08:30 - 09:00 *Registration*

09:00 - 09:10 *Opening*

09:10 - 10:30 *Oral long paper presentations*

Are Frequent Phrases Directly Retrieved like Idioms? An Investigation with Self-Paced Reading and Language Models
Giulia Rambelli, Emmanuele Chersoni, Marco S. G. Senaldi, Philippe Blache and Alessandro Lenci

A Survey of MWE Identification Experiments: The Devil is in the Details
Carlos Ramisch, Abigail Walsh, Thomas Blanchard and Shiva Taslimipoor

The Better Your Syntax, the Better Your Semantics? Probing Pretrained Language Models for the English Comparative Correlative
Leonie Weissweiler, Valentin Hofmann, Abdullatif Koksal and Hinrich Schütze

Predicting Compositionality of Verbal Multiword Expressions in Persian
Mahtab Sarlak, Yalda Yarandi and Mehrnoush Shamsfard

10:30 - 11:15 *Morning coffee break*

11:15 - 12:15 *Keynote Talk, Leo Wanner: Lexical collocations: Explored a lot, still a lot more to explore*

12:15 - 12:50 *Oral paper presentations*

Romanian Multiword Expression Detection Using Multilingual Adversarial Training and Lateral Inhibition
Andrei Avram, Verginica Barbu Mititelu and Dumitru-Clementin Cercel

PARSEME corpus release 1.3
Agata Savary, Cherifa Ben Khelil, Carlos Ramisch, Voula Giouli, Verginica Barbu Mititelu, Najet Hadj Mohamed, Cvetana Krstev, Chaya Liebeskind, Hongzhi Xu, Sara Stymne, Tunga Güngör, Thomas Pickard, Bruno Guillaume, Eduard Bejček, Archna Bhatia, Marie Candito, Polona Gantar, Uxoa Iñurrieta, Albert Gatt, Jolanta Kovalevskaite, Timm Lichte, Nikola Ljubešić, Johanna Monti, Carla Parra Escartín, Mehrnoush Shamsfard, Ivelina Stoyanova, Veronika Vincze and Abigail Walsh

12:50 - 14:15 *Lunch Break*

Saturday, May 6, 2023 (continued)

14:15 - 14:45 *Keynote Talk, Asma Abacha and Goran Nenadic: MWEs in ClinicalNLP and Healthcare Text Analytics*

14:45 - 15:15 *Oral short paper presentations*

Detecting Idiomatic Multiword Expressions in Clinical Terminology using Definition-Based Representation Learning
François Remy, Alfiya Khabibullina and Thomas Demeester

Investigating the Effects of MWE Identification in Structural Topic Modelling
Dimitrios Kokkinakis, Ricardo Sánchez, Sebastianus Bruinsma and Mia-Marie Hammarlin

15:15 - 15:45 *Panel discussion: Multiword Expressions in Knowledge-intensive Domains: Clinical Text as a Case Study*

15:45 - 16:30 *Afternoon coffee break*

16:30 - 17:15 *Poster session*

Idioms, Probing and Dangerous Things: Towards Structural Probing for Idiomaticity in Vector Space
Filip Klubička, Vasudevan Nedumpozhimana and John Kelleher

Simple and Effective Multi-Token Completion from Masked Language Models
Oren Kalinsky, Guy Kushilevitz, Alexander Libov and Yoav Goldberg

Annotation of lexical bundles with discourse functions in a Spanish academic corpus
Eleonora Guzzi, Margarita Alonso-Ramos, Marcos Garcia and Marcos García Salido

Enriching Multiword Terms in Wiktionary with Pronunciation Information
Lenka Bajcetic, Thierry Declerck and Gilles Sérasset

Automatic Generation of Vocabulary Lists with Multiword Expressions
John Lee and Adilet Uvaliyev

A MWE lexicon formalism optimised for observational adequacy
Adam Lion-Bouton, Agata Savary and Jean-Yves Antoine

Saturday, May 6, 2023 (continued)

17:15 - 17:45 *Oral short paper presentations*

Token-level Identification of Multiword Expressions using Pre-trained Multilingual Language Models
Raghuraman Swaminathan and Paul Cook

Graph-based multi-layer querying in Parseme Corpora
Bruno Guillaume

17:45 - 18:00 *Closing*

Token-level Identification of Multiword Expressions using Pre-trained Multilingual Language Models

Raghuraman Swaminathan and **Paul Cook**
Faculty of Computer Science
University of New Brunswick
{rswamina,paul.cook}@unb.ca

Abstract

In this paper, we consider novel cross-lingual settings for multiword expression (MWE) identification (Ramisch et al., 2020) and idiomaticity prediction (Tayyar Madabushi et al., 2022) in which systems are tested on languages that are unseen during training. Our findings indicate that pre-trained multilingual language models are able to learn knowledge about MWEs and idiomaticity that is not language-specific. Moreover, we find that training data from other languages can be leveraged to give improvements over monolingual models.

1 Introduction

Multiword expressions (MWEs) are combinations of lexical items that exhibit some degree of idiomaticity (Baldwin and Kim, 2010). For example, *ivory tower* exhibits semantic idiomaticity because its meaning of a place where people are isolated from real-world problems is not transparent from the literal meanings of its component words.

Multiword expressions can be ambiguous in context with similar-on-the-surface literal combinations. For example, *red flag* is ambiguous between an MWE meaning a warning sign and a literal combination. Knowledge of MWEs can enhance the performance of natural language processing systems for downstream tasks such as machine translation (Carpuat and Diab, 2010) and opinion mining (Berend, 2011). Much work has therefore focused on recognizing MWEs in context, by identifying which tokens in a text correspond to MWEs (e.g., Schneider and Smith, 2015; Gharbieh et al., 2017; Ramisch et al., 2018, 2020) and by distinguishing idiomatic and literal usages of potentially-idiomatic expressions (e.g., Fazly et al., 2009; Salton et al., 2016; Haagsma et al., 2018; Liu and Hwa, 2018; King and Cook, 2018; Kurfalı and Östling, 2020).

One interesting line of investigation in such work is the ability of models to generalize to expressions that were not observed during training. For example, this was a focus in the evaluation of Ramisch et al. (2020). Fakharian and Cook (2021) further explore the ability of language models to encode information about idiomaticity that is not specific to a particular language by considering cross-lingual idiomaticity prediction, in which the idiomaticity of expressions in a language that was not observed during training is predicted. In this paper we further consider cross-lingual idiomaticity prediction.

SemEval 2022 task 2 subtask A (Tayyar Madabushi et al., 2022) is a binary sentence-level classification task of whether a sentence containing a potentially-idiomatic expression includes an idiomatic or literal usage of that expression. In this subtask, the training data consists of English and Portuguese, while the model is evaluated on English, Portuguese, and Galician. As such, the shared task considered evaluation on Galician, which was not observed during training. In this paper, we examine cross-lingual settings further, conducting experiments which limit the training data to one of English or Portuguese, to further assess the cross-lingual capabilities of models for idiomaticity prediction.

PARSEME 1.2 is a sequence labelling task in which tokens which occur in verbal MWEs, and the corresponding categories of those MWEs (e.g., light-verb construction, verb-particle construction), are identified (Ramisch et al., 2020). This shared task considered a monolingual experimental setup for fourteen languages; separate models were trained and tested on each language. In this work, we consider two different experimental setups: a multilingual setting in which a model is trained on the concatenation of all languages, and a cross-lingual setting in which, for each language, a model is trained on training data from all other languages, and is then tested on that language that was held out during training.

For each task considered, we use models based

Proceedings of the 19th Workshop on Multiword Expressions (MWE 2023), pages 1–6

on multilingual language models (e.g., mBERT). Our findings in cross-lingual experimental setups indicate that language models are able to capture information about MWEs that is not restricted to a specific language. Moreover, we find that knowledge from other languages can be leveraged to improve over monolingual models for MWE identification and idiomaticity prediction.

2 Models

For SemEval 2022 task 2 subtask A we apply BERT (Devlin et al., 2019) models for sequence classification. In the initial shared task, a multilingual BERT (mBERT) model is used for the baseline. We consider this, and also more-powerful models, including XLM-RoBERTa (Conneau et al., 2019) and mDeBERTa (He et al., 2021).

For PARSEME 1.2, we use the MTLB-STRUCT system (Taslimipoor et al., 2020), which performed best overall in the shared task. MTLB-STRUCT simultaneously learns MWEs and dependency trees by creating a dependency tree CRF network (Rush, 2020) using the same BERT weights for both tasks.

3 Materials and methods

In this section, we describe our datasets and experimental setup (Section 3.1), implementation and parameter settings (Section 3.2), and evaluation metrics (Section 3.3).

3.1 Datasets and experimental setup

The SemEval 2022 task 2 subtask A dataset is divided into train, dev, eval, and test sets. We train models on the train set and evaluate on the test set, which was used for the final evaluation in the shared task. The dataset includes instances in three languages: English (en), Portuguese (pt) and Galician (gl). We only consider the "zero-shot" setting from the shared task in which models are evaluated on MWE types that are not seen in the training data. For this setting, the training data consists of English and Portuguese, while the test data includes these languages and also Galician. In this work, we consider further cross-lingual experiments in which a model is evaluated on expressions in a language which was not observed during training. Specifically, we explore models that are trained on one of English or Portuguese. We evaluate on the test dataset, and focus on results for languages that were not observed during training (e.g., when training on English, we focus on results for Portuguese and Galician). The train data consists of 3327 English instances and 1164 Portuguese instances. The test data consists of 916, 713, and 713 English, Portuguese and Galician instances, respectively.

For PARSEME 1.2, the shared task dataset contains sentences with token-level annotations for verbal MWEs (VMWEs) in fourteen languages. (The set of languages is shown in Table 2.) The data for each language is divided into train, dev, and test sets. The average number of sentences in the train and test sets, over all languages, is roughly $12.5k$ and $6k$, respectively. In the initial shared task, experiments were conducted in a monolingual setting, i.e., models were trained on the train set for a particular language, and then tested on the test set for that same language. In this work, we consider further multilingual and cross-lingual settings. In the first setting, referred to as "all", we train a multilingual model on the concatenation of the training data for all languages, and then test on each language. In the second setting, referred to as "heldout", for each language, a model is trained on training data from all other languages, and is then tested on that language that was held out during training.

3.2 Implementation and parameter settings

We use Huggingface (Wolf et al., 2020) implementations of mBERT, XLM-RoBERTa and mDeBERTa. Specifically, we use the bert-base-multilingual-cased, xlm-roberta-base and mdeberta-v3-base implementations. mBERT is pre-trained on the 104 languages with the largest Wikipedias. XLM-RoBERTa and mDeBERTa are pre-trained on 2.5TB of CommonCrawl data covering 100 languages. We use mBERT, XLM-RoBERTa, and mDeBERTa for the SemEval task and mBERT for the PARSEME task.

For the SemEval task, for testing, since the gold standard for the test data was not publicly available when we conducted our experiments, we uploaded our models' predictions to the competition website to obtain results over the test data.

For the MTLB-STRUCT system for the PARSEME task, we use the "multi-task" setting, where the loss of the model is back-propagated based on learning of MWE and dependency parse tags (Taslimipoor et al., 2019). For both the multilingual and cross-lingual settings (described in Section 3.1), we use the default parameter settings of MTLB-STRUCT, where the number of epochs

Model	Train	Test			
		en	pt	gl	ALL
mBERT	en	0.717	0.583	0.420	0.587
	pt	0.355	0.578	0.478	0.482
	en+pt	0.700	0.662	0.550	0.665
RoBERTa	en	0.697	0.590	0.390	0.571
	pt	0.555	0.553	0.440	0.531
	en+pt	0.706	0.668	0.526	0.651
mDeBERTa	en	0.700	0.523	0.304	0.526
	pt	0.582	0.567	0.499	0.556
	en+pt	0.720	0.644	0.495	0.635
Baseline		0.345	0.391	0.434	0.389

Table 1: Macro F1 score for each model, training and testing on the indicated language(s). Results for a most-frequent class baseline are also shown.

is 10 and the batch size is 3×10^{-5}.

3.3 Evaluation metrics

For the SemEval task, the classes are imbalanced. We follow the shared task and evaluate using macro F1 score.

For the PARSEME task, we also use the shared task evaluation metrics: global token-based F1 score, global MWE-based F1 score, and unseen MWE-based F1 score. The global token-based evaluation measures the precision and recall of the predicted VMWE boundaries. The global MWE-based evaluation measures the precision and recall of complete VMWEs, including their type (e.g., LVC, VPC). The unseen MWE-based evaluation considers only VMWEs that are not observed in the training (or development) data. Note that in the case of cross-lingual experiments in the heldout setting, in which systems are evaluated on expressions in a language that was not observed during training, all test expressions are unseen during training.

For both tasks we compare against a most-frequent class baseline. For the PARSEME task, for each language, we label each token as the most-frequent class of VMWE observed in the training data for that language. Although this most-frequent class baseline performs relatively poorly for the PARSEME task, it provides a point of comparison to determine whether cross-lingual models capture information about idiomaticity.

4 Results

Here we present results on the SemEval (Section 4.1) and then PARSEME (Section 4.2) tasks.

4.1 SemEval

Results are shown in Table 1. We focus on cross-lingual settings, i.e., when the model is tested on a different language than it is trained on.

When testing on English, and training on Portuguese, each model improves over the most-frequent class baseline, although the difference is quite small for mBERT. When testing on Portuguese, and training on English, the findings are similar in that all models again improve over the baseline. It is also interesting to note that for mBERT and RoBERTa, results for training on English and testing on Portuguese are in fact higher than for training and testing on Portuguese. This somewhat counter-intuitive finding could be due to the larger number of training instances for English compared to Portuguese (Section 3.1). When testing on Galician, results for models trained on English do not improve over the baseline. Models trained on Portuguese perform better than those trained on English, and show small improvements over the baseline. Despite differences in training data size for English and Portuguese, models trained on Portuguese could perform better on Galician than those trained on English because Portuguese and Galician are both Romance languages. Training on the concatenation of the English and Portuguese training data gives the best results on Galician, and improves over the results for models trained on only Portuguese for mBERT and RoBERTa. This finding suggests that models for predicting idiomaticity can be improved with additional training data from other languages.

Overall, these findings indicate that the models are able to learn information about idiomaticity that is not language-specific. These findings are in line with those of Fakharian and Cook (2021).

4.2 PARSEME

Results on the PARSEME task are shown in Table 2. The monolingual approach ("Mono" in Table 2) is our reproduction of the MTLB-STRUCT system on the shared task. In this setting, a monolingual model is trained and tested on each language. In the "all" setting, a model is trained on the concatenation of the training data for all languages. For "heldout", for a given target language, a model is trained on all other languages, and then evaluated on the target language, which was held out during training. When calculating the unseen MWE-based F1 score ("Unseen" in Table 2), for each setting,

Language	Setting	MWE	Token	Unseen
DE	Mono	0.699	0.734	0.398
	All	0.729	0.738	0.434
	Heldout	0.269	0.423	0.207
EL	Mono	0.732	0.776	0.420
	All	0.743	0.776	0.423
	Heldout	0.407	0.415	0.147
EU	Mono	0.804	0.832	0.346
	All	0.815	0.839	0.380
	Heldout	0.194	0.258	0.112
FR	Mono	0.802	0.830	0.431
	All	0.797	0.825	0.437
	Heldout	0.501	0.560	0.196
GA	Mono	0.311	0.465	0.210
	All	0.422	0.483	0.301
	Heldout	0.111	0.133	0.069
HE	Mono	0.482	0.527	0.215
	All	0.491	0.536	0.219
	Heldout	0.141	0.146	0.064
HI	Mono	0.729	0.785	0.504
	All	0.759	0.796	0.549
	Heldout	0.376	0.452	0.278
IT	Mono	0.632	0.673	0.227
	All	0.618	0.656	0.200
	Heldout	0.376	0.437	0.160
PL	Mono	0.815	0.826	0.400
	All	0.808	0.815	0.380
	Heldout	0.361	0.382	0.144
PT	Mono	0.736	0.758	0.358
	All	0.807	0.821	0.397
	Heldout	0.486	0.500	0.183
RO	Mono	0.903	0.908	0.299
	All	0.898	0.900	0.275
	Heldout	0.481	0.502	0.092
SV	Mono	0.721	0.731	0.425
	All	0.769	0.751	0.467
	Heldout	0.303	0.413	0.215
TR	Mono	0.701	0.716	0.430
	All	0.708	0.718	0.457
	Heldout	0.394	0.416	0.189
ZH	Mono	0.696	0.725	0.605
	All	0.705	0.732	0.618
	Heldout	0.121	0.188	0.148
Average	Mono	0.699	0.738	0.380
	All	0.722	0.746	0.400
	Heldout	0.331	0.381	0.169
	Baseline	0.002	0.067	0.001

Table 2: MWE-based, token-based, and unseen F1 score for the monolingual (mono), "all", and "heldout", experimental settings, for each language.

we report results over the instances that are unseen based on the monolingual training and development data. This enables comparisons between settings for this evaluation metric. However, in the heldout setting, all test instances are in fact unseen during training.

For each of the three evaluation metrics, we see that the average F1 score for the all setting is higher than that for the monolingual setting. This indicates that information from other languages can be leveraged to give improvements over a monolingual approach. This is inline with the findings on the SemEval task from Section 4.1. We also see that, for all languages, and all evaluation metrics, the F1 score for the heldout setting is less than that for the monolingual setting. This is perhaps unsurprising; a model that has access to language-specific training data is able to outperform one that does not. However, the results in the heldout setting are higher than the baseline on average (Table 2) and for each language (results not shown). This indicates that models are able to learn information about MWEs that is not language specific. This is again inline with the findings on the SemEval task from Section 4.1 and the findings of Fakharian and Cook (2021).

Category	Mono	All	Heldout
IAV	0.4929	0.5408	0.0000
IRV	0.6945	0.7188	0.3135
LS.ICV	0.0000	0.0000	0.0000
LVC.cause	0.3965	0.4429	0.0994
LVC.full	0.6392	0.6661	0.3495
MVC	0.4707	0.4853	0.0000
VID	0.5147	0.5335	0.2320
VPC.full	0.5799	0.5825	0.0565
VPC.semi	0.4363	0.4712	0.0052

Table 3: Per-category MWE-based F1 score across languages which have instances of these categories.

In an effort to better understand the performance in the heldout setting and the knowledge about idiomaticity that is learned, we report results for each category of VMWE in Table 3. The best results for the heldout setting are for (full) light-verb constructions (LVC.full), inherently-reflexive verbs (IRV), and verbal idioms (VID). Although not all languages have instances of all of these categories, they are by far the most frequent categories of VMWEs in the PARSEME 1.2 data (Ramisch et al., 2020), which could be why the model performs relatively well on these categories in the heldout setting.

5 Conclusions

In this paper, we considered new cross-lingual settings for the SemEval 2022 task 2 subtask A and PARSEME 1.2 shared tasks, in which models are evaluated on languages that are not seen during training. Our findings indicate that language models are able to learn information about MWEs and idiomaticity that is not language-specific. Our findings further show that additional training data from other languages can be leveraged to give improvements over monolingual models for identifying MWEs and predicting idiomaticity.

In future work, we intend to further explore the influence of language families and categories of multiword expressions on the ability of idiomaticity prediction and MWE identification models to generalize to unseen languages. We further plan to explore the ability of these models to generalize to languages that were unseen during language model pre-training (Muller et al., 2021).

Acknowledgements

This work is financially supported by the Natural Sciences and Engineering Research Council of Canada and the University of New Brunswick.

References

Timothy Baldwin and Su Nam Kim. 2010. Multiword expressions. In Nitin Indurkhya and Fred J. Damerau, editors, *Handbook of Natural Language Processing*, 2nd edition. CRC Press, Boca Raton, USA.

Gábor Berend. 2011. Opinion expression mining by exploiting keyphrase extraction. In *Proceedings of 5th International Joint Conference on Natural Language Processing*, pages 1162–1170, Chiang Mai, Thailand. Asian Federation of Natural Language Processing.

Marine Carpuat and Mona Diab. 2010. Task-based evaluation of multiword expressions: a pilot study in statistical machine translation. In *Human Language Technologies: The 2010 Annual Conference of the North American Chapter of the Association for Computational Linguistics*, pages 242–245, Los Angeles, California. Association for Computational Linguistics.

Alexis Conneau, Kartikay Khandelwal, Naman Goyal, Vishrav Chaudhary, Guillaume Wenzek, Francisco Guzmán, Edouard Grave, Myle Ott, Luke Zettlemoyer, and Veselin Stoyanov. 2019. Unsupervised cross-lingual representation learning at scale. *arXiv preprint arXiv:1911.02116*.

Jacob Devlin, Ming-Wei Chang, Kenton Lee, and Kristina Toutanova. 2019. BERT: Pre-training of deep bidirectional transformers for language understanding. In *Proceedings of the 2019 Conference of the North American Chapter of the Association for Computational Linguistics: Human Language Technologies, Volume 1 (Long and Short Papers)*, pages 4171–4186, Minneapolis, Minnesota. Association for Computational Linguistics.

Samin Fakharian and Paul Cook. 2021. Contextualized embeddings encode monolingual and cross-lingual knowledge of idiomaticity. In *Proceedings of the 17th Workshop on Multiword Expressions (MWE 2021)*, pages 23–32, Online. Association for Computational Linguistics.

Afsaneh Fazly, Paul Cook, and Suzanne Stevenson. 2009. Unsupervised type and token identification of idiomatic expressions. *Computational Linguistics*, 35(1):61–103.

Waseem Gharbieh, Virendrakumar Bhavsar, and Paul Cook. 2017. Deep learning models for multiword expression identification. In *Proceedings of the 6th Joint Conference on Lexical and Computational Semantics (*SEM 2017)*, pages 54–64, Vancouver, Canada. Association for Computational Linguistics.

Hessel Haagsma, Malvina Nissim, and Johan Bos. 2018. The other side of the coin: Unsupervised disambiguation of potentially idiomatic expressions by contrasting senses. In *Proceedings of the Joint Workshop on Linguistic Annotation, Multiword Expressions and Constructions (LAW-MWE-CxG-2018)*, pages 178–184, Santa Fe, New Mexico, USA. Association for Computational Linguistics.

Pengcheng He, Jianfeng Gao, and Weizhu Chen. 2021. Debertav3: Improving deberta using electra-style pretraining with gradient-disentangled embedding sharing. *arXiv preprint arXiv:2111.09543*.

Milton King and Paul Cook. 2018. Leveraging distributed representations and lexico-syntactic fixedness for token-level prediction of the idiomaticity of English verb-noun combinations. In *Proceedings of the 56th Annual Meeting of the Association for Computational Linguistics (Volume 2: Short Papers)*, pages 345–350, Melbourne, Australia. Association for Computational Linguistics.

Murathan Kurfalı and Robert Östling. 2020. Disambiguation of potentially idiomatic expressions with contextual embeddings. In *Proceedings of the Joint Workshop on Multiword Expressions and Electronic Lexicons*, pages 85–94, online. Association for Computational Linguistics.

Changsheng Liu and Rebecca Hwa. 2018. Heuristically informed unsupervised idiom usage recognition. In *Proceedings of the 2018 Conference on Empirical Methods in Natural Language Processing*, pages 1723–1731, Brussels, Belgium. Association for Computational Linguistics.

Benjamin Muller, Antonios Anastasopoulos, Benoît Sagot, and Djamé Seddah. 2021. When being unseen from mBERT is just the beginning: Handling new languages with multilingual language models. In *Proceedings of the 2021 Conference of the North American Chapter of the Association for Computational Linguistics: Human Language Technologies*, pages 448–462, Online. Association for Computational Linguistics.

Carlos Ramisch, Silvio Cordeiro, Agata Savary, Veronika Vincze, Verginica Barbu Mititelu, Archna Bhatia, Maja Buljan, Marie Candito, Polona Gantar, Voula Giouli, et al. 2018. Edition 1.1 of the parseme shared task on automatic identification of verbal multiword expressions. In *Proceedings of the Joint Workshop on Linguistic Annotation, Multiword Expressions and Constructions (LAW-MWE-CxG-2018)*, pages 222–240. Association for Computational Linguistics.

Carlos Ramisch, Agata Savary, Bruno Guillaume, Jakub Waszczuk, Marie Candito, Ashwini Vaidya, Verginica Barbu Mititelu, Archna Bhatia, Uxoa Iñurrieta, Voula Giouli, Tunga Güngör, Menghan Jiang, Timm Lichte, Chaya Liebeskind, Johanna Monti, Renata Ramisch, Sara Stymne, Abigail Walsh, and Hongzhi Xu. 2020. Edition 1.2 of the PARSEME shared task on semi-supervised identification of verbal multiword expressions. In *Proceedings of the Joint Workshop on Multiword Expressions and Electronic Lexicons*, pages 107–118, online. Association for Computational Linguistics.

Alexander Rush. 2020. Torch-struct: Deep structured prediction library. In *Proceedings of the 58th Annual Meeting of the Association for Computational Linguistics: System Demonstrations*, pages 335–342, Online. Association for Computational Linguistics.

Giancarlo Salton, Robert Ross, and John Kelleher. 2016. Idiom token classification using sentential distributed semantics. In *Proceedings of the 54th Annual Meeting of the Association for Computational Linguistics (Volume 1: Long Papers)*, pages 194–204, Berlin, Germany. Association for Computational Linguistics.

Nathan Schneider and Noah A. Smith. 2015. A corpus and model integrating multiword expressions and supersenses. In *Proceedings of the 2015 Conference of the North American Chapter of the Association for Computational Linguistics: Human Language Technologies*, pages 1537–1547, Denver, Colorado. Association for Computational Linguistics.

Shiva Taslimipoor, Sara Bahaadini, and Ekaterina Kochmar. 2020. MTLB-STRUCT @parseme 2020: Capturing unseen multiword expressions using multitask learning and pre-trained masked language models. In *Proceedings of the Joint Workshop on Multiword Expressions and Electronic Lexicons*, pages 142–148, online. Association for Computational Linguistics.

Shiva Taslimipoor, Omid Rohanian, and Le An Ha. 2019. Cross-lingual transfer learning and multitask learning for capturing multiword expressions. In *Proceedings of the Joint Workshop on Multiword Expressions and WordNet (MWE-WN 2019)*, pages 155–161, Florence, Italy. Association for Computational Linguistics.

Harish Tayyar Madabushi, Edward Gow-Smith, Marcos Garcia, Carolina Scarton, Marco Idiart, and Aline Villavicencio. 2022. SemEval-2022 task 2: Multilingual idiomaticity detection and sentence embedding. In *Proceedings of the 16th International Workshop on Semantic Evaluation (SemEval-2022)*, pages 107–121, Seattle, United States. Association for Computational Linguistics.

Thomas Wolf, Lysandre Debut, Victor Sanh, Julien Chaumond, Clement Delangue, Anthony Moi, Pierric Cistac, Tim Rault, Rémi Louf, Morgan Funtowicz, et al. 2020. Transformers: State-of-the-art natural language processing. In *Proceedings of the 2020 conference on empirical methods in natural language processing: system demonstrations*, pages 38–45.

Romanian Multiword Expression Detection Using Multilingual Adversarial Training and Lateral Inhibition

Andrei-Marius Avram[1], **Verginica Barbu Mititelu**[2], **Dumitru-Clementin Cercel**[1]
[1]University Politehnica of Bucharest, Faculty of Automatic Control and Computers
[2]Romanian Academy Research Institute for Artificial Intelligence
andrei_marius.avram@stud.acs.upb.ro, vergi@racai.ro, dumitru.cercel@upb.ro

Abstract

Multiword expressions are a key ingredient for developing large-scale and linguistically sound natural language processing technology. This paper describes our improvements in automatically identifying Romanian multiword expressions on the corpus released for the PARSEME v1.2 shared task. Our approach assumes a multilingual perspective based on the recently introduced lateral inhibition layer and adversarial training to boost the performance of the employed multilingual language models. With the help of these two methods, we improve the F1-score of XLM-RoBERTa by approximately 2.7% on unseen multiword expressions, the main task of the PARSEME 1.2 edition. In addition, our results can be considered SOTA performance, as they outperform the previous results on Romanian obtained by the participants in this competition.

1 Introduction

The correct identification and handling of multiword expressions (MWEs) are important for various natural language processing (NLP) applications, such as machine translation, text classification, or information retrieval. For example, in machine translation, if an MWE is not recognized as such and is literally translated rather than as an expression, the resulting translation either is confusing or has the wrong meaning (Zaninello and Birch, 2020). In text classification, MWEs recognition can provide important information about the topic or sentiment of a text (Catone et al., 2019), while in information retrieval, MWEs can clarify the meaning of a query and improve the accuracy of search results (Englmeier and Contreras, 2021).

The PARSEME COST Action[1] organized three editions Savary et al. (2017); Ramisch et al. (2018, 2020) of a shared task that aimed at improving the identification of verbal MWEs (VMWEs) in text. This work improves the results obtained in PARSEME 1.2 (Ramisch et al., 2020) for the Romanian language. We investigate the advantages of using Romanian monolingual Transformer-based (Vaswani et al., 2017) language models together with merging all the datasets for each language presented at the competition in a single corpus and then fine-tuning several multilingual language models on it. Additionally, for the latter, we aim to enhance the overall system's performance by generating language-independent features, with the help of two techniques, namely the lateral inhibition layer (Păiș, 2022) on top of the language models and adversarial training (Lowd and Meek, 2005) between languages.

Our experiments show that by employing these two algorithms, the results of the cross-lingual robustly optimized BERT approach (XLM-RoBERTa) (Conneau et al., 2020) improve by 2.7% on unseen MWEs when trained on the combined dataset. Additionally, we report state-of-the-art (SOTA) results with the monolingual training of Romanian Bidirectional Encoder Representations from Transformer (RoBERT) (Dumitrescu et al., 2020) in comparison with the results obtained at the PARSEME 1.2 edition, achieving an F1-score of 60.46%, an improvement of over 20%.

2 Dataset

The PARSEME multilingual corpus was annotated with several types of VMWEs, to serve as training and testing material for the shared task. The quality of the manual annotation was further enhanced by a semi-automatic way of ensuring annotation consistency. For edition 1.2, the corpus contained 14 languages: Basque, Chinese, French, German, Hebrew, Hindi, Irish, Italian, Modern Greek, Polish, Portuguese, Romanian, Swedish, and Turkish.

The types of VMWEs (i.e., universal, quasi-universal, and language-specific types) annotated

[1]https://typo.uni-konstanz.de/parseme/.

Proceedings of the 19th Workshop on Multiword Expressions (MWE 2023), pages 7–13
May 6, 2023 ©2023 Association for Computational Linguistics

therein are described in the annotation guidelines[2]. The types of VMWEs annotated for Romanian are as follows: VID (verbal idiom) like "fura somnul" (eng., "steal sleep-the", "fall asleep"), LVC.full (light verb construction with a semantically bleached verb) like "da citire" (eng., "give reading", "read"), LVC.cause (light verb construction in which the verb has a causative meaning) like "da foc" (eng., "give fire", "put on fire"), and IRV (inherently reflexive verb) like "se gândi" (eng., "Refl.Cl. think", "think").

The whole corpus version 1.2 contains 5.5 million tokens with 68k VMWEs annotations, split into train, dev, and test sets, on the one hand for controlling the distribution of unseen VMWEs both in dev with respect to test and in test with respect to train+dev, and on the other hand in ensuring a sufficient number of unseen VMWEs in the test set for each language. The Romanian training corpus contains 195k tokens in which 1,218 VMWEs are annotated. The Romanian dev set contains 134,340 tokens and 818 annotated VMWEs; the Romanian test set includes 685,566 tokens and 4,135 annotated VMWEs. The frequency of occurrence of VMWEs in Romanian ranges from 8% (for LVC.full) to 22% (for LVC.cause), with an average of 12%, thus being quite redundant (Barbu Mititelu et al., 2019).

3 System Description

3.1 Monolingual Training

We experiment with four BERT-based models (first two monolingual and last two multilingual) for MWE identification using only the Romanian part of the PARSEME 1.2 corpus, namely the RoBERT, the Distilled Romanian BERT (Distil-RoBERT) (Avram et al., 2022a), the multilingual BERT (M-BERT) (Kenton and Toutanova, 2019), and the XLM-RoBERTa (Conneau et al., 2020). We follow the standard sequence tagging procedure described in the original BERT model and fine-tune the embeddings produced by the last layer for the input tokens to predict the corresponding MWE labels using a feed-forward layer.

3.2 Multilingual Training

Our second and principal line of work here combines all the training sets of the corpora. Therefore, we train the two multilingual language models on the resulting dataset and then evaluate the models on the Romanian test set of the PARSEME 1.2 shared task. In addition, we improve the performance of the system by forcing the embeddings of the respective language models to depend less on their source language and more on the semantic specificities of an MWE using a lateral inhibition layer and adversarial training.

The general architecture of our multilingual training methodology is depicted in Figure 1. It is divided into three major components: a multilingual BERT model that acts as a feature extractor F and produces the embeddings of the tokens, a classifier C whose role is to identify the MWEs in the given texts, and a language discriminator LG whose role is to recognize the language of the input. We employ the lateral inhibition layer before feeding the embeddings to C and adversarially train LG by reversing its gradient before backpropagating through F. Further details on these two methods are given below.

3.3 Lateral Inhibition

The neural inhibitory layer, modelled after the biological process of lateral inhibition in the brain, has been successfully used for the named entity recognition (NER) task in the past (Păiș, 2022; Avram et al., 2022b; Mitrofan and Păiș, 2022). We envisage that since the terms recognised by NER are just a subset of the MWEs identification, both being grounded in sequence tagging, introducing this layer into our model would also bring improvements in the final performance of our system. However, in the previous work, the neural inhibitory layer was mainly used to enhance the quality of the extracted named entities. In contrast, in this work, we employ it to achieve language-independent embeddings out of the multilingual transformer models.

The main idea behind the lateral inhibitory layer is quite simple. Given the embeddings X produced by a language model and a weight matrix W with a bias b, the output Y of this layer is described in the following formula:

$$Y = X * Diag(H(X * ZeroDiag(W) + b)) \quad (1)$$

where $Diag$ is a function that creates a matrix whose main diagonal is the vector given as input, $ZeroDiag$ is a function that sets a given matrix with the zero value on the main diagonal, and H is the Heaviside step function.

[2] https://parsemefr.lis-lab.fr/parseme-st-guidelines/1.2/.

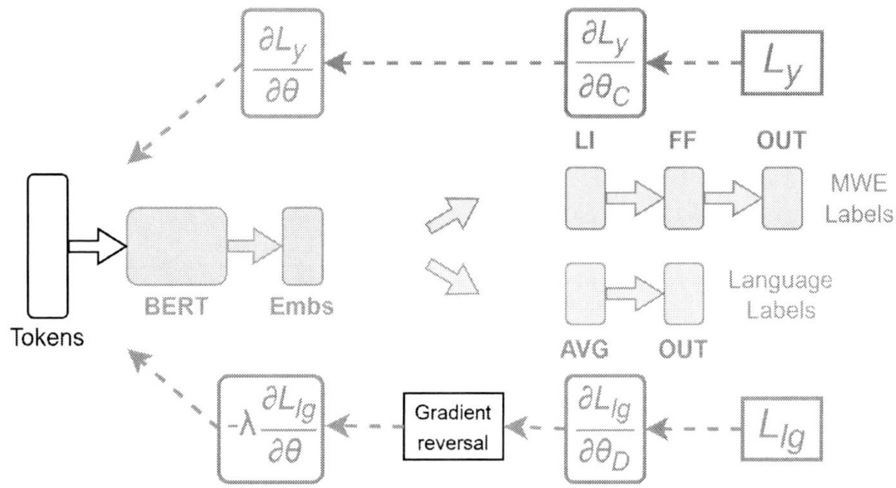

Figure 1: The multilingual training architecture. We use a multilingual BERT-based model to extract the embeddings from the input tokens (green). All these embeddings are fed into a classifier with a lateral inhibition layer to predict the MWE labels (blue) and into an adversarially trained language discriminator (orange). The block arrow depicts the forward pass, and the dotted arrow the backward pass.

Equation 1 works well for the forward pass. However, since the Heaviside step function is not differentiable, the lateral inhibition layer approximates the respective gradients with the gradients of the parameterized Sigmoid function (Wunderlich and Pehle, 2021), a technique known as surrogate gradient learning (Neftci et al., 2019).

3.4 Adversarial Training

Adversarial training of neural networks has been a highly influential area of research in recent years, particularly in fields such as computer vision with generative unsupervised models (Gui et al., 2021). Adversarial training has also been used to train predictive models (Zhao et al., 2022), and in recent research, both multilingual and cross-lingual adversarial neural networks were introduced (Hu et al., 2019; Guzman-Nateras et al., 2022). These networks are designed to learn discriminative representations that are invariant to language. In this study, we utilize the same methodology to learn task-specific representations in a multilingual setting, trying to improve the predictive capabilities of the employed multilingual transformer models.

Our methodology closely follows the domain adversarial neural network algorithm (DANN) (Ganin et al., 2016), the difference here being that instead of reversing the gradient to create domain-independent features, we reverse it to generate language-independent embeddings out of the multilingual transformer models. As is the case for our system, DANN has in its composition a feature extractor F, a label classifier C, and a domain classifier D that is replaced in our work with a language classifier LG. Thus, the gradient computation of each component can be formalized in the following equations:

$$
\begin{aligned}
\theta_C &= \theta_C - \alpha \frac{\partial L_y}{\partial \theta_C} \\
\theta_{LG} &= \theta_{LG} - \alpha \frac{\partial L_{lg}}{\partial \theta_{LG}} \\
\theta_F &= \theta_F - \alpha \left(\frac{\partial L_y}{\partial \theta_F} - \lambda \frac{\partial L_{lg}}{\partial \theta_F} \right)
\end{aligned}
\tag{2}
$$

where θ_C are the parameters of the label classifier, L_y is the loss obtained by the label classifier when predicting the class labels y, θ_{LG} are the parameters of the language classifier, L_{lg} is the loss obtained by the language classifier when predicting the language labels d, θ_F are the parameters of the feature extractor, λ is the hyperparameter used to reverse the gradients, and α is the learning rate.

4 Results

4.1 Monolingual Training

Table 1 shows the results of our monolingual training. We report both the overall scores (called global MWE) and the scores of the identified MWEs that do not appear in the training set (called unseen

Model	Global MWE			Unseen MWE		
	P	R	F1	P	R	F1
MTLB-STRUCT	89.88	91.05	90.46	28.84	41.47	34.02
TRAVIS-mono	**90.80**	91.39	91.09	33.05	51.51	40.26
RoBERT	90.73	**93.74**	**92.21**	**52.97**	**70.69**	**60.56**
Distil-RoBERT	87.56	90.40	88.96	41.06	62.77	49.65
M-BERT	90.39	90.11	90.25	46.82	51.09	48.86
XLM-RoBERTa	90.72	91.46	91.09	51.54	62.77	56.61

Table 1: The results of the models trained on the monolingual Romanian set.

Model	Global MWE			Unseen MWE		
	P	R	F1	P	R	F1
M-BERT	**91.34**	88.46	**89.88**	**49.90**	48.12	48.99
M-BERT + LI	90.78	88.85	89.81	45.06	45.15	45.10
M-BERT + Adv	89.14	**90.13**	89.63	46.27	**56.44**	**50.85**
M-BERT + LI + Adv	89.95	88.78	89.36	45.44	50.30	47.74
XLM-RoBERTa	**91.23**	92.53	**91.87**	52.92	**64.55**	58.16
XLM-RoBERTa + LI	91.12	92.02	91.02	52.11	61.19	56.28
XLM-RoBERTa + Adv	89.45	**92.87**	91.12	54.91	63.96	59.09
XLM-RoBERTa + Adv + LI	90.49	92.61	91.53	**55.01**	64.47	**59.36**

Table 2: The results of the multilingual models trained on the multilingual combined dataset and evaluated on the Romanian set. LI means lateral inhibition, and Adv means multilingual adversarial training.

MWE), as well as the results of the best overall system (MTLB-STRUCT) (Taslimipoor et al., 2020) and the results of the best system on Romanian (TRAVIS-mono) (Kurfalı, 2020). All our monolingual models outperform the MTLB-STRUCT and TRAVIS-mono systems by more than 8% on unseen MWE, with RoBERT achieving an improvement of more than 20%. We believe that this is due to the more intensive hyperparameter search that we performed and the text preprocessing which consisted of things like replacing the letters with diacritics in Romanian to the standard used in pretraining or making sure that the tokenizer produces cased subtokens[3].

Both the highest global MWE and unseen MWE performance were achieved by the monolingual RoBERT model, with F1-scores of 92.21% and 60.56%, respectively. The second highest performance was obtained by the XLM-RoBERTa model, although it is a multilingual model. Thus, XLM-RoBERTa outperformed the other monolingual model, Distil-RoBERT, by 2.1% on global MWE and 7% on unseen MWE. This phenomenon has also been noticed by Conneau et al. (2020), showing the raw power of multilingual models pretrained on a large amount of textual data.

4.2 Multilingual Training

Table 2 shows the results for the multilingual training of both M-BERT and XLM-RoBERTa. As in the monolingual training case, XLM-RoBERTa achieves better performance, coming out on top with an F1-score of 58.16% in comparison with the 48.99% F1-score obtained by M-BERT. We also notice that the simple multilingual training (i.e., without lateral inhibition and adversarial training) improves the results of the two models when trained on the monolingual Romanian set.

The adversarial training improves the performance of both M-BERT and XLM-RoBERTa in multilingual training. At the same time, the lateral inhibition layer brought improvements only to the later when it was combined with adversarial training. Thus, by merging the two methodologies, we outperform the XLM-RoBERTa's results trained

[3]These text preprocessing techniques are suggested at `https://github.com/dumitrescustefan/Romanian-Transformers`.

on monolingual data (i.e., around 2.7% on unseen MWEs), which was the main target of the competition, being behind RoBERT with only 1.2%.

5 Conclusions

The detection and processing of MWEs play an important role in various areas of NLP. This paper made notable improvements in unseen Romanian MWE identification by employing a lateral inhibition layer and adversarial training to multilingual large language models like XLM-RoBERTa. This way, we were able to improve the results of XLM-RoBERTa. In addition, we achieved SOTA results on this task with a simple fine-tuning of RoBERT that involved a better hyperparameter search and text preprocessing pipeline, respectively.

Future work considers an analysis of the language-independent embeddings produced in the multilingual training, together with more experiments on other languages, to validate the generalization of this approach. In addition, we intend to add these results in LiRo - the public benchmark for Romanian NLP models (Dumitrescu et al., 2021).

References

Andrei-Marius Avram, Darius Catrina, Dumitru-Clementin Cercel, Mihai Dascalu, Traian Rebedea, Vasile Pais, and Dan Tufis. 2022a. Distilling the knowledge of Romanian BERTs using multiple teachers. In *Proceedings of the Thirteenth Language Resources and Evaluation Conference*, pages 374–384, Marseille, France. European Language Resources Association.

Andrei-Marius Avram, Vasile Păiș, and Maria Mitrofan. 2022b. Racai@ smm4h'22: Tweets disease mention detection using a neural lateral inhibitory mechanism. In *Proceedings of The Seventh Workshop on Social Media Mining for Health Applications, Workshop & Shared Task*, pages 1–3.

Verginica Barbu Mititelu, Mihaela Cristescu, and Mihaela Onofrei. 2019. The Romanian corpus annotated with verbal multiword expressions. In *Proceedings of the Joint Workshop on Multiword Expressions and WordNet (MWE-WN 2019)*, pages 13–21, Florence, Italy. Association for Computational Linguistics.

Maria Carmela Catone, Mariacristina Falco, Alessandro Maisto, Serena Pelosi, and Alfonso Siano. 2019. Automatic text classification through point of cultural interest digital identifiers. In *International Conference on P2P, Parallel, Grid, Cloud and Internet Computing*, pages 211–220. Springer.

Alexis Conneau, Kartikay Khandelwal, Naman Goyal, Vishrav Chaudhary, Guillaume Wenzek, Francisco Guzmán, Édouard Grave, Myle Ott, Luke Zettlemoyer, and Veselin Stoyanov. 2020. Unsupervised cross-lingual representation learning at scale. In *Proceedings of the 58th Annual Meeting of the Association for Computational Linguistics*, pages 8440–8451.

Stefan Dumitrescu, Andrei-Marius Avram, and Sampo Pyysalo. 2020. The birth of romanian bert. In *Findings of the Association for Computational Linguistics: EMNLP 2020*, pages 4324–4328.

Stefan Daniel Dumitrescu, Petru Rebeja, Beata Lorincz, Mihaela Gaman, Andrei Avram, Mihai Ilie, Andrei Pruteanu, Adriana Stan, Lorena Rosia, Cristina Iacobescu, et al. 2021. Liro: Benchmark and leaderboard for romanian language tasks. In *Thirty-fifth Conference on Neural Information Processing Systems Datasets and Benchmarks Track (Round 1)*.

Kurt Englmeier and Pedro Contreras. 2021. Aspect fusion as design paradigm for legal information retrieval. In *International Conference on Intelligent Human Systems Integration*, pages 547–553. Springer.

Yaroslav Ganin, Evgeniya Ustinova, Hana Ajakan, Pascal Germain, Hugo Larochelle, François Laviolette, Mario Marchand, and Victor Lempitsky. 2016. Domain-adversarial training of neural networks. *The journal of machine learning research*, 17(1):2096–2030.

Jie Gui, Zhenan Sun, Yonggang Wen, Dacheng Tao, and Jieping Ye. 2021. A review on generative adversarial networks: Algorithms, theory, and applications. *IEEE Transactions on Knowledge and Data Engineering*.

Luis Guzman-Nateras, Minh Van Nguyen, and Thien Nguyen. 2022. Cross-lingual event detection via optimized adversarial training. In *Proceedings of the 2022 Conference of the North American Chapter of the Association for Computational Linguistics: Human Language Technologies*, pages 5588–5599.

Ke Hu, Hasim Sak, and Hank Liao. 2019. Adversarial training for multilingual acoustic modeling. *arXiv preprint arXiv:1906.07093*.

Jacob Devlin Ming-Wei Chang Kenton and Lee Kristina Toutanova. 2019. Bert: Pre-training of deep bidirectional transformers for language understanding. In *Proceedings of NAACL-HLT*, pages 4171–4186.

Murathan Kurfalı. 2020. Travis at parseme shared task 2020: How good is (m) bert at seeing the unseen? In *Proceedings of the Joint Workshop on Multiword Expressions and Electronic Lexicons*, pages 136–141.

Daniel Lowd and Christopher Meek. 2005. Adversarial learning. In *Proceedings of the eleventh ACM SIGKDD international conference on Knowledge discovery in data mining*, pages 641–647.

Maria Mitrofan and Vasile Păiș. 2022. Improving romanian bioner using a biologically inspired system. In *Proceedings of the 21st Workshop on Biomedical Language Processing*, pages 316–322.

Emre O Neftci, Hesham Mostafa, and Friedemann Zenke. 2019. Surrogate gradient learning in spiking neural networks: Bringing the power of gradient-based optimization to spiking neural networks. *IEEE Signal Processing Magazine*, 36(6):51–63.

Vasile Păiș. 2022. Racai at semeval-2022 task 11: Complex named entity recognition using a lateral inhibition mechanism. In *Proceedings of the 16th International Workshop on Semantic Evaluation (SemEval-2022)*, pages 1562–1569.

Carlos Ramisch, Silvio Ricardo Cordeiro, Agata Savary, Veronika Vincze, Verginica Barbu Mititelu, Archna Bhatia, Maja Buljan, Marie Candito, Polona Gantar, Voula Giouli, Tunga Güngör, Abdelati Hawwari, Uxoa Iñurrieta, Jolanta Kovalevskaitė, Simon Krek, Timm Lichte, Chaya Liebeskind, Johanna Monti, Carla Parra Escartín, Behrang QasemiZadeh, Renata Ramisch, Nathan Schneider, Ivelina Stoyanova, Ashwini Vaidya, Abigail Walsh, Cristina Aceta, Itziar Aduriz, Jean-Yves Antoine, Špela Arhar Holdt, Gözde Berk, Agnė Bielinskienė, Goranka Blagus, Loic Boizou, Claire Bonial, Valeria Caruso, Jaka Čibej, Matthieu Constant, Paul Cook, Mona Diab, Tsvetana Dimitrova, Rafael Ehren, Mohamed Elbadrashiny, Hevi Elyovich, Berna Erden, Ainara Estarrona, Aggeliki Fotopoulou, Vassiliki Foufi, Kristina Geeraert, Maarten van Gompel, Itziar Gonzalez, Antton Gurrutxaga, Yaakov Ha-Cohen Kerner, Rehab Ibrahim, Mihaela Ionescu, Kanishka Jain, Ivo-Pavao Jazbec, Teja Kavčič, Natalia Klyueva, Kristina Kocijan, Viktória Kovács, Taja Kuzman, Svetlozara Leseva, Nikola Ljubešić, Ruth Malka, Stella Markantonatou, Héctor Martínez Alonso, Ivana Matas, John McCrae, Helena de Medeiros Caseli, Mihaela Onofrei, Emilia Palka-Binkiewicz, Stella Papadelli, Yannick Parmentier, Antonio Pascucci, Caroline Pasquer, Maria Pia di Buono, Vandana Puri, Annalisa Raffone, Shraddha Ratori, Anna Riccio, Federico Sangati, Vishakha Shukla, Katalin Simkó, Jan Šnajder, Clarissa Somers, Shubham Srivastava, Valentina Stefanova, Shiva Taslimipoor, Natasa Theoxari, Maria Todorova, Ruben Urizar, Aline Villavicencio, and Leonardo Zilio. 2018. Annotated corpora and tools of the PARSEME shared task on automatic identification of verbal multiword expressions (edition 1.1). LINDAT/CLARIAH-CZ digital library at the Institute of Formal and Applied Linguistics (ÚFAL), Faculty of Mathematics and Physics, Charles University.

Carlos Ramisch, Bruno Guillaume, Agata Savary, Jakub Waszczuk, Marie Candito, Ashwini Vaidya, Verginica Barbu Mititelu, Archna Bhatia, Uxoa Iñurrieta, Voula Giouli, Tunga Güngör, Menghan Jiang, Timm Lichte, Chaya Liebeskind, Johanna Monti, Renata Ramisch, Sara Stymme, Abigail Walsh, Hongzhi Xu, Emilia Palka-Binkiewicz, Rafael Ehren, Sara Stymne, Matthieu Constant, Caroline Pasquer, Yannick Parmentier, Jean-Yves Antoine, Carola Carlino, Valeria Caruso, Maria Pia Di Buono, Antonio Pascucci, Annalisa Raffone, Anna Riccio, Federico Sangati, Giulia Speranza, Renata Ramisch, Silvio Ricardo Cordeiro, Helena de Medeiros Caseli, Isaac Miranda, Alexandre Rademaker, Oto Vale, Aline Villavicencio, Gabriela Wick Pedro, Rodrigo Wilkens, Leonardo Zilio, Monica-Mihaela Rizea, Mihaela Ionescu, Mihaela Onofrei, Jia Chen, Xiaomin Ge, Fangyuan Hu, Sha Hu, Minli Li, Siyuan Liu, Zhenzhen Qin, Ruilong Sun, Chenweng Wang, Huangyang Xiao, Peiyi Yan, Tsy Yih, Ke Yu, Songping Yu, Si Zeng, Yongchen Zhang, Yun Zhao, Vassiliki Foufi, Aggeliki Fotopoulou, Stella Markantonatou, Stella Papadelli, Sevasti Louizou, Itziar Aduriz, Ainara Estarrona, Itziar Gonzalez, Antton Gurrutxaga, Larraitz Uria, Ruben Urizar, Jennifer Foster, Teresa Lynn, Hevi Elyovitch, Yaakov Ha-Cohen Kerner, Ruth Malka, Kanishka Jain, Vandana Puri, Shraddha Ratori, Vishakha Shukla, Shubham Srivastava, Gozde Berk, Berna Erden, and Zeynep Yirmibeşoğlu. 2020. Annotated corpora and tools of the PARSEME shared task on semi-supervised identification of verbal multiword expressions (edition 1.2). LINDAT/CLARIAH-CZ digital library at the Institute of Formal and Applied Linguistics (ÚFAL), Faculty of Mathematics and Physics, Charles University.

Agata Savary, Carlos Ramisch, Silvio Ricardo Cordeiro, Federico Sangati, Veronika Vincze, Behrang QasemiZadeh, Marie Candito, Fabienne Cap, Voula Giouli, Ivelina Stoyanova, Antoine Doucet, Kübra Adalı, Verginica Barbu Mititelu, Eduard Bejček, Ismail El Maarouf, Gülşen Eryiğit, Luke Galea, Yaakov Ha-Cohen Kerner, Chaya Liebeskind, Johanna Monti, Carla Parra Escartín, Jolanta Kovalevskaitė, Simon Krek, Lonneke van der Plas, Cristina Aceta, Itziar Aduriz, Jean-Yves Antoine, Greta Attard, Kirsty Azzopardi, Loic Boizou, Janice Bonnici, Mert Boz, Ieva Bumbulienė, Jael Busuttil, Valeria Caruso, Manuela Cherchi, Matthieu Constant, Monika Czerepowicka, Anna De Santis, Tsvetana Dimitrova, Tutkum Dinç, Hevi Elyovich, Ray Fabri, Alison Farrugia, Jamie Findlay, Aggeliki Fotopoulou, Vassiliki Foufi, Sara Anne Galea, Polona Gantar, Albert Gatt, Anabelle Gatt, Carlos Herrero, Uxoa Iñurrieta, Glorianna Jagfeld, Milena Hnátková, Mihaela Ionescu, Natalia Klyueva, Svetla Koeva, Viktória Kovács, Taja Kuzman, Svetlozara Leseva, Sevi Louisou, Teresa Lynn, Ruth Malka, Héctor Martínez Alonso, John McCrae, Helena de Medeiros Caseli, Ayşenur Miral, Amanda Muscat, Joakim Nivre, Michael Oakes, Mihaela Onofrei, Yannick Parmentier, Caroline Pasquer, Maria Pia di Buono, Belem Priego Sanchez, Annalisa Raffone, Renata Ramisch, Erika Rimkutė, Monica-Mihaela Rizea, Katalin Simkó, Michael Spagnol, Valentina Stefanova, Sara Stymne, Umut Sulubacak, Nicole Tabone, Marc Tanti, Maria Todorova, Zdenka Urešová, Aline Villavicencio, and Leonardo Zilio. 2017. Annotated corpora and tools of the PARSEME shared task on automatic identification of verbal multiword expressions (edition 1.0).

LINDAT/CLARIAH-CZ digital library at the Institute of Formal and Applied Linguistics (ÚFAL), Faculty of Mathematics and Physics, Charles University.

Shiva Taslimipoor, Sara Bahaadini, and Ekaterina Kochmar. 2020. Mtlb-struct@ parseme 2020: Capturing unseen multiword expressions using multi-task learning and pre-trained masked language models. In *Proceedings of the Joint Workshop on Multiword Expressions and Electronic Lexicons*, pages 142–148.

Ashish Vaswani, Noam Shazeer, Niki Parmar, Jakob Uszkoreit, Llion Jones, Aidan N Gomez, Łukasz Kaiser, and Illia Polosukhin. 2017. Attention is all you need. *Advances in neural information processing systems*, 30.

Timo C Wunderlich and Christian Pehle. 2021. Event-based backpropagation can compute exact gradients for spiking neural networks. *Scientific Reports*, 11(1):12829.

Andrea Zaninello and Alexandra Birch. 2020. Multiword expression aware neural machine translation. In *Proceedings of the 12th Language Resources and Evaluation Conference*, pages 3816–3825.

Weimin Zhao, Sanaa Alwidian, and Qusay H Mahmoud. 2022. Adversarial training methods for deep learning: A systematic review. *Algorithms*, 15(8):283.

Predicting Compositionality of Verbal Multiword Expressions in Persian

Mahtab Sarlak* and **Yaldasadat Yarandi*** and **Mehrnoush Shamsfard**
NLP Research Laboratory, Shahid Beheshti University
{ma.sarlak, y.yarandi}@mail.sbu.ac.ir
{m-shams}@sbu.ac.ir

Abstract

The identification of Verbal Multiword Expressions (VMWEs) presents a greater challenge compared to non-verbal MWEs due to their higher surface variability. VMWEs are linguistic units that exhibit varying levels of semantic opaqueness and pose difficulties for computational models in terms of both their identification and the degree of compositionality. In this study, a new approach to predicting the compositional nature of VMWEs in Persian is presented. The method begins with an automatic identification of VMWEs in Persian sentences, which is approached as a sequence labeling problem for recognizing the components of VMWEs. The method then creates word embeddings that better capture the semantic properties of VMWEs and uses them to determine the degree of compositionality through multiple criteria. The study compares two neural architectures for identification, BiLSTM and ParsBERT, and shows that a fine-tuned BERT model surpasses the BiLSTM model in evaluation metrics with an F1 score of 89%. Next, a word2vec embedding model is trained to capture the semantics of identified VMWEs and is used to estimate their compositionality, resulting in an accuracy of 70.9% as demonstrated by experiments on a collected dataset of expert-annotated compositional and non-compositional VMWEs.

1 Introduction

In today's world, multiword expression detection and embedding are trending topics, particularly among the research conducted on natural language processing. Multiword expressions (MWEs) are word combinations that display some form of idiomaticity, in which the semantics of some of the MWEs cannot be predicted from the semantics of their component. These expressions comprised of at least two words, inclusive of a headword and syntactically related words that display some degree of lexical, morphological, syntactic, and/or semantic idiosyncrasy (Sag et al., 2002). In this paper, we focus on verbal MWE (VMWE) which is a multiword expression such that its syntactic head is a verb and its other components are directly dependent on the verb (Sag et al., 2002). Identifying a VMWE in a Persian sentence poses many challenges, like in other languages(Constant et al., 2017). One of the primary ones is the violation of the compositionality principle, leading to the inability to deduce the semantic meaning of the VMWE from the meanings of its individual components as shown in (1).

(1) دست روی دست گذاشتن
lit. put hand on hand
doing nothing

Discontiguous VMWEs pose an extra challenge, as shown in the example (2).

(2) او اقدام به خودکشی کرد
lit. he attempt to suicide did
he **attempted** suicide

In (2), identifying the compound verb "اقدام کرد" (attempt did => attempted suicide) becomes challenging through traditional approaches. Finally, the assignment of grammatical roles to certain word sequences can be entirely dependent on the sense of the words and the context in which they are used.

* These two authors contributed equally to this work

Proceedings of the 19th Workshop on Multiword Expressions (MWE 2023), pages 14–23
May 6, 2023 ©2023 Association for Computational Linguistics

(3) او دستش را بلند کرد
lit. he his hand tall did
He **raised** his hand

(4) او آثار هنری را بلند کرد
lit. He artworks tall did
He **stole** the artworks

For instance, in (3) and (4), although the sense of the word "بلند" (tall) is the same in both examples, the expressions "بلند کرد" (I did tall) have different meaning depending on the context (raised and stole, respectively). Furthermore, representing VMWEs as unified units in embeddings is challenging due to the limitation of traditional static embeddings generating one embedding per token, while VMWEs consist of multiple tokens. Alternative representation methods need exploration. Additionally, as previously mentioned, VMWEs can possess both idiomatic and literal meanings, leading to syntactic ambiguity. This creates a problem for the generation of embedding vectors that accurately capture the semantic meaning of such expressions. **Contribution:** The contributions of this paper are two-fold. First, we propose non-contextual and contextual methods to identify VMWEs. For the non-contextual strategy, we use a VMWE dataset based on Persian WordNet, while LSTM and BERT models are used as the contextual methods. Though the BERT model uses contextual embedding for each word, our LSTM model has a non-contextual embedding layer in its network. In our second contribution, we aim to measure the degree of compositionality of a VMWE by analyzing the semantic similarity between its components and the expression as a whole. To do this, we utilize two word-level and character-level embedding methods: word2vec and fasttext, which capture the semantic meaning of the VMWEs by concatenating detected VMWEs in the training corpus. We then determine the compositionality of a VMWE by using six different metrics. Finally, we have gathered a dataset that includes around 55 VMWEs, which have been tagged as either compositional or non-compositional, to evaluate the accuracy of our predictions.

In Section 2, a review of existing methods is presented. The proposed algorithm for identification and prediction of compositionality is detailed in Section 3 and 4, respectively. The effectiveness of the introduced approaches is assessed through experiments, the results of which are presented in Section 5. Finally, in Section 6, the results are discussed and concluding remarks are drawn.

2 Related Work

VMWEs identification: There are generally two types of methods to identify VMWEs in a sentence: language-dependent and language-independent methods. In terms of language-dependent methods, (Chaghari and Shamsfard, 2013) introduced an unsupervised method to identify Persian VMWEs by defining a set of linguistic rules. (Saljoughi Badlou, 2016) also introduced a language-dependent method to identify Persian MWEs by creating regular expressions by Persian linguistic rules and searching extracted MWEs from Wikipedia article titles and FarsNet (Shamsfard, 2007). Moreover, (Salehi et al., 2012) introduced a method that utilized a bilingual parallel corpus and evaluated the efficacy of seven linguistically-informed features in automatically detecting Persian LVCs with the aid of two classifiers.

In recent years, deep learning has demonstrated remarkable success in sequence tagging tasks, including MWE identification (Ramisch et al., 2018; Taslimipoor and Rohanian, 2018). RNNs and ConvNets have shown significant progress in this area. (Gharbieh et al., 2017) achieved their best results on the DiMSUM (Schneider et al., 2016) dataset using a ConvNet architecture to identify MWEs. (Taslimipoor and Rohanian, 2018) proposed a language-independent LSTM architecture to identify VMWEs, which includes both convolutional and recurrent layers, and an optional high-level CRF layer. Additionally, (Rohanian et al., 2020) focused on using MWEs to identify verbal metaphors and proposed a deep learning model based on attention-guided GCNs, which incorporate both syntactic dependencies and information about VMWEs.

Supervised techniques like deep learning require vast amounts of labeled data. The fine-tuning step of the BERT model has the capability to tackle this issue, making it a powerful tool. ParsBERT, developed by (Farahani et al., 2021), is a monolingual Persian language model based on Google's BERT architecture that utilizes the same BERT-Base settings. It was trained on over 2 million diverse documents, allowing it to perform various tasks, including sentiment analysis, text classification, and named entity recognition.

VMWEs compositionality prediction: Compositionality prediction of MWEs has garnered considerable attention in recent years. One popular method for measuring the compositionality of MWEs is through the use of word embeddings. (Salehi et al., 2015) were among the first to explore this approach by comparing the performance of two embedding models, word2vec and MSSG, in predicting the degree of compositionality of MWEs in English and German datasets. Their hypothesis was that the similarity between MWEs and their component words' embedding vectors would be indicative of the MWEs' compositionality. They then found that combining string similarity with the word embedding approach was comparable to existing state-of-the-art methods (Salehi and Cook, 2013). A study by (Nandakumar et al., 2018) provides a similar examination, using word-level, character-level, and document-level embeddings to calculate the compositionality of MWEs in English. Their results suggest that the word2vec (Mikolov et al., 2013) model, followed by fasttext (Bojanowski et al., 2017) and infersent(Conneau et al., 2017), outperformed other embedding models. (Cordeiro et al., 2019) improved that method and proposed that multi-word expressions (MWEs) should be preprocessed into a single unit prior to model training. This has a drawback that a comprehensive list of MWEs be available beforehand to accurately identify and consolidate them into a single token. Additionally, any alterations to the set of MWEs would mandate retraining of the model. Consequently, this study aims to determine the degree of compositionality of each VMWE by first identifying them and training an embedding model to capture their semantic information. The resulting embedding vectors are then utilized to predict the compositionality of each VMWE.

Despite numerous studies on predicting MWEs compositionality, much of the research has been concentrated on English and European language corpora. To the best of our knowledge, there has been no investigation on compositionality prediction of VMWEs in Persian, which is a low-resource language. Thus, in this work, we aim to address these two issues by leveraging the methods established in previous MWE studies.

3 VMWE Identification

In this section, we first present the datasets utilized in the proposed approach for VMWE identification, followed by a detailed description of the methods and models employed for this task. To detect VMWEs, a combination of a non-contextual method and two deep learning models are employed. These deep learning models treat the VMWE detection task as a sequence labelling problem, where the goal is to assign a relevant tag to each token in the sequence. To accomplish this, an IOB-like labelling format was used to tag the VMWEs in sentences, where the beginning component of the expression is tagged as 'B', its other components are tagged as 'I', and the words in the sentence that do not belong to any VMWE receive an 'O' tag. Additionally, sentences containing two VMWEs with mixed components were removed for simplicity (e.g. 5). The two deep learning models used are an LSTM-based architecture and a BERT-based model.

(5) در تمام طول زندگی اش نقش بازی کرد
lit. in all length his life role play did
He impersonated during all his life
VMWE1 : بازی کرد (play did => play)
VMWE2 : نقش بازی کرد (role play did => impersonate)

3.1 Dataset for the identification of VMWE

In terms of datasets, the Parseme Corpus (Savary et al., 2017) serves as the annotated corpus of tagged VMWEs, comprising 3226 sentences. The VMWEs in this corpus were manually annotated by a single annotator per file. Every verb-particle construction (VPC) that is fully non-compositional, where the particle modifies the meaning of the verb, is tagged, and a number bonds the components of the VMWE. Additionally, Persian Dependency Treebank (PerDT) contains 30 thousand tagged sentences (Rasooli et al., 2013). PerDT was tagged using both rule-based and manual strategies. The first strategy utilized the dependency tree to identify the components of VMWEs by extracting words with LVP[1], NVE[2], and VPRT [3] tags and their connected verbs, resulting in the detection of 32056 VMWEs in the training set of the corpus. A manual annotation of VMWEs was also performed on 1000 sentences of

[1] Light Verb Particle

[2] Non-Verbal Element

[3] Verb-Particle Construction

the corpus. Although this method resulted in fewer tagged sentences, it was more accurate and reliable compared to the previous strategy. We evaluated our non-contextual method on the Parseme Corpus and trained neural networks on both corpora.

3.2 Non-contextual method

The first strategy for identifying VMWEs

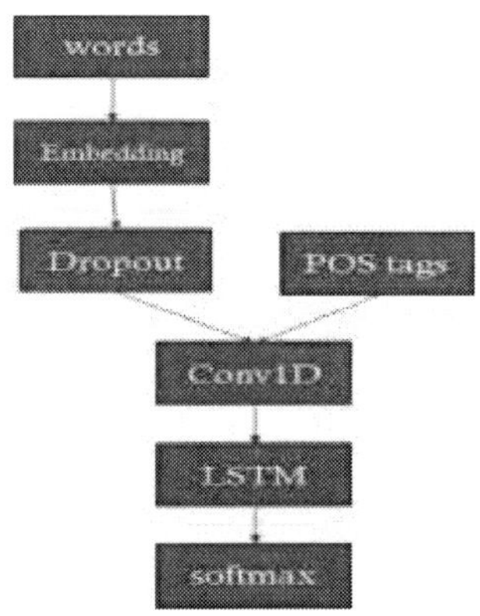

Figure 1: The architecture of ConvNet + LSTM

involves a straightforward approach that seeks to identify such expressions within a sentence. To achieve this, a dataset of VMWEs was created by collecting all compound verbs in FarsNet, which is the Persian wordnet With 100,000 words developed by the natural language processing laboratory at Shahid Beheshti University. We extracted 21462 VMWEs from FarsNet. To identify VMWEs in a sentence, the n-grams (for n=2,3,4) were extracted and searched for the presence of all components of a multi-word verb within the n-gram. Not all cases that are found are VMWEs, and not all VMWEs can be found in this way, especially if there are intermediate words. However, this approach can help identify potential VMWEs. The effectiveness of this approach will be evaluated in the evaluation section.

3.3 Long Short-Term Memory (LSTM)

A neural network architecture comprised of a convolution network and an LSTM network was utilized. The network was designed with an embedding layer as the initial component, which is demonstrated to produce better results than utilizing a standalone embedding model. To enhance the accuracy of predictions, the inputs to the network were augmented with POS tags. The architecture of the layers is illustrated in Figure 1. The first layer encompasses a combination of token vectors derived from the embedding layer, concatenated with 50-dimension features and a dropout rate of 0.2. The output of this layer and the POS tags were then concatenated as a numerical code at the end of the embedding vector of each word and then, fed into a ConvNet layer containing 200 neurons and a filter size of 1. No dropout was applied to the ConvNet layer and the activation function used was Rectified Linear Unit (ReLU). The output of the convolutional layer was then fed into a bi-directional LSTM network with 100 neurons and a recurrent dropout rate of 0.5.

3.4 BERT

BERT (Bidirectional Encoder Representations from Transformers) is a pre-trained neural model based on self-attention blocks. It has achieved state-of-the-art results on various natural language processing tasks, such as question answering (Devlin et al., 2018) and Multi-Genre Natural Language Inference (Nangia et al., 2017), due to its ability to embed each token in a sentence contextually, it can capture the meaning of each token within its context. The advantage of BERT is that it is a general architecture that can be applied to multiple problems, and its pre-training on raw, unlabeled texts minimizes the need for labeled data. Additionally, BERT has been pre-trained in 104 languages, including Persian. In this study, we utilize the ParsBERT model, pre-trained on Persian text, to identify VMWEs in Persian sentences. The ParsBERT model is fine-tuned on datasets specifically for the task of tagging tokens that are part of a VMWE.

4 Predicting the Compositionality of VMWEs

The primary objective of this paper is to predict the compositionality of VMWEs. Our assumption is that the degree of compositionality of a multiword expression can be determined by evaluating the semantic similarity between its constituent components and the expression itself. This evaluation is conducted by comparing the similarity of the embedding vectors of the corresponding word tokens. To accomplish this, we follow the studies of (Salehi et al., 2015) and (Nandakumar et al., 2018) and investigate six metrics to determine the compositionality of

VMWEs. In this section, the criteria for the task and a description of the datasets are presented.

4.1 Methodology

One of the defining challenges of VMWEs is their compositional nature, where the semantic meaning of a VMWE can be dissimilar from the meanings of its individual components. Therefore, the objective of this research is to determine the degree of compositional property by analyzing the embedding vectors of both the VMWEs and their components.

We begin with the preparation of four different corpora for training embedding models. The detected VMWEs are pre-processed by removing all spaces and semi-spaces[4], and replacing them with an underscore symbol to consider the VMWE as a single word. Two word-level and character-level embedding models, namely word2vec and fasttext, are then trained on the processed corpora.

To assess the compositionality of the VMWEs, six different criteria are leveraged to predict the compositionality of the VMWEs based on the generated VMWE-specific embedding vectors. It is assumed that the compositionality of an MWE can be captured by computing the relative similarity between the MWE's component embedding vectors and the embedding vector of the MWE. Consequently, the majority of the proposed metrics focus on calculating this similarity, followed by the determination of a threshold that indicates whether a VMWE is compositional or not based on the computed metric value. We compare the performance of different criteria in distinguishing compositional and non-compositional VMWEs. All similarity calculations between two vectors are performed using cosine similarity. Additionally, the embedding models are trained on the original corpora to obtain the embedding vectors of all VMWE components. In this study, the overall compositionality of VMWEs is computed using six metrics. In order to evaluate the used embedding vectors, we introduced a new metric called Syn_sim. This is in addition to two previously introduced metrics, Direct_pre and Direct_post, by Salehi et al. (2015) and Nandakumar et al. (2018). Furthermore, (Rossyaykin and Loukachevitch, 2019) and (Loukachevitch and Parkhomenko, 2018) proposed DFsing and DFsum, while Loukachevitch and Parkhomenko (2018) suggested DFcomp. These criteria are explained in more detail.

Syn_sim: Intuitively, we can demonstrate that an embedding effectively captures the semantic meaning of a VMWE if it's similar to the embedding vector of that VMWE's synonymous simple verb, which is extracted through Farsnet. We directly compare two different similarity metrics: (1) the similarity between the VMWE's embedding vector and that of the synonymous simple verb; and (2) the similarity between the synonymous verb and 'combined' vector, which is computing an element-wise sum over VMWE's components embedding vector. We calculate these two similarities of the embeddings of the VMWE and its synonymous simple verb using the following three formulas:

$$combined_{vector} = \sum_{i=1}^{N} w_i \quad (1)$$

$$sim\_syn\_vmwe = cos(vmwe,\ syn\_verb_1) \quad (2)$$

$$sim\_syn\_combined = \cos(combined_{vector},\ syn\_verb_1) \quad (3)$$

Where: vmwe, w_i, and syn_verb_1 are the embeddings for the VMWE, i-th components of VMWE, and synonymous simple verb, respectively. In all cases, if the sim_syn_vmwe is greater than the sim_syn_combined, it means that the constructed VMWE's vector provides a better representation than the combined vector; Thus, the use of the introduced embedding model leads to a better result as it produces better semantic-aware representation for VMWEs.

Direct_pre: Assuming that compositional VMWEs tend to have a similar context with their components, we compare the vector embedding of the VMWE with the 'combined' vector of its components by calculating the cosine similarity between them. Formally:

$$direct\_pre = cos(vmwe, combined_{vector}) \quad (4)$$

Direct_post: The similarity between the vector embedding of a VMWE and each of its components is first measured. Then the overall compositionality of the VMWE is computed by combining the similarity scores below.

$$direct_{post} = \alpha\ cos(vmwe, w1) + (1-\alpha) * \cos(vmwe, w2) \quad (5)$$

[4] In Persian typography, a semi-space is a zero-width-space character that separates two sides without leaving any space between them.

Where w1 and w2 denote the embedding for the first and second component of the VMWE, respectively. Here, we assume that the VMWE consists of two components as most of Persian VMWEs are light verb constructions (LVCs), but the formula can be easily generalized to concider more than two components.

DFsum: The similarity between the vector embedding of a VMWE and the element-wise sum of normalized vectors of its components is computed. Formally:

$$combined\_vector\_norm = \sum_{i=1}^{N} \frac{w_i}{|w_i|} \quad (6)$$

$$DFsum = cos(vmwe, combined\_vector\_norm) \quad (7)$$

DFcomp: The similarity between the VMWE's components' word vectors is computed. Formally:

$$DFcomp = cos(w_1, w_2) \quad (8)$$

DFsing: The similarity between the vector embedding of a VMWE and the vector of the most similar single word (sim_word) is calculated as below :

$$DFsing = cos(vmwe, sim\_word) \quad (9)$$

4.2 Dataset for compositionality prediction

For our experiment, we use four current Persian corpora, namely Bijankhan, HmBlogs, PARSEME, and PerDT to statistically study the occurrences of VMWES in Persian texts.

Bijankhan: The dataset of Bijankhan is a tagged corpus that is gathered from daily news and common texts (Bijankhan, 2004). This corpus contains about 2.6 million tagged words with 550 Persian part-of-speech tags.

HmBlogs: A tokenized corpus of 500 million sentences and 6.5 billion tokens is gathered by (Khansari and Shamsfard, 2021) We use the first 1 million sentences of it.

Compositional and non-compositional VMWE dataset: A self-gathered dataset of compositional and non-compositional verbs was identified by linguists, which annotated for compositionality on a binary scale. According to (Karimi, 1997) and (Sharif, 2017), 33 compositional and 22 non-compositional verbs were extracted in an infinitive form.

5 Results and Discussion

This section showcases the evaluation outcomes achieved during the testing phase for identifying VMWEs and predicting their compositionality. The evaluation was performed on the Parseme corpus test-set for all identification techniques.

5.1 VMWE Identification Evaluation

We trained our identification networks using the Parseme and PerDT corpora, identifying 2451 VMWEs and 1669 unique ones in Parseme, and using IOB format for tagging. We also tagged and used VMWEs from PerDT for the train set. Table 1 and Table 2 specify the results. The first row of Table 1 shows the results of the non-contextual

	Token_based			**VMWE_based**			**Sentence_based**
	p	r	**fl**	**p**	**r**	**fl**	**accuracy**
Non-Contextual	-	-	-	34.19%	43.71 %	38.36%	-
LSTM	61.50% 69.95% 63.39%	49.23 % 50.40 % 51.03 %	54.71 % 58.59 % 56.54 %	72.00% 85.52% 72.34%	60.07 % 63.67 % 61.07 %	65.50% 72.99% 66.23%	51.11% 58.05% 53.61%
BERT	94.04% 90.34% 94.88%	84.25 % 74.54 % 77.86 %	88.87 % 81.68 % 85.53 %	92.37% 91.43% 93.25%	85.99 % 77.90 % 79.09 %	89.07% 84.13% 85.59%	71.38% 63.88% 68.61%

Table 1: VMWE Identification Results

method on the Parseme dataset. For the other rows, the first row of each method was trained on Parseme corpus, while the other rows used both corpora to train the models. However, the second and third rows consider the rule-based and manually tagged PerDT, respectively. It is not surprising that contextual methods utilizing neural networks exhibit a substantial improvement over non-contextual methods. The LSTM model performs relatively better with a train-set size increase, achieving about 73% F1-score. The BERT model has the highest F1-score of 89.07% on the PARSEME train-set. The BERT model performs better on PARSEME due to inaccuracies in manual and rule-based tagging methods, caused by the absence of expert annotators and limited expert evaluation. Additionally, BERT's sensitivity to incorrect data is higher than the LSTM model as it is pre-trained on Persian, resulting in lower performance for the second and third rows.

	Seen proportion	**CDSV**	**CDUV**
1	33.33%	89.00%	62.56%
2	73.12%	80.42%	46.75%

Table 2: Proportion of seen VMWEs in Parseme and the percentage of correct detection of seen(CDSV) and unseen verbs(CDUV)

We also analyzed the results based on seen and unseen verbs. Table 2 shows the evaluation results of the best model (BERT fine-tuned on Parseme) on seen and unseen verbs by two approaches.

- We considered seen verbs as verbs whose exact forms (like their persons, tenses etc.) exist in the train set.
- For finding seen verbs, we turn the core (the main verb) of all verbal expressions in the test and train set to their infinitive form and then check whether the expression exists in the train set.

5.2 Compositionality Prediction of VMWEs

Criterion	**threshold**	**accuracy**
Direct pre	0.23	**0.709**
Direct post	0.27	0.655
DFcomp	0.23	0.618
DFsum	0.23	**0.709**

Table 3: Evaluation results of the criteria

The experiments began with analysing the top most similar words or expressions to some of the frequent VMWEs to find the best embedding model capable of capturing VMWE's semantics. By increasing the corpus size, we observe that the top most similar expressions of a VMWE are closer to the meaning of that VMWE. Take for example, the meaning of similar top expressions using word embedding models trained on relatively more minor corpora such as Parseme and PerDT is far different from the semantic meaning of the verb. Besides, most of the VMWEs in Persian are considered Light verb constructions (LVCs), which consist of a semantically reduced verb and a NVE. Also, a limited set of light verbs, around 20 Persian full verbs (Family, 2006), can be combined with an NVE to form a VMWE. Most of the top most similar expressions obtained using fasttext generated embedding vectors have a similar verbal

VMWE	**syn_verb**	**sim_syn_vmwe**	**sim_syn_combined**
در_نظر_گرفتند (in consider got => considered)	شمردن (considering)	0.81	0.62
خشمگین_شده (angry become => get angry)	برافروختن (getting angry)	0.88	0.63
بیان_می_کرد expression was doing => was) (expressing	فرمودن (saying)	0.83	0.50

Table 4:The degree of similarity with a synonymous simple verb

element with different NVE due to the character-level attitude of fasttext embedding models. Therefore, the semantics of the VMWE is not well-captured by fasttext. This being the case, for analyzing the compositionality of VMWE, only the word2vec model trained on Hmblog, which is the largest corpus, is considered. To assess the compositional nature of a verb in the dataset, the median value of each proposed criterion is calculated for the five most frequently occurring inflections of the verb. This median value is then used to determine the degree of compositionality of the infinitive verb, as measured by the given metric. Table 3 presents our experiment results for Direct_pre, Direct_post, DFsum, and DFcomp using the optimal threshold. The most accurate threshold was determined for each criterion within the calculated range of values. Direct_pre and DFsum achieved the highest accuracy of 70.9% among the proposed metrics, distinguishing between compositional and non-compositional verbs. A Direct_pre criterion value or DFsum above 0.23 indicates a compositional verb, while a value below indicates a non-compositional verb. Although Direct_post is also accurate, DFcomp had the lowest accuracy and did not effectively separate the two categories.

5.3 Analysis of Proposed Criteria

Further analysis Syn_sim reveals that out of 75152 non repetitive VMWE in the corpus, synonymous simple verbs for 4384 VMWE have been extracted; among them, for 3558 VMWE, the similarity of the synonymous simple verb to the VMWE is greater than the similarity of the synonymous simple verb to the combined vector (Table 4). Therefore, in 81% of VMWEs, the VMWE embedding vector constructed by the proposed method provides a better representation than the combined vector. Table 5 shows Direct_pre results for various VMWEs, where the values are highly similar to those of the DFsum metric. Non-compositional verbs in column one typically have a lower calculated criterion than compositional verbs in column five. However, some non-compositional verbs such as "چشم_زدن" (eye hitting => jinxing) have unexpectedly high calculated values due to their low occurrence frequency. This shows that higher occurrence frequency is likely to result in a more accurate calculated value, and should be taken into consideration when predicting compositionality. Moreover, DFcomp overestimates non-compositional verbs compared to compositional ones, and DFsing is unsuitable as the most similar expressions are often compound verbs.

non-compositional	Direct_pre	DFcomp	freq	compositional	DFcomp	Direct_pre	freq
چشم_زدن (eye hitting => jinxing)	**0.23**	0.22	7	نگاه_کنید (look do => look)	0.30	0.37	296
فریب_خورده (deception ate => deceived)	**0.25**	0.40	28	تغییر_کند (change do => change)	0.33	0.43	130
دوست_دارم (friend have => to like)	**0.10**	0.56	1032	خاک_کرد (soil did => buried)	0.16	0.23	3
شکست_خورده (failure ate => failed)	0.17	0.51	132	فکر_کنید (think do => think)	0.24	0.40	258
زمین_خوردن (land eating => falling down)	0.13	0.29	50	قرار_دادن (put have => putting up)	0.32	0.38	1806
چانه_زدن (chin hiting => to bargaining)	0.14	0.4	62	آمده_به_دنیا (to world came => born)	0.25	0.51	105

Table 5: Samples of Direct_pre and DFcomp results

6 Conclusion

To conclude, this paper presented an approach to predicting the compositional nature of VMWEs in Persian. The proposed method utilized automatic identification of VMWEs, followed by the creation of word embeddings that better capture the semantic properties of these expressions, and multiple criteria to determine their degree of compositionality. The study compared two neural architectures, BiLSTM and ParsBERT, and found that a fine-tuned BERT model outperformed the BiLSTM model with an F1 score of 89%. Moreover, the paper demonstrated the effectiveness of a word2vec embedding model in capturing the semantics of identified VMWEs and used criteria, resulting in an accuracy of 70.9% on a collected dataset of expert-annotated compositional and non-compositional VMWEs. These findings have important implications for further research in predicting the compositional nature of multiword expressions.

Limitations

The limitations of our approach are mainly attributed to the limited annotated dataset of compositional and non-compositional VMWEs used in our experiments, which may not be representative of the full population of VMWEs in the Persian language. Moreover, the high prevalence of VMWEs in Persian and the varying perspectives among linguists on their compositional status add to the limitations of our results. Furthermore, the reliance on word embeddings for our approach may lead to potential inaccuracies in capturing the semantic information of words, especially for Persian which is a low-resource language. The limited data available for training word embeddings may not accurately reflect the language usage, resulting in a higher risk of inaccuracies for common words in the language that may not appear frequently in the training corpus. Moreover, as a further research we should evaluate the rule-based method against neural network-based models thoroughly, which requires more expert- annotated dataset. In addition, for future research endeavors, it is imperative to conduct a comprehensive evaluation of rule-based approaches in comparison to neural network-based models. However, such an evaluation would necessitate a more substantial dataset annotated by domain experts. Given these limitations, the results should be interpreted with caution, and further research is needed to fully understand the complexities of VMWEs in the Persian language.

References

Mahmood Bijankhan. 2004. The role of the corpus in writing a grammar: An introduction to a software. *Iranian Journal of Linguistics*, 19(2):48–67.

Piotr Bojanowski, Edouard Grave, Armand Joulin, and Tomas Mikolov. 2017. Enriching word vectors with subword information. *Transactions of the association for computational linguistics*, 5:135–146.

A Chaghari and Mehrnoush Shamsfard. 2013. Identification of verbs in Persian language sentences. *Journal of Computer Science and Engineering*.

Alexis Conneau, Douwe Kiela, Holger Schwenk, Loic Barrault, and Antoine Bordes. 2017. Supervised learning of universal sentence representations from natural language inference data. *arXiv preprint arXiv:1705.02364*.

Mathieu Constant, Gülşen Eryiğit, Johanna Monti, Lonneke Van Der Plas, Carlos Ramisch, Michael Rosner, and Amalia Todirascu. 2017. Multiword expression processing: A survey. *Computational Linguistics*, 43(4):837–892.

Silvio Cordeiro, Aline Villavicencio, Marco Idiart, and Carlos Ramisch. 2019. Unsupervised compositionality prediction of nominal compounds. *Computational Linguistics*, 45(1):1–57.

Jacob Devlin, Ming-Wei Chang, Kenton Lee, and Kristina Toutanova. 2018. Bert: Pre-training of deep bidirectional transformers for language understanding. *arXiv preprint arXiv:1810.04805*.

Neiloufar Family. 2006. *Explorations of semantic space: The case of light verb constructions in Persian*. PhD Thesis, Paris, EHESS.

Mehrdad Farahani, Mohammad Gharachorloo, Marzieh Farahani, and Mohammad Manthouri. 2021. Parsbert: Transformer-based model for persian language understanding. *Neural Processing Letters*, 53:3831–3847.

Waseem Gharbieh, Virendrakumar Bhavsar, and Paul Cook. 2017. Deep learning models for multiword expression identification. In *Proceedings of the 6th Joint Conference on Lexical and Computational Semantics (* SEM 2017)*, pages 54–64.

Simin Karimi. 1997. Persian complex verbs: Idiomatic or compositional. *LEXICOLOGY-BERLIN-*, 3:273–318.

Hamzeh Motahari Khansari and Mehrnoush Shamsfard. 2021. HmBlogs: A big general Persian corpus. *arXiv preprint arXiv:2111.02362.*

Natalia Loukachevitch and Ekaterina Parkhomenko. 2018. Recognition of multiword expressions using word embeddings. In *Russian Conference on Artificial Intelligence*, pages 112–124. Springer.

Tomas Mikolov, Ilya Sutskever, Kai Chen, Greg S. Corrado, and Jeff Dean. 2013. Distributed representations of words and phrases and their compositionality. *Advances in neural information processing systems*, 26.

Navnita Nandakumar, Bahar Salehi, and Timothy Baldwin. 2018. A comparative study of embedding models in predicting the compositionality of multiword expressions. In *Proceedings of the Australasian Language Technology Association Workshop 2018*, pages 71–76.

Nikita Nangia, Adina Williams, Angeliki Lazaridou, and Samuel R. Bowman. 2017. The repeval 2017 shared task: Multi-genre natural language inference with sentence representations. *arXiv preprint arXiv:1707.08172.*

Carlos Ramisch, Silvio Cordeiro, Agata Savary, Veronika Vincze, Verginica Barbu Mititelu, Archna Bhatia, Maja Buljan, Marie Candito, Polona Gantar, and Voula Giouli. 2018. Edition 1.1 of the PARSEME shared task on automatic identification of verbal multiword expressions. In *Proceedings of the Joint Workshop on Linguistic Annotation, Multiword Expressions and Constructions (LAW-MWE-CxG-2018)*, pages 222–240. Association for Computational Linguistics.

Mohammad Sadegh Rasooli, Manouchehr Kouhestani, and Amirsaeid Moloodi. 2013. Development of a Persian syntactic dependency treebank. In *Proceedings of the 2013 Conference of the North American Chapter of the Association for Computational Linguistics: Human Language Technologies*, pages 306–314.

Omid Rohanian, Marek Rei, Shiva Taslimipoor, and Le Ha. 2020. Verbal multiword expressions for identification of metaphor. In ACL.

P. O. Rossyaykin and N. V. Loukachevitch. 2019. Measure clustering approach to MWE extraction. In *Komp'juternaja Lingvistika i Intellektual'nye Tehnologii*, pages 562–575.

Ivan A. Sag, Timothy Baldwin, Francis Bond, Ann Copestake, and Dan Flickinger. 2002. Multiword expressions: A pain in the neck for NLP. In *Computational Linguistics and Intelligent Text Processing: Third International Conference, CICLing 2002 Mexico City, Mexico, February 17–23, 2002 Proceedings 3*, pages 1–15. Springer.

Bahar Salehi, Narjes Askarian, and Afsaneh Fazly. 2012. Automatic identification of Persian light verb constructions. In *International Conference on Intelligent Text Processing and Computational Linguistics*, pages 201–210. Springer.

Bahar Salehi and Paul Cook. 2013. Predicting the compositionality of multiword expressions using translations in multiple languages. In *Second Joint Conference on Lexical and Computational Semantics (* SEM), Volume 1: Proceedings of the Main Conference and the Shared Task: Semantic Textual Similarity*, pages 266–275.

Bahar Salehi, Paul Cook, and Timothy Baldwin. 2015. A word embedding approach to predicting the compositionality of multiword expressions. In *Proceedings of the 2015 Conference of the North American Chapter of the Association for Computational Linguistics: Human Language Technologies*, pages 977–983.

Pourya Saljoughi Badlou. 2016. *Recognizing MultiWord Expressions in Persian*. Ph.D. thesis, Shahid Beheshti University.

Agata Savary, Carlos Ramisch, Silvio Ricardo Cordeiro, Federico Sangati, Veronika Vincze, Behrang Qasemi Zadeh, Marie Candito, Fabienne Cap, Voula Giouli, and Ivelina Stoyanova. 2017. The PARSEME shared task on automatic identification of verbal multiword expressions. In *The 13th Workshop on Multiword Expression at EACL*, pages 31–47.

Nathan Schneider, Dirk Hovy, Anders Johannsen, and Marine Carpuat. 2016. SemEval-2016 task 10: Detecting minimal semantic units and their meanings (DiMSUM). In *Proceedings of the 10th International Workshop on Semantic Evaluation (SemEval-2016)*, pages 546–559.

Mehrnoush Shamsfard. 2007. Developing FarsNet: A lexical ontology for Persian. *GWC 2008*:413.

Babak Sharif. 2017. Persian Compound Verb Formation from a Cognitive Grammar Viewpoint. *Language Related Research*, 8(2):149–170.

Shiva Taslimipoor and Omid Rohanian. 2018. Shoma at parseme shared task on automatic identification of vmwes: Neural multiword expression tagging with high generalisation. *arXiv preprint arXiv:1809.03056.*

PARSEME Corpus Release 1.3

Agata Savary
Paris-Saclay Univ,
CNRS, LISN, France
agata.savary@universite-paris-saclay.fr

Cherifa Ben Khelil
Univ of Tours, LIFAT, France
cherifa.bk@gmail.com

Carlos Ramisch
Aix Marseille U, CNRS,
LIS, France
carlos.ramisch@lis-lab.fr

Voula Giouli
ILSP
ATHENA Res Centre, Greece

Verginica Barbu Mititelu
RACAI
Romanian Academy

Najet Hadj Mohamed
U Tours, LIFAT, France
U Sfax, MIRACL, Tunisia

Cvetana Krstev
Univ of Belgrade, Serbia

Chaya Liebeskind
Jerusalem College of Technology
Israel

Hongzhi Xu
SISU, ICSA,
Shanghai, China

Menghan Jiang
MSU-BIT U Shenzhen China

Sara Stymne
Uppsala Univ, Sweden

Tunga Güngör
Boğaziçi Univ, Turkey

Thomas Pickard
University of Sheffield, UK

Bruno Guillaume
Univ de Lorraine, CNRS,
Inria, LORIA, France

Archna Bhatia
IHMC, USA

Alexandra Butler
Univ California, USA

Marie Candito
Univ Paris Diderot, France

Apolonija Gantar
Univ Ljubljana, Slovenia

Uxoa Iñurrieta
Univ Basque Country, Spain

Albert Gatt
Utrecht Univ, Netherlands

Jolanta Kovalevskaite
VMU, Lithuania

Simon Krek
Jožef Stefan Inst, Slovenia

Timm Lichte
Univ Tübingen, Germany

Nikola Ljubešić
Jožef Stefan Inst, Slovenia

Johanna Monti
UNIOR NLP Res Group
U Naples L'Orientale, Italy

Carla Parra Escartín
Dublin City U, Ireland

Mehrnoush Shamsfard
Shahid Beheshti Univ, Iran

Ivelina Stoyanova
IBL, BAS, Bulgaria

Veronika Vincze
ELKH-SZTE
Research Group on AI, Hungary

Abigail Walsh
ADAPT Centre, Dublin City
Univ, Ireland

Abstract

We present version 1.3 of the PARSEME multilingual corpus annotated with verbal multiword expressions. Since the previous version, new languages have joined the undertaking of creating such a resource, some of the already existing corpora have been enriched with new annotated texts, while others have been enhanced in various ways. The PARSEME multilingual corpus represents 26 languages now. All monolingual corpora therein use Universal Dependencies v.2 tagset. They are (re-)split observing the PARSEME v.1.2 standard, which puts impact on unseen VMWEs. With the current iteration, the corpus release process has been detached from shared tasks; instead, a process for continuous improvement and systematic releases has been introduced.

1 Introduction

The difficulty in automatically identifying multiword expressions (MWEs) in texts has been acknowledged for a while (Sag et al., 2002; Baldwin and Kim, 2010), and confirmed through results of experiments, many of which conducted as part of shared tasks (Schneider et al., 2016; Savary et al., 2017; Ramisch et al., 2018, 2020). MWEs, especially verbal ones (VMWEs), have been the focus of the PARSEME community since the homony-

Proceedings of the 19th Workshop on Multiword Expressions (MWE 2023), pages 24–35
May 6, 2023 ©2023 Association for Computational Linguistics

mous COST Action took place[1] and are now paid further attention, in correlation with syntactic annotation and language typology, within the UniDive COST Action[2].

Training, tuning, and testing the systems that are able to identify VMWEs in texts need corpora annotated with such expressions. Within PARSEME, guidelines for annotating VMWEs were created and then improved with feedback provided during annotation. When we compare the differences between v. 1.0 of the guidelines[3] and their v. 1.1[4], we notice that the latter came with a refined VMWEs typology and an enhanced decision tree ensuring the consistent treatment of the phenomenon in a multilingual environment.

The guidelines contain the following types[5] of VMWEs, established with respect to their pervasiveness in the languages under study.
Universal types include: (i) VID (verbal idiom) e.g. (de) ***schwarz fahren*** (lit. 'black drive') 'take a ride without a ticket', (ii) LVC (light verb construction), which has two subtypes: LVC.full, e.g. (hr, sr) ***držati govor*** (lit. 'hold a speech') 'give a talk' and LVC.cause, e.g. (ro) ***da bătăi de cap*** (lit. 'give strikes of head') 'give a hard time'.
Quasi-universal types contain: (i) IRV (inherently reflexive verbs), e.g. (pt) ***se queixar*** 'complain', (ii) VPC (verb-particle construction), with two subtypes: VPC.full, e.g. (en) ***do in*** and VPC.semi, e.g. (en) ***eat up***, (iii) MVC (multi-verb construction), e.g. (fr) ***laisser tomber*** (lit. 'let fall') 'give up'.
Language-specific types - so far, only Italian has defined such a type: ICV (inherently clitic verb): (it) ***smetterla*** (lit. 'quit it') 'knock it off'.
Experimental category – IAV (inherently adpositional verbs), e.g. (es) ***entender de*** *algo* (lit. 'understand of something') 'know about something' – is annotated optionally. Whenever language-specific characteristics demand it, the decision trees are adjusted to reflect those characteristics, as in the case of Italian or Hindi.

The initiative of collecting and annotating corpora following common guidelines was initially joined by 18 language teams. With each new edition of the corpus, some teams remained active, some others were on standby and some new teams joined. In total, until edition 1.2, corpora for 26 were created but not unified within one single edition.

With this new release (v.1.3) which is the topic of this paper, our objectives are: (i) to release all past 26 languages[6] in a unified format, i.e. morphosyntactic annotation in Universal Dependencies[7] (UD) (Nivre et al., 2020) format, (ii) to detach the corpus releases from shared tasks, and (iii) to define a process of continuous improvement and systematic releasing (following the UD model).

This describes the novelties concerning the annotated data (Sec. 2–4), their underlying morphosyntactic annotation layers (Sec. 5), and their split (Sec. 6). Then, the statistics of the resulting corpus are provided (Sec. 7). We also describe recent developments of the technical infrastructure at the service of the corpus development (Sec. 5–9). We provide results of two VMWE identifiers trained on the new release, which establishes new state of the art for many languages (Sec. 10). We finally conclude and evoke perspectives for future work (Sec. 11). The corpus is available for download at `http://hdl.handle.net/11372/LRT-5124`.

2 New languages

We have two new languages on board: Arabic and Serbian.

The previous dataset for **Arabic** was created by Hawwari in PARSEME 1.1 (Ramisch et al., 2018). However, this corpus has never been published under an open license, being restricted to the Shared Task participants. The Arabic corpus in PARSEME 1.3 is a new corpus created from scratch. More than 4,700 VMWEs have been annotated in about 7,500 sentences taken from the UD corpus Prague Arabic Dependency Treebank (PADT) (Hajic et al., 2004), containing newspaper articles. This new annotated corpus is already available in the PARSEME repository under the CC-BY v4 license.

The **Serbian** language was not represented in the previous versions of the PARSEME corpus. The

[1] `https://typo.uni-konstanz.de/parseme/`

[2] `https://unidive.lisn.upsaclay.fr/`

[3] `https://parsemefr.lis-lab.fr/parseme-st-guidelines/1.0/?page=home`

[4] `https://parsemefr.lis-lab.fr/parseme-st-guidelines/1.1/?page=home`

[5] For their definition and examples in various languages, please see the guidelines: `https://parsemefr.lis-lab.fr/parseme-st-guidelines/1.3/?page=home`

[6] The 26 languages and their corresponding language codes are: Arabic (ar), Bulgarian (bg), Czech (cs), German (de), Greek (el), English (en), Spanish (es), Basque (eu), Farsi (fa), French (fr), Irish (ga), Hebrew (he), Croatian (hr), Hungarian (hu), Hindi (hi), Italian (it), Lithuanian (lt), Maltese (mt), Polish (pl), Portuguese (pt), Romanian (ro), Slovene (sl), Swedish (sv), Serbian (sr), Turkish (tr), Chinese (zh).

[7] `universaldependencies.org`

first step in preparing the Serbian PARSEME corpus consisted of the preparation of the large set of examples required for the guidelines.[8] Through this work, it became clear that the types of VMWEs to be encoded in Serbian texts were: LVC (full and cause), VID, and IRV. The Serbian corpus in PARSEME 1.3 consists of 3,586 sentences of newspaper texts covering mostly daily politics, and a small part dealing with fashion. The morphosyntactic annotation of texts was done using UDPipe (Straka, 2018). More than 1,300 VMWEs (approx. 640 different types) were annotated in it by one annotator. For the next edition of the corpus, we will try to recruit at least one more annotator for the same text.

3 Enlarged corpora

Three of the languages already present in previous editions were further enhanced with new annotated data: Greek, Swedish, and Chinese.

In the first edition of the PARSEME corpus, the **Greek** (EL) dataset was rather small and we have been committed since to adding new data in view of ultimately providing a corpus of adequate size. The new dataset comprises newswire texts (c. 26K sentences) also from sources that are characterized as bearing an informal register, lifestyle magazines, and newspapers, in order to account for new types of VMWEs. Only a fraction of the Greek dataset bears manual annotations at the lemma, POS, and dependency levels, namely the one originating from the UD initiative; the rest was completed automatically using UDpipe. VMWEs annotation was performed by two annotators; during the annotation process, extensive discussions were aimed at manually correcting common errors and avoiding inconsistencies.

The **Swedish** data set is expanded in comparison to PARSEME release 1.2. The Swedish annotations now cover the complete UD Swedish-Talbanken treebank, increasing the total size from 4,304 to 6,026 sentences. The Swedish corpus includes the manual morphosyntactic annotations from UD, now updated from version 2.5 to version 2.11. The new annotations were done in connection to the PARSEME 1.2 annotation campaign, by two trained annotators. As an extra decision support, the annotators were given access to the report from the consistency check for Swedish PARSEME 1.2, which both annotators reported as being very useful.

In this edition, the **Chinese** data includes 9,000 newly annotated sentences from the CoNLL 2017 Shared Task (Zeman et al., 2017). The columns were updated with the new UDPipe model to make the data consistent with the standard of UD 2.11. All the sentences were double annotated and the decisions were made by a trained linguistics student for the disagreed ones.

4 Enhancements of the existing data

The **Croatian** PARSEME annotations were, long overdue, transferred to the source hr500k dataset (Ljubešić et al., 2016)[9]. Sentences in hr500k that were annotated with PARSEME annotations are those that are annotated with gold UD linguistic annotation. With the PARSEME annotation transfer into hr500k, we enabled the gold UD annotations, which are being continuously improved, to be transferred back to the Croatian PARSEME dataset. The percentage of sentences that went through some change is rather staggering: from 3828 sentences, only 374 (9.8%) stayed identical as in PARSEME version 1.1, while the remaining sentences went through some sort of improvement in the linguistic annotation, either UD error correction or UD standard enhancement.

The **Romanian** corpus contained annotation of the VID, LVC.full, LVC.cause, and IRV types of MWEs in its previous releases. The new version contains annotation of IAVs, a type that was experimental in the Shared Task 1.2. Working with this type raised a few challenges, given that the class of such verbs seems to be heterogeneous with respect to the presence of the preposition in various syntactic structures in which the verb occurs. On the other hand, the test for identifying this type has proven insufficient in the case of some verbs, which shows the need for revisiting it. Given the frequency of this type in the corpus (a third of all VMWEs in the Romanian corpus is represented by IAVs, see Table 2), we consider it important to decide upon a common way of treating it in various languages.

In some languages, manual revision of previous annotations was performed. Thus, in **English**, the 1.1 version of the corpus went through a thorough process of consistency checks (Savary et al., 2018). In **Polish**, a number of controversial or inconsistent annotations were spotted by a new team member.

[8] Andjela Antić and Isidora Jaknić, master students at the University of Belgrade, helped in this task.

[9] http://hdl.handle.net/11356/1183

Grew-Match was also used to identify potential errors. Revealed errors were manually fixed. In the **Irish** corpus, a controversial category was removed (IRV), with MWEs of this type re-categorised as IAV or VID. Morphosyntactic annotations were also updated to be consistent with UD v2.11.

The **Turkish** corpus was improved in its morphosyntactic annotations. It was manually reviewed by one annotator and the incorrect annotations from the previous release were corrected. This resulted in changes in the form, lemma, UPOS, and XPOS fields in, respectively, 15, 2480, 1250, and 1266 tokens. The number of morphological features changed in the features field is 6451.

For two languages, **Czech** and **Maltese**, PARSEME corpora were released in version 1.0 only. The 1.0-to-1.1 upgrade of the PARSEME annotation guidelines[10] involved a few major changes, including a redesigned set of VMWE categories. Thus, upgrading 1.0 corpora to version 1.1 requires some manual intervention. Further upgrades to versions 1.2 and 1.3 were minor and mostly automatically applicable. For the present release, we could achieve a partial upgrade from version 1.0 to 1.3 in Czech and Maltese. Future work includes manual annotation of the LVC.cause category, which emerged in v 1.1.

5 Compatibility with Universal Dependencies

Syntactic and semantic properties of MWEs are deeply intertwined.[11] Therefore, the PARSEME corpus has, since its beginnings, been released with annotations for both VMWEs and morphosyntax for most languages. The morphosyntactic annotations have not been produced by PARSEME annotators but rather extracted from existing treebanks or generated by parsers.

To this end, we have been increasingly relying on the UD framework (de Marneffe et al., 2021), treebank collection (Nivre et al., 2020) and UDPipe parser (Straka, 2018), as PARSEME largely shares UD's objectives and principles of universality and diversity. Since edition 1.1, the PARSEME corpus uses the `.cupt` format, which extends the UD' CoNLL-U format with a VMWE annotation layer.[12] Since edition 1.2, we have strongly advocated compatibility with UD version 2.

This objective has been finally achieved in the current 1.3 edition. In 11 languages, we have at least partly manual morphosyntactic annotations. When those stem from UD treebanks, we synchronised them with the most recent UD release (2.11 from November 2022)[13]. In 16 languages, at least part of the morphosyntactic data had been automatically generated and we updated them using the most recent UDPipe models (mostly v 2.10).[14] Whenever several models per language existed, tagging/parsing performances and the genre of the training corpus were used as choice criteria.

As a result, all 26 language corpora now use the UD-2 tagsets (most often in the 2.11 version) for POS, morphological features, and dependency relations.[15] The README files were updated with details of the above updates and a change log now documents the history of releases.

In the future, the procedure for synchronising morphosyntactic annotations with recent UD releases or updating them with UDPipe should be made fully automatic. In the long run, we plan gradual convergence with UD, so as to possibly integrate the PARSEME annotations into UD treebanks (Savary et al., 2023).

6 Corpus re-split

The PARSEME Shared Task edition 1.2 involved dividing the annotated corpora provided by the task organizers into three subsets: training, development, and test (train/dev/test). The training data is used to train the MWE identification systems, the development data is used to perform model selection and fine-tuning, and the test data is used to evaluate the performance of the final models. Since new languages were added and others updated, we decided to follow the 1.2 standard (Ramisch et al., 2020) to re-split the annotated corpus for each language participating in the 1.3 release. This splitting method is based on two key parameters: the number of unseen VMWEs in the test data compared to the combined train and dev data, and the number of unseen VMWEs in the dev data compared to the

[10] `https://parsemefr.lis-lab.fr/parseme-st-guidelines/`

[11] In particular, PARSEME approximates semantic non-compositionality of MWE by their lexical and morphosyntactic inflexibility.

[12] `.cupt` is an instantiation of the CoNLL-U Plus Format.

[13] Exceptions are: (i) Czech, English, Polish, and Basque, where tracing PARSEME sentences to UD treebanks should be simplified, (ii) Italian, where the source treebank is not part of UD and did not evolve.

[14] `https://ufal.mff.cuni.cz/udpipe/2/models`

[15] Maltese lacks annotations for morphological features.

train data. The latter ensures that the dev data is similar to the test data, thereby making it possible for systems that are tuned on the dev data to perform well on the test data. Just as in the Shared Task 1.2, we set the number of unseen VMWEs in the test to 300 and the number of unseen VMWEs in the dev to 100. This configuration has been established to ensure a balanced split that meets the input specifications while preserving the natural distribution of the data, particularly the ratio of unseen to all VMWEs. This particular attention paid to unseen VMWE is motivated by the observation from Shared Task 1.1 that the performances of the VMWE identification systems correlate weakly with the size of the training data but strongly with the proportion of unseen VMWE in the test data. The statistics for the train/dev/test splits across 26 languages can be found in Table 2.

7 Statistics of the corpus

Table 2 presents the corpus statistics, including the number of annotated VMWEs per category. In total, the corpus amounts to over 9 million tokens in over 455,000 sentences, with an average of about 20 tokens per sentence.

Over 127,000 VMWEs are annotated across all 26 languages. The most frequent categories are LVC.full, IRV and VID. The universality (understood as existence in all languages under study) is confirmed for VIDs and LVC.full. LVC.cause, deemed universal, is not annotated in Czech and Turkish. In Czech this is due to the fact that the corpus development was on standby since edition 1.0 in which the LVC.cause category was not defined (cf. Sec. 4). In Turkish we might face a language-specific understanding of the guidelines.

The (quasi-universal) IRV category is present in all Slavic and Romance languages of the collection. Among Germanic languages, IRVs are present in German and Swedish but not in English. VPC.full is a pervasive category in Hungarian and in all 3 Germanic languages. It also occurs in Arabic, Greek, Hebrew, Irish, and Italian. VPC.semi is the dominating category in Chinese and is observed in Germanic languages, Hungarian, Irish, and Italian. IAVs are present in some languages and not others – this is not due to the nature of the language but rather to the fact that this category is considered experimental and has been annotated optionally. MVCs are pervasive in Chinese and in Hindi. Their high frequency in Spanish is probably due to a language-specific understanding of the guidelines.[16] Finally, LS.ICV is an Italian-specific category and obviously occurs in this language only.

All corpora are currently being released under various flavors of the Creative Commons license. Their publication via the LINDAT/CLARIN platform is upcoming.

8 Annotation guidelines

One important aspect of the PARSEME guidelines is the database of examples in multiple languages. Currently, the guidelines feature 232 example identifiers, each covering up to 28 languages. However, not all languages have examples for all example identifiers: we have a total of 1,980 examples, whereas, in theory, we could include up to $232 \times 28 = 6,496$ examples. In edition 1.2, the guidelines contained 1,801 examples; the newly added examples concern mostly Serbian and Arabic, i.e. the languages for which new corpora have been created for this release. Figure 1 shows a histogram with the number of examples per language, ranging from 188 for Spanish to only 1 example for Turkish, Hebrew, and Lithuanian.[17]

The examples in the guidelines are complex, including their form in the original language, lexicalised components in bold, literal, and idiomatic translations, as well as explanations, comments, negative counter-examples, etc. Their addition by language experts is a time-consuming and error-prone process that required much energy. One of the latest improvements on the PARSEME guidelines is a system for online example editing. The original XML language used to edit the examples on a shared online spreadsheet was replaced by an online editing system illustrated in Figure 2. We expect that this system will allow for a much quicker and more autonomous editing of examples by language teams.

9 Versioning, documenting and querrying

In order to help the maintenance of the different corpora, a new infrastructure was set up. All existing corpora, gathered from different previous releases were put in the same GitLab group[18], with each language having its own repository. Now, all

[16]The MVC category in Spanish seems to be used to signal compositional modal verb constructions.

[17]Statistics based on a dump of the examples database on September 14, 2022.

[18]`https://gitlab.com/parseme`

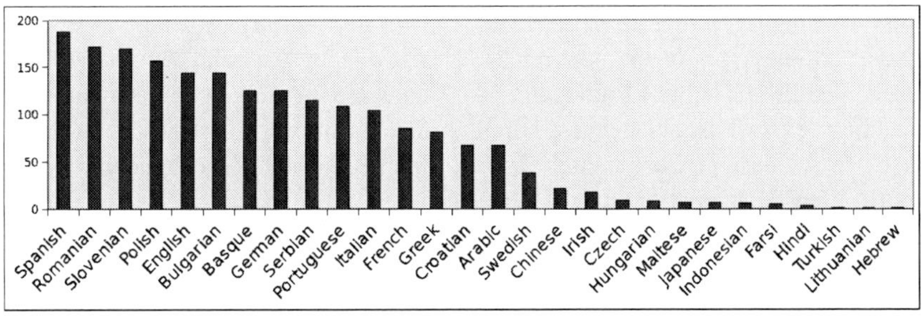

Figure 1: Number of examples per language in PARSEME 1.3 guidelines.

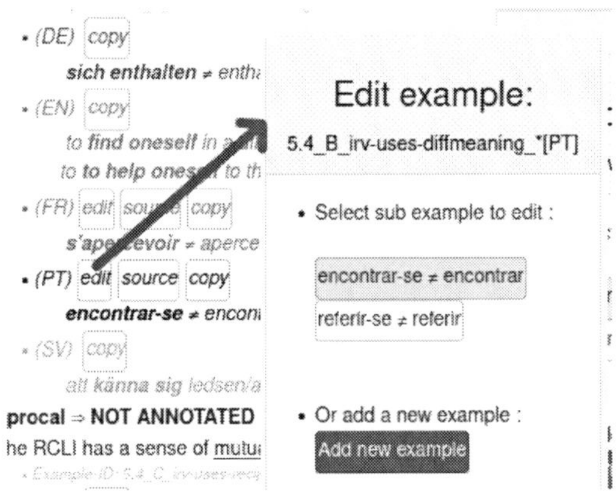

Figure 2: Screenshot of example editing GUI.

new updates on treebanks and new data are stored in this unique place. A rich collection of Wiki pages, available from the same GitLab space, gathers rich documentation of the PARSEME corpora and shared task initiatives, the corresponding tools and procedures, etc.

The Grew-match (Guillaume, 2021) tool has a new instance[19] which gives access to the PARSEME corpora. With this tool, it is possible to make graph-based queries to observe the annotated data; both PARSEME annotations and the underlying UD annotations can be used in queries. Data from each release is available. Moreover, thanks to a continuous integration system, data synchronized with the current development state of each of the 26 corpora (i.e. the data available on the `master` branch of each GitLab repository) can be accessed in Grew-match and the corresponding consistency checks web page is updated automatically when data changes[20].

As an example of Grew-match usage, a simple request[21] can be used to observe what verb lemmas are used in LVC.full annotation in a given corpus (the English one in the example).

10 System results

We began training two state-of-the-art systems, namely Seen2Seen (Pasquer et al., 2020) and MTLB-STRUCT (Taslimipoor et al., 2020), on each corpus of release 1.3. Ranked first in the PARSEME Shared Task edition 1.2 closed track (as far as the global MWE-based F-measure is concerned), Seen2Seen reads all annotated VMWEs in the train and then extracts from the test all candidate occurrences of the same multi-sets of lemmas. The system subsequently runs these candidates through a sequence of morpho-syntactic filters. In total, 8 filters are defined, and Seen2Seen chooses which filter to activate for each language during the training phase based on its performance on the dev corpus. MTLB-STRUCT is a semi-supervised system based on pre-trained BERT models that offers two learning approaches, single-task (where only VMWE annotations are used) or multi-task (where VMWE tags and dependency parse trees are learned jointly), to achieve semi-supervised training. This system has the best global MWE-based F-measure in the PARSEME Shared Task edition 1.2 open track and demonstrated the best performance for detecting unseen VMWEs. The training and evaluation process for MTLB-STRUCT has been completed only for the multi-task version of MTLB-STRUCT, and we report on this version only. The training of the single-task version is still ongoing.

Table 1 provides a comparison of the performance of Seen2Seen and of the multi-task version fo MTLB-STRUCT in identifying VMWEs, including their precision, recall, and F-measure

[19] `http://parseme.grew.fr`

[20] All the links to these services are available in the page: `https://gitlab.com/parseme/corpora/-/wikis/home`

[21] `http://parseme.grew.fr/?custom=63edd82034bea`

scores across 14 languages of the Shared Task edition 1.2 and 26 languages of the new release 1.3. For Seen2Seen, the F-score significantly increased in edition 1.3 for Basque, Hebrew, Hindi, and Swedish. In the case of Basque and Hindi, where no new VMWE annotations were added, this enhancement is certainly due to re-annotating the corpora with a recent version of UDPipe, which must have enhanced the quality of lemmas, used by Seen2Seen to extract VMWE candidates. In Swedish, the corpus size significantly grew, while in Hebrew its quality improved with consistency checks.

For MTLB-STRUCT, the evaluation of the release 1.3 models for Irish, Croatian, Hungarian and Romanian could not be performed for technical reasons. Among the other 10 languages covered both in release 1.2 and 1.3, the increase of the global F-measure is the most significant in Swedish. Also Basque, French, Portuguese and Turkish benefit from the data enhancements. For other languages, the F-measure is lower than in version 1.2, likely due to switching to the multi-task version of the model.

The primary focus of Figure 3 is to showcase how the F-score changes as the number of VMWE tokens in the training corpus varies between releases 1.2 and 1.3. By analyzing the F-scores of different languages, we can observe the effect of the number of VMWE tokens in the training corpus on the performance of the Seen2Seen and MTLB-STRUCT systems. For instance, the increase of the Swedish (SV) and Basque (EU) datasets brought about a higher F-score. Conversely, the F-score for Chinese (ZH) significantly decreased despite the increase in the number of VMWE annotations. This might be attributed to the increased number of unseen VMWEs in the larger corpus. Interestingly, the Turkish dataset decreased in edition 1.3 but the global F-score for both systems increase, which might stem from the higher quality of the 1.3 release data. For Seen2Seen, a large increase of the dataset brings a significant decrease of the F-score, which might indicate a biased nature of the 1.2 release, balanced in version 1.3.

Note that we restrict our comparison to edition 1.2. It would be less meaningful to compare the scores of editions 1.0 and 1.1 with the current version since the splitting methods used in those editions did not prioritize unseen VMWEs. But, even restricted to releases 1.2 and 1.3, the comparison may not be fully reliable, since: (i) each corpus was re-split into train, dev and test sets, i.e. the systems are not trained and evaluated with the same data partitions, (ii) only teh multi-task version of MTLB-STRUCT is examined for release 1.3.

11 Future work

This paper summarises the first release of the PARSEME corpora out of the context of a shared task. This fourth release (v.1.3) is the first one to cover the union of all the languages included in the previous three releases. Moreover, 2 new languages were included, a significant amount of additional data was added for 3 languages, and annotations for many languages were enhanced in various ways.

The future of the PARSEME corpus collection relies on the interests and availability of its volunteer contributors for each language. From the infrastructure perspective, we would like to consolidate the release methodology so that future yearly releases can smoothly integrate and make available the upgrades performed throughout the year by language teams. This includes further automation of procedures, in the spirit of CI/CD[22], including updates of the UD morpho-syntactic annotations, validating the file formats and MWE annotations, and checking the `README.md` documentation.

Another important goal of PARSEME is the extension of its guidelines to (a) non-verbal MWEs, (b) verbal MWEs not covered in the current guidelines, and (c) improved cross-lingual account of phenomena that are currently biased by the set of languages covered in the corpora.

Finally, we envisage synergies with the UD community so that the MWE layer and the morpho-syntactic annotations become gradually even more compatible. The challenges to achieving this goal include reaching compatible tokenisation decisions, unified terminology, reduction of redundancy (e.g. MWEs annotated as subrelations of syntactic dependencies), and syntactic connectiveness of annotated MWEs.

Acknowledgements

This work has been funded by the French Agence Nationale pour la Recherche, through the SELEX-INI project (ANR-21-CE23-0033-01). We thank Quentin Barrouyer and Baptiste Souche for their contribution to the editable annotation guidelines.

[22]Continuous integration and continuous deliver are concepts stemming from the domain of software engineering.

Lang	Seen2Seen						MTLB-STRUCT					
	Shared Task 1.2			*Release 1.3*			*Shared Task 1.2*			*Release 1.3*		
	P	R	F1	P	R	F1	P	R	F1	P	R	F1
AR				58.33	45.29	50.99				59.54	61.47	60.49
BG				61.69	70.4	65.76				72.53	75.31	73.89
CS				71.54	77.02	74.18				84.99	83.56	84.27
DE	86.21	57.65	69.09	82.87	62.74	71.41	77.11	75.24	76.17	72.58	73.35	72.96
EL	73.55	61.4	66.93	65.81	**66.83**	66.31	72.54	72.69	72.62	71.83	71.48	71.66
EN				78.96	48.33	59.96				66.61	64.72	65.65
ES				57	54.27	55.6				55.45	56.27	55.86
EU	83.15	71.58	76.94	**85.15**	**79.42**	**82.18**	80.72	79.36	80.03	80.49	**80.9**	**80.69**
FA				86.56	61.49	71.9				87.3	85.46	86.37
FR	84.52	73.51	78.63	84.02	**74.17**	**78.79**	80.04	78.81	79.42	**81.57**	**79.18**	**80.36**
GA	77.17	16.28	26.89	36.21	**21.11**	26.67	37.72	25	30.07	*	*	*
HE	65.84	31.81	42.9	57.43	**39.64**	**46.91**	56.2	42.35	48.3	**58.1**	37.48	45.56
HI	86.56	39.23	53.99	**89.9**	**43.58**	**58.7**	72.25	75.04	73.62	**72.51**	72.64	72.57
HR				83.27	68.87	75.39				*	*	*
HU				95.6	19.23	32.02				*	*	*
IT	67.76	62.31	64.92	**67.82**	**62.5**	**65.05**	67.68	60.27	63.76	66.63	**60.37**	63.35
LT				78.03	35.66	48.95				62.47	47.75	54.12
MT				17.92	15.36	16.54				19.29	10.61	13.69
PL	91.15	74.28	81.85	**93.16**	74.07	**82.53**	82.94	79.18	81.02	82.2	78.88	80.51
PT	75.81	69.99	72.79	**79.71**	69.16	**74.06**	73.93	72.76	73.34	73.85	**74.04**	**73.95**
RO	82.69	81.81	82.25	65.74	**86.93**	74.87	89.88	91.05	90.46	*	*	*
SL				33.87	54.73	41.84				41.29	31.66	35.84
SR				87.46	48.11	62.08				69.09	62.4	65.57
SV	86.07	59.96	70.68	**93.27**	**73.56**	**82.25**	69.59	73.68	71.58	**73.94**	**80.44**	**77.06**
TR	61.69	65.33	63.46	60.24	**70.74**	65.07	68.41	70.55	69.46	66.48	**75.54**	**70.72**
ZH	44.84	54.71	49.28	25.47	56.3	35.07	68.56	70.74	69.63	64.5	61.92	63.18

Table 1: Comparing Seen2Seen and MTLB-STRUCT performance across 14 languages (Shared Task 1.2) and 26 languages (Release 1.3): Global MWE-based Precision (P), Recall (R), and F-measure (F1).

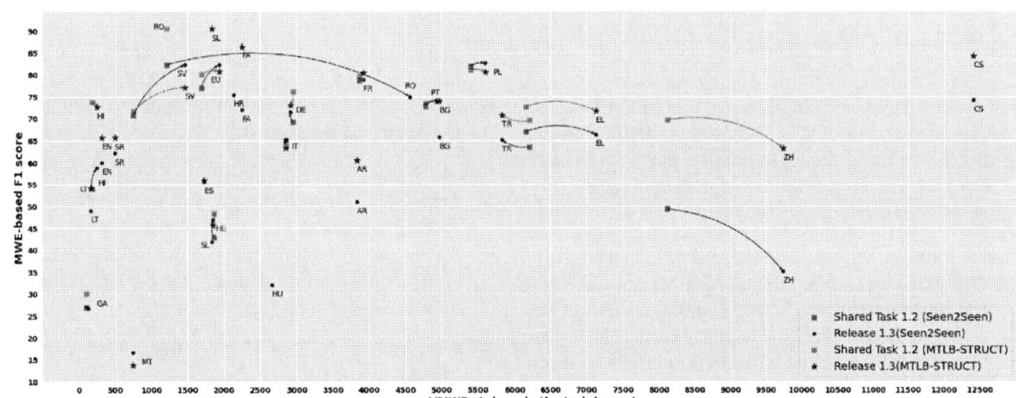

Figure 3: Seen2Seen and (multi-task) MTLB-SRUCT performance: A Comparison of MWE-based F1-Scores and VMWEs tokens in the training set between Shared Task 1.2 and release 1.3

Two other initiatives which contributed to the outcomes presented here are the CA21167 COST action UniDive (Universality, diversity and idiosyncrasy in language technology) and the Dagstuhl Seminar 21351 (Universals of Linguistic Idiosyncrasy in Multilingual Computational Linguistics).

References

Timothy Baldwin and Su Nam Kim. 2010. Multiword expressions. In Nitin Indurkhya and Fred J. Damerau, editors, *Handbook of Natural Language Processing, Second Edition*, pages 267–292. CRC Press, Taylor and Francis Group, Boca Raton, FL. ISBN 978-1420085921.

Marie-Catherine de Marneffe, Christopher D. Manning, Joakim Nivre, and Daniel Zeman. 2021. Universal Dependencies. *Computational Linguistics*, 47(2):255–308.

Bruno Guillaume. 2021. Graph matching and graph rewriting: GREW tools for corpus exploration, maintenance and conversion. In *Proceedings of the 16th Conference of the European Chapter of the Association for Computational Linguistics: System Demonstrations*, pages 168–175, Online. Association for Computational Linguistics.

Jan Hajic, Otakar Smrz, Petr Zemánek, Jan Šnaidauf, and Emanuel Beška. 2004. Prague arabic dependency treebank: Development in data and tools. In *Proc. of the NEMLAR Intern. Conf. on Arabic Language Resources and Tools*, volume 1.

Nikola Ljubešić, Filip Klubička, Željko Agić, and Ivo-Pavao Jazbec. 2016. New inflectional lexicons and training corpora for improved morphosyntactic annotation of Croatian and Serbian. In *Proceedings of the Tenth International Conference on Language Resources and Evaluation (LREC'16)*, pages 4264–4270, Portorož, Slovenia. European Language Resources Association (ELRA).

Joakim Nivre, Marie-Catherine de Marneffe, Filip Ginter, Jan Hajič, Christopher D. Manning, Sampo Pyysalo, Sebastian Schuster, Francis Tyers, and Daniel Zeman. 2020. Universal Dependencies v2: An evergrowing multilingual treebank collection. In *Proceedings of the Twelfth Language Resources and Evaluation Conference*, pages 4034–4043, Marseille, France. European Language Resources Association.

Caroline Pasquer, Agata Savary, Carlos Ramisch, and Jean-Yves Antoine. 2020. Verbal multiword expression identification: Do we need a sledgehammer to crack a nut? In *Proceedings of the 28th International Conference on Computational Linguistics*, pages 3333–3345.

Carlos Ramisch, Silvio Ricardo Cordeiro, Agata Savary, Veronika Vincze, Verginica Barbu Mititelu, Archna Bhatia, Maja Buljan, Marie Candito, Polona Gantar, Voula Giouli, Tunga Güngör, Abdelati Hawwari, Uxoa Iñurrieta, Jolanta Kovalevskaitė, Simon Krek, Timm Lichte, Chaya Liebeskind, Johanna Monti, Carla Parra Escartín, Behrang QasemiZadeh, Renata Ramisch, Nathan Schneider, Ivelina Stoyanova, Ashwini Vaidya, and Abigail Walsh. 2018. Edition 1.1 of the PARSEME shared task on automatic identification of verbal multiword expressions. In *Proceedings of the Joint Workshop on Linguistic Annotation, Multiword Expressions and Constructions (LAW-MWE-CxG-2018)*, pages 222–240, Santa Fe, New Mexico, USA. Association for Computational Linguistics.

Carlos Ramisch, Agata Savary, Bruno Guillaume, Jakub Waszczuk, Marie Candito, Ashwini Vaidya, Verginica Barbu Mititelu, Archna Bhatia, Uxoa Iñurrieta, Voula Giouli, Tunga Güngör, Menghan Jiang, Timm Lichte, Chaya Liebeskind, Johanna Monti, Renata Ramisch, Sara Stymne, Abigail Walsh, and Hongzhi Xu. 2020. Edition 1.2 of the PARSEME shared task on semi-supervised identification of verbal multiword expressions. In *Proceedings of the Joint Workshop on Multiword Expressions and Electronic Lexicons*, pages 107–118, online. Association for Computational Linguistics.

Ivan A. Sag, Timothy Baldwin, Francis Bond, Ann Copestake, and Dan Flickinger. 2002. Multiword Expressions: A Pain in the Neck for NLP. In *Proceedings of the 3rd International Conference on Intelligent Text Processing and Computational Linguistics (CICLing-2002)*, pages 1–15, Mexico City, Mexico.

Agata Savary, Marie Candito, Verginica Barbu Mititelu, Eduard Bejček, Fabienne Cap, Slavomír Čéplö, Silvio Ricardo Cordeiro, Gülşen Eryiğit, Voula Giouli, Maarten van Gompel, Yaakov HaCohen-Kerner, Jolanta Kovalevskaitė, Simon Krek, Chaya Liebeskind, Johanna Monti, Carla Parra Escartín, Lonneke van der Plas, Behrang QasemiZadeh, Carlos Ramisch, Federico Sangati, Ivelina Stoyanova, and Veronika Vincze. 2018. PARSEME multilingual corpus of verbal multiword expressions. In Stella Markantonatou, Carlos Ramisch, Agata Savary, and Veronika Vincze, editors, *Multiword expressions at length and in depth: Extended papers from the MWE 2017 workshop*, pages 87–147. Language Science Press., Berlin.

Agata Savary, Carlos Ramisch, Silvio Cordeiro, Federico Sangati, Veronika Vincze, Behrang QasemiZadeh, Marie Candito, Fabienne Cap, Voula Giouli, Ivelina Stoyanova, and Antoine Doucet. 2017. The PARSEME shared task on automatic identification of verbal multiword expressions. In *Proceedings of the 13th Workshop on Multiword Expressions (MWE 2017)*, pages 31–47, Valencia, Spain. Association for Computational Linguistics.

Agata Savary, Sara Stymne, Verginica Mititelu, Nathan Schneider, Carlos Ramisch, and Joakim Nivre. 2023. PARSEME meets Universal Dependencies: Getting on the same page in representing multiword expressions. *Northern European Journal of Language Technology*, to appear.

Nathan Schneider, Dirk Hovy, Anders Johannsen, and Marine Carpuat. 2016. SemEval-2016 Task 10: Detecting Minimal Semantic Units and their Meanings (DiMSUM). In *Proceedings of the 10th International Workshop on Semantic Evaluation (SemEval-2016)*, pages 546–559, San Diego, California. Association for Computational Linguistics.

Milan Straka. 2018. UDPipe 2.0 prototype at CoNLL 2018 UD shared task. In *Proceedings of the CoNLL 2018 Shared Task: Multilingual Parsing from Raw Text to Universal Dependencies*, pages 197–207, Brussels, Belgium. Association for Computational Linguistics.

Shiva Taslimipoor, Sara Bahaadini, and Ekaterina Kochmar. 2020. Mtlb-struct@ parseme 2020: Capturing unseen multiword expressions using multi-task learning and pre-trained masked language models. *arXiv preprint arXiv:2011.02541*.

Daniel Zeman, Martin Popel, Milan Straka, Jan Hajic, Joakim Nivre, Filip Ginter, Juhani Luotolahti, Sampo Pyysalo, Slav Petrov, Martin Potthast, Francis Tyers, Elena Badmaeva, Memduh Gokirmak, Anna Nedoluzhko, Silvie Cinkova, Jan Hajic jr., Jaroslava Hlavacova, Václava Kettnerová, Zdenka Uresova, Jenna Kanerva, Stina Ojala, Anna Missilä, Christopher D. Manning, Sebastian Schuster, Siva Reddy, Dima Taji, Nizar Habash, Herman Leung, Marie-Catherine de Marneffe, Manuela Sanguinetti, Maria Simi, Hiroshi Kanayama, Valeria dePaiva, Kira Droganova, Héctor Martínez Alonso, Çağrı Çöltekin, Umut Sulubacak, Hans Uszkoreit, Vivien Macketanz, Aljoscha Burchardt, Kim Harris, Katrin Marheinecke, Georg Rehm, Tolga Kayadelen, Mohammed Attia, Ali Elkahky, Zhuoran Yu, Emily Pitler, Saran Lertpradit, Michael Mandl, Jesse Kirchner, Hector Fernandez Alcalde, Jana Strnadová, Esha Banerjee, Ruli Manurung, Antonio Stella, Atsuko Shimada, Sookyoung Kwak, Gustavo Mendonca, Tatiana Lando, Rattima Nitisaroj, and Josie Li. 2017. Conll 2017 shared task: Multilingual parsing from raw text to universal dependencies. In *Proceedings of the CoNLL 2017 Shared Task: Multilingual Parsing from Raw Text to Universal Dependencies*, pages 1–19, Vancouver, Canada. Association for Computational Linguistics.

A Full corpus statistics and system results

Lang-split	Sentences	Tokens	Avg. length	VMWE	VID	IRV	LVC.full	LVC.cause	VPC.full	VPC.semi	IAV	MVC	LS.ICV
AR-train	6091	252456	41.4	3841	955	0	2178	236	0	0	468	4	0
AR-dev	342	14746	43.1	228	54	0	121	15	0	0	38	0	0
AR-test	1050	44541	42.4	680	173	0	379	52	0	0	75	1	0
AR-Total	7483	311743	41.6	4749	1182	0	2678	303	0	0	581	5	0
BG-train	15950	353748	22.1	4969	922	2421	1401	157	0	0	68	0	0
BG-dev	1380	30980	22.4	431	88	179	138	22	0	0	4	0	0
BG-test	4269	95685	22.4	1304	250	623	370	43	0	0	18	0	0
BG-Total	21599	480413	22.2	6704	1260	3223	1909	222	0	0	90	0	0
CS-train	42288	711213	16.8	12405	1353	8576	2476	0	0	0	0	0	0
CS-dev	1725	28697	16.6	523	68	357	98	0	0	0	0	0	0
CS-test	5418	93283	17.2	1608	192	1067	349	0	0	0	0	0	0
CS-Total	49431	833193	16.8	14536	1613	10000	2923	0	0	0	0	0	0
DE-train	6475	125081	19.3	2912	1015	230	222	23	1277	145	0	0	0
DE-dev	628	12046	19.1	281	103	25	22	6	119	6	0	0	0
DE-test	1893	36434	19.2	848	319	67	67	4	348	43	0	0	0
DE-Total	8996	173561	19.2	4041	1437	322	311	33	1744	194	0	0	0
EL-train	21983	587001	26.7	7128	2368	1	4430	154	127	0	0	48	0
EL-dev	1077	28833	26.7	348	107	0	228	9	4	0	0	0	0
EL-test	3115	82590	26.5	1032	366	0	635	16	12	0	0	3	0
EL-Total	26175	698424	26.6	8508	2841	1	5293	179	143	0	0	51	0
EN-train	2150	35534	16.5	317	44	0	98	12	112	16	22	13	0
EN-dev	1302	21660	16.6	199	35	0	63	10	62	7	13	9	0
EN-test	3984	67009	16.8	598	108	0	172	29	194	30	36	29	0
EN-Total	7436	124203	16.7	1114	187	0	333	51	368	53	71	51	0
ES-train	3424	112906	32.9	1732	200	433	259	54	0	0	328	458	0
ES-dev	521	17333	33.2	256	31	73	36	2	0	0	47	67	0
ES-test	1570	52125	33.2	751	96	208	97	25	1	0	136	188	0
ES-Total	5515	182364	33	2739	327	714	392	81	1	0	511	713	0
EU-train	5033	70017	13.9	1932	392	0	1444	96	0	0	0	0	0
EU-dev	1441	20957	14.5	560	130	0	404	26	0	0	0	0	0
EU-test	4684	66833	14.2	1754	358	0	1304	92	0	0	0	0	0
EU-Total	11158	157807	14.1	4246	880	0	3152	214	0	0	0	0	0
FA-train	2364	40110	16.9	2249	11	1	2237	0	0	0	0	0	0
FA-dev	321	5430	16.9	303	1	0	302	0	0	0	0	0	0
FA-test	932	16028	17.1	901	5	0	896	0	0	0	0	0	0
FA-Total	3617	61568	17	3453	17	1	3435	0	0	0	0	0	0
FR-train	14540	364414	25	3921	1529	1024	1286	63	0	0	0	19	0
FR-dev	1580	40107	25.3	437	157	123	146	11	0	0	0	0	0
FR-test	4841	121321	25	1297	471	354	446	23	0	0	0	3	0
FR-Total	20961	525842	25	5655	2157	1501	1878	97	0	0	0	22	0
GA-train	330	7104	21.5	127	25	0	43	19	3	6	31	0	0
GA-dev	318	7680	24.1	134	24	0	42	21	4	2	41	0	0
GA-test	1057	24123	22.8	398	57	0	115	78	21	12	115	0	0
GA-Total	1705	38907	22.8	659	106	0	200	118	28	20	187	0	0
HE-train	14035	283984	20.2	1855	848	0	740	158	109	0	0	0	0
HE-dev	1296	26766	20.6	171	59	0	90	10	12	0	0	0	0
HE-test	3869	77731	20	507	201	0	219	55	32	0	0	0	0
HE-Total	19200	388481	20.2	2533	1108	0	1049	223	153	0	0	0	0
HI-train	399	8641	21.6	242	13	0	155	7	0	0	0	67	0
HI-dev	322	6786	21	200	15	0	123	4	0	0	0	58	0
HI-test	963	20003	20.7	592	33	0	363	15	0	0	0	181	0
HI-Total	1684	35430	21	1034	61	0	641	26	0	0	0	306	0
HR-train	3357	77599	23.1	2131	161	657	476	81	0	0	756	0	0
HR-dev	672	15329	22.8	439	35	132	90	20	0	0	162	0	0
HR-test	2104	50018	23.7	1332	97	404	314	46	1	0	470	0	0
HR-Total	6133	142946	23.3	3902	293	1193	880	147	1	0	1388	0	0
HU-train	2139	54658	25.5	2664	39	0	400	130	1755	340	0	0	0
HU-dev	1000	25205	25.2	1259	19	0	173	69	843	155	0	0	0
HU-test	3020	76473	25.3	3837	46	0	570	202	2558	461	0	0	0
HU-Total	6159	156336	25.3	7760	104	0	1143	401	5156	956	0	0	0
IT-train	10641	292065	27.4	2854	999	783	502	112	74	2	343	19	20
IT-dev	1202	32652	27.1	324	109	81	52	18	11	0	44	4	5
IT-test	3885	106072	27.3	1032	376	280	180	44	20	0	110	10	12
IT-Total	15728	430789	27.3	4210	1484	1144	734	174	105	2	497	33	37
LT-train	2281	42782	18.7	163	53	0	102	8	0	0	0	0	0
LT-dev	2181	41421	18.9	161	66	0	91	4	0	0	0	0	0
LT-test	6642	124309	18.7	488	189	0	286	13	0	0	0	0	0
LT-Total	11104	208512	18.7	812	308	0	479	25	0	0	0	0	0
MT-train	6460	154979	23.9	749	311	0	434	1	3	0	0	0	0
MT-dev	975	22924	23.5	119	53	0	65	0	0	0	0	1	0
MT-test	3165	74382	23.5	358	154	1	201	0	1	0	0	1	0
MT-Total	10600	252285	23.8	1226	518	1	700	1	4	0	0	2	0
PL-train	18037	303628	16.8	5595	637	2832	1881	245	0	0	0	0	0
PL-dev	1421	23865	16.7	430	54	199	163	14	0	0	0	0	0
PL-test	4089	68647	16.7	1288	142	657	434	55	0	0	0	0	0
PL-Total	23547	396140	16.8	7313	833	3688	2478	314	0	0	0	0	0

Lang-split	Sentences	Tokens	Avg. length	VMWE	VID	IRV	LVC.full	LVC.cause	VPC.full	VPC.semi	IAV	MVC	LS.ICV
PT-train	24594	557486	22.6	4926	999	782	3031	99	0	0	0	15	0
PT-dev	1867	42855	22.9	375	72	64	229	10	0	0	0	0	0
PT-test	5601	127728	22.8	1125	235	175	694	18	0	0	0	3	0
PT-Total	32062	728069	22.7	6426	1306	1021	3954	127	0	0	0	18	0
RO-train	26889	479681	17.8	4562	806	1799	246	87	0	0	1624	0	0
RO-dev	7668	139314	18.1	1257	222	516	64	22	0	0	433	0	0
RO-test	22107	395913	17.9	3689	616	1511	206	73	0	0	1283	0	0
RO-Total	56664	1014908	17.9	9508	1644	3826	516	182	0	0	3340	0	0
SL-train	15220	321377	21.1	1834	390	885	135	37	0	0	387	0	0
SL-dev	3054	64429	21	376	79	189	27	8	0	0	73	0	0
SL-test	9551	200381	20.9	1153	255	552	77	19	0	0	250	0	0
SL-Total	27825	586187	21	3363	724	1626	239	64	0	0	710	0	0
SR-train	1382	33839	24.4	492	100	212	158	22	0	0	0	0	0
SR-dev	544	13558	24.9	203	49	91	53	10	0	0	0	0	0
SR-test	1660	39970	24	609	120	261	191	37	0	0	0	0	0
SR-Total	3586	87367	24.3	1304	269	564	402	69	0	0	0	0	0
SV-train	2795	44904	16	1466	189	106	197	3	681	290	0	0	0
SV-dev	765	12328	16.1	421	66	29	54	2	199	71	0	0	0
SV-test	2466	39588	16	1268	186	102	166	5	581	228	0	0	0
SV-Total	6026	96820	16	3155	441	237	417	10	1461	589	0	0	0
TR-train	16730	248697	14.8	5824	3140	0	2679	0	0	0	0	5	0
TR-dev	1396	20679	14.8	466	250	0	216	0	0	0	0	0	0
TR-test	4180	62793	15	1439	751	0	688	0	0	0	0	0	0
TR-Total	22306	332169	14.8	7729	4141	0	3583	0	0	0	0	5	0
ZH-train	44103	738713	16.7	9744	877	0	1101	158	0	4177	0	3431	0
ZH-dev	1215	19936	16.4	274	23	0	26	7	0	117	0	101	0
ZH-test	3611	61698	17	801	73	0	87	12	0	335	0	294	0
ZH-Total	48929	820347	16.7	10819	973	0	1214	177	0	4629	0	3826	0
Total	455629	9264811	20.3	127498	26214	29062	40933	3238	9164	6443	7375	5032	37

Table 2: Statistics of the 1.3 release of the PARSEME corpus

Investigating the Effects of MWE Identification in Structural Topic Modelling

Dimitrios Kokkinakis
University of Gothenburg and Centre for Ageing and Health (AgeCap), Sweden
dimitrios.kokkinakis@gu.se

Ricardo Muñoz Sánchez
University of Gothenburg, Sweden
ricardo.munoz.sanchez@gu.se

Sebastianus C. J. Bruinsma
Chalmers University of Technology, Sweden
sebastianus.bruinsma@chalmers.se

Mia-Marie Hammarlin
Lund University and Birgit Rausing Centre for Medical Humanities (BRCMH), Sweden
mia-marie.hammarlin@kom.lu.se

Abstract

Multiword expressions (MWEs) are common word combinations which exhibit idiosyncrasies in various linguistic levels. For various downstream natural language processing applications and tasks, the identification and discovery of MWEs has been proven to be potentially practical and useful, but still challenging to codify. In this paper we investigate various, relevant to MWE, resources and tools for Swedish, and, within a specific application scenario, we apply structural topic modelling to investigate whether there are any interpretative advantages of identifying MWEs.

1 Introduction

Multiword expressions (MWEs) are common word combinations which exhibit idiosyncrasies on a variety of lexical, syntactic, semantic, pragmatic and/or statistical levels. In this paper we investigate the impact of multiword expression (MWE) identification as a text preprocessing step prior to the application of a structural topic modeling (STM) approach (Roberts et al., 2019). As a case scenario, for investigating the feasibility of this experimental set-up, we provide an exploratory comparison of the STM analysis on a dataset that contains Swedish social medial posts about novel vaccines (mRNA, Novavax), *with* and *without* the identification of MWEs. The aim of this work is to answer the following research question: *in a mixed-method research design can MWE identification enhance the interpretability and explainability of the generated topics and themes?*

We start by applying both available MWE lexical resources for Swedish (lexicons and processing tools) and standard extraction techniques (e.g., n-gram collocations) to preprocess the vaccine-related narratives by keeping one version of the dataset intact, i.e., without any MWEs identified. Then, we apply STM in the two versions of the same dataset, to uncover the most prevalent discussion topics. As a methodological step, we utilize an exploratory mixed quantitative-qualitative approach (Ivankova et al., 2016) to investigate, compare, discuss, and loosely evaluate these topics with respect to the specific application scenario at hand (cf. Section 2). The motivation behind the application is based on the fact that multiword expressions can improve topic coherence, which is positively correlated with human assessment and readability of topics (Aletras & Stevenson, 2013). MWEs can also be used to reduce ambiguity, for example, by recognizing multiword terms/names as opposed to single word tokens could prevent an incorrect interpretation in many domains; for instance, *autoimmun reaction* 'autoimmune reaction' (instead of *autoimmun* and *reaction* separately) or *vitamin D-brist* 'vitamin D deficiency' (instead of *vitamin* and *D-brist* separately) (cf. Spasic & Button, 2020; Kochmar et al., 2020).

2 Application scenario: Swedish social media data about novel vaccines

We use vaccine skepticism as the application scenario for our case study. Vaccine skepticism can be triggered by anxiety about possible side effects and concerns related to novel vaccine technologies, such as the messenger RNA (mRNA) which can be used as a reason for not

Proceedings of the 19th Workshop on Multiword Expressions (MWE 2023), pages 36–44
May 6, 2023 ©2023 Association for Computational Linguistics

receiving (the COVID-19) vaccine (Leong et al., 2022). For instance, the University of Lund study: "Intracellular Reverse Transcription of Pfizer BioNTech COVID-19 mRNA Vaccine BNT162b2 In Vitro in Human Liver Cell Line" (Aldén et al., 2022), published on February 2022, has been frequently cited since its release, as a confirmation for vaccine skepticism and hesitancy, highlighting a potential misconception that the mRNA vaccine alters the human DNA.

2.1 Dataset: Swedish social media data on novel vaccines and vaccination

Having the aforementioned study as one of our starting points, we extracted Swedish tweets downloaded from February 10, 2022 (two weeks before the Lund study was published) to November 10, 2022 (nine months in total). The tweets were collected using the rtweet package (v1.1.0), which provides access to the Twitter API from R[1]. The final tweet data set consisted of 1,870 unique tweets from 858 different users (26,000 tokens without punctuation and with stop words removed). Furthermore, we extracted 8,900 unique social media posts (80,000 tokens; again, without punctuation and with stop words removed), from the popular Swedish forum Flashback[2]. These posts originate from Flashback vaccine-related threads published around the same period as above.

Two versions of the whole dataset were produced, the first version we name *sv-socialMedia-original* (without any labelled MWEs) and the second *sv-socialMedia-mwe* (the version with labelled MWEs; *cf.* 2.2).

2.2 Swedish MWE resources

For the MWE exploration in STM we decided to use as a preprocessing step any, as far as possible, available, Swedish resources for MWE annotation. We applied the following resources:

i. available multiword lists and lexicons with multiword entries, such as Swedish lexicalized idioms[3] (e.g., *vind i seglen* 'wind in your sails' [i.e., to have success] and *käppar i hjulet* 'stand in the way') and phrasal verbs, including inflected forms[4] (e.g., *komma ihåg* 'to remember' and *bryta ner* 'break down');
ii. named entity recognition for Swedish (Kokkinakis et al., 2014). Named entities that are composed of more than one token were kept and marked as a MWE; e.g., *Robert Malone; Falun Gong* and *Bill Gates foundation*);
iii. function words, mainly adverbs and prepositions[5] (e.g., *till följd av* 'as a result of' and *på grund av* 'because of');
iv. medical terminology, particularly names of symptoms[6] from ICD-10, and disease names. Technical and medical terms usually form non-compositional compound terms because of the need for specificity. Combining such terms into single token compounds may result in improved specificity / comprehensibility in the topics (cf. Boyd-Graber et al., 2017). E.g., *försämrat immunförsvar* 'impaired immune system';
v. statistically significant n-gram collocations [7] (basically bigrams and some trigrams) after manual selection of the top-400 strongest collocations. For instance, some of the highly ranked n-grams, acquired from the dataset, include: *kognitiv förmåga* 'cognitive ability'; *fertil ålder* 'fertile age'; *plötsligt hjärtstopp* 'sudden cardiac arrest'; *naturlig*

[1] The keywords that were used included the pattern: (m-?[Rr][Nn][Aa]|[Nn]ovavax).* ('?' the preceding character is optional; '|' disjunction and '.*' ≥ 0 characters following) or the hashtags #mRNA / #novavax and lang:sv (Swedish).

[2] `https://www.flashback.org/`.

[3] The lexicalized idioms (ca 4,000) originate from the NEO lexicon: `https://spraakbanken.gu.se/en/resources/neo-idiom`.

[4] Collection from various Internet sources e.g., the Swedish Wiktionary `https://sv.wiktionary.org/wiki/Kategori:Svenska/Partikelverb`; and the manually annotated Swedish verbal MWEs in the 1.2 edition of the PARSEME Shared Task, particularly the categories; Verb-particle constructions (VPC.full) and the inherently reflexive verbs (IRV) `https://lindat.mff.cuni.cz/repository/xmlui/handle/11234/1-3367`.

[5] `https://sv.wiktionary.org/wiki/Appendix:Svenska_flerordiga_prepositioner`.

[6] ICD-10-SE: International Statistical Classification of Diseases and Related Health Problems 10th Revision. R00-R99: Symptoms, signs and abnormal clinical and laboratory findings: `https://www.socialstyrelsen.se/statistik-och-data/klassifikationer-och-koder/icd-10/`.

[7] Using the R package `quanteda` (v. 0.9.9-65).

immunitet 'natural immunity' and *villkorat godkännande* 'conditional authorization'.

2.3 Data Preprocessing

Data preprocessing is a critical step in the raw text analysis process. Maier et al. (2018) emphasize the fact that appropriate preprocessing of the text collection is one of the major challenges researchers need to tackle for topic modeling application to textual data. This procedure involves a series of actions to clean and normalize text with the goals of removing potential noise and consequently obtain a better quality of the data and the topics for the dataset (cf. Section 2.1). The *sv-socialMedia-mwe* dataset is preprocessed with the annotation of the resources described in Section 2.2, in which multiword tokens are concatenated by an underscore character to a single token for uniformity (e.g., *Robert_Malone*). However, before annotation, both versions of the social media textual content were normalized. Basically, letters were converted from uppercase to lowercase; punctuations were stripped off and stop-words were removed (for the *sv-socialMedia-mwe* stop-words were removed after the MWE recognition).

In addition to the standard stop-words, we stripped off the top-10 most frequent and corpus-specific words, e.g., *vaccin* 'vaccine'; *vaccinera* 'to vaccinate'; *biverkning* 'side effect' and *sjukdom* 'disease'. These are repeated words that negatively affect the quality of topic models, leaving less representational power for the remaining text and, consequently, most likely yield less coherent topics (Almgerbi et al., 2021). As in other studies (cf. Duraivel & Lavanya, 2021) we neither stemmed nor lemmatized the dataset since stemming can alter the context of some of the words important for model building and interpretability. Moreover, we didn't lemmatize since we wanted to also investigate whether inflection could bring some valuable interpretative information. We are aware that this is a threshold hard to meet since lemmatization can also dilute useful information regarding a single concept into several inflected forms. To avoid missing out important information, we kept the corpus unstemmed and unlemmatized for the analysis. The identified MWEs during the preprocessing phase are replaced with single tokens before running the SMT, which does not induce any additional complexity to the models used in SMT. The distribution of the MWE types (relative frequency) is shown in Figure 1; moreover, in absolute values there were 3,926 bigrams; 628 trigrams and 26 tetragrams in the data.

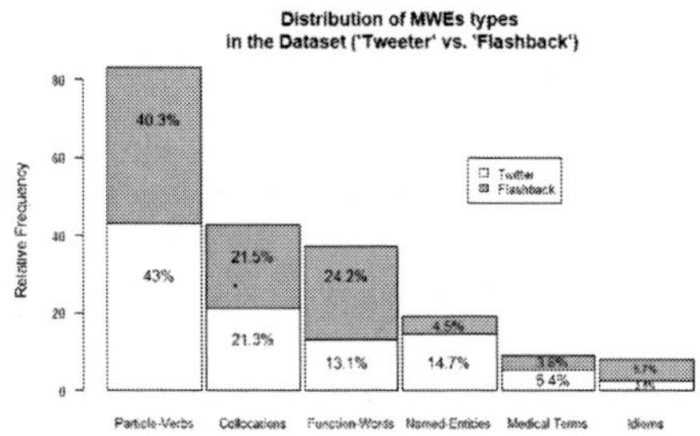

Figure 1: Distribution of the relative frequency of the MWE types in the dataset.

3 Related work

Latent Dirichlet Allocation (LDA) (Blei et al., 2002), is a popular topic modeling method that uses the statistical analysis of textual data to identify themes or topics that occur in a document collection. Although topic modelling can identify the topics contained in text, the original bag of words approach used by LDA models ignores the order of the words which limits the deeper understanding of the content. Therefore, during the last years researchers try to enhance the various flavors of topic models with the addition of n-gram features to improve the results and reduce the complexity of the models. Particularly, phrase-based topic modeling has shown significant improvement, especially on short text data (Kherwa & Bansal, 2020; Nokel & Loukachevitch, 2016); and several studies acknowledge the fact LDA results can be improved when MWE expressions are included during processing (Wang et al., 2016; Guarino & Santoro 2018; Cheevaprawatdomrong et al., 2022).

4 Structural Topic Modeling

Structural topic model (STM) has emerged as an extension to LDA allowing the integration of covariates into the prior distributions for document-topic compositions and topic-word proportions. Thereby, STM can be used to model how the content of a collection of documents changes as a function of document-level covariates such as day and time, and gain insights and understanding on how topics evolve (Lebryk 2021).

We apply STM to automatically detect latent topics in the dataset which can be used to investigate the nature of these topics reflected in the novel vaccine discussions (Scannell et al., 2021). We use a sequential explanatory mixed methods approach which consists of a quantitative phase (collection, cleaning, and natural language processing of the data), followed by a qualitative phase (in-depth analysis of the results from the quantitative phase). This type of design provides greater analysis depth than either singular analysis would (Fetters et al., 2013).

4.1 STM parameters

Since there is no "correct" solution for determining the optimal number of topics *k* that should be generated during the model selection process, several diagnostic aspects of the topic modeling were evaluated to decide the number of topics, *k*, to use. The *stm* package implements several evaluation metrics, such as the spread of *semantic coherence* (Mimno et al., 2011) and *exclusivity*, which both capture what humans qualitatively perceive as good topics (Roberts, et al., 2019). After preprocessing of the data, a document-term matrix was created and used for modeling, while the best model yielded 6 topics. This number was chosen after running multiple STM models, ranging from 2 to 40 topics (Roberts et al., 2019). We then used a combination of quantitative (exclusivity and semantic coherence) and qualitative methods to decide on the final numbers of topics (Appendix A), in order to evaluate the performance of structural topic modelling algorithm. The semantic coherence score measures the degree of semantic similarity between high-scoring words in the topic and ranges from $-\infty$ to 0. High semantic coherence measurements help distinguish between topics that are semantically interpretable while low scored topics are usually artifacts of statistical inference. Exclusivity measures the extent to which the top words for each topic do not appear as top words in other topics. Exclusivity ranges from 0 to $+\infty$. These quantitative metrics measure to what degree topics contain many overlapping words, and to what degree words that occur in the same topic also occur in the same context. For simplification reasons during the comparison between the two dataset versions, we set the number of topics to be the same. Figure 2 shows the semantic coherence vs the exclusivity of the models (40 topics), while Appendix B shows the temporal evolution of the identified topics.

5 Results and discussion

We have hypothesized that the identification of multiword expressions can provide us with better and more targeted insights and enhance the interpretability and explainability of the generated topics and themes. The characterization of the multiword expression types which are recognized and applied in this experimental setup follows the order given in Section 2.2.

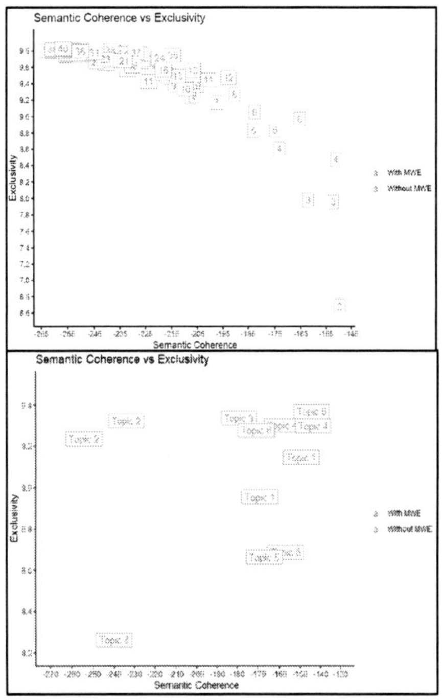

Figure 2. Comparison of the number of topics. Semantic coherence vs exclusivity of the generated models in the 2 versions of the dataset (top fourty topics and bottom six).

We extracted a list of keywords for each topic that have the highest association with that certain topic. For this association, we base ourselves on the FREX (frequency and exclusive) value of each word. This value combines the exclusivity of each word (meaning that a word occurs more often in that topic than in others) while also correcting for its overall frequency (Airoldi and Bischof 2016). To better understand and label the topics and to label them, we also extracted the top

30 most representative posts for each topic.

This qualitative evaluation shows that the proposed method provides only *slightly* better performance of SMT on the *sv-socialMedia-mwe* dataset. Moreover, the FREX metric helps us to assign intuitive labels to the subject matter. FREX is defined as the ratio of word frequency, and subject to word-topic exclusivity. Balancing these two measurements is important as frequent words can often be uninformative, while completely exclusive words can be very rare and not informative. The FREX example below, for instance, taken from the *sv-socialMedia-mwe* version (of topic 2 'women's health issues'), illustrates that three of the tokens, among the top 12, are multiwords: *mensrubbning* 'menstrual disorder'; *polio* 'polio'; *missfall* 'miscarriage'; *fertilitet* 'fertility'; *graviditet* 'pregnancy'; *stelkramp*, 'tetanus'; *klimakteriet* 'menopause'; *rubbning* 'disturbance'; *[gravid_kvinna]* 'pregnant woman'; *menstruation* 'menstruation'; *[röda_hund]* 'rubella'; and *[fertil_ålder]* 'fertile age'.

6 Conclusions and Future Work

The results suggest that the STM models perform only *slightly* better without MWE than with. One reason could be that the vocabulary is larger without MWEs included, so the number of topics capture more words. Still, the differences are quite small, and the comparisons of the models based on the two datasets are not 100% fair, since the MWE accounts for about 600 "terms" more and is therefore kind-of another dataset altogether as far as the STM is concerned.

Still, there is some indication that MWE identification leads to better interpretability of the STM, as calculated by the semantic coherence, which was higher for the dataset with MWEs. Therefore, we could conclude that the identification of MWEs can slightly enhance the explainability of the generated topics and themes, which could lead to a more appropriate labeling of the topic itself during the qualitative interpretation of the generated topics, i.e., incorporating multiword expressions into the models, creates slightly more informative resulting topics.

In general, the major differences between the two versions of the topics are also shown in the graphs of Appendix B which show the prevalence over time for the topics of the two dataset versions – without stating anything about their quality. Major differences for some of the generated topics, that needs further investigation.

As a future work it would be also interesting to verify the efficacy of our resources and our method on different domains and types of datasets and explore more resources for multiword recognition for Swedish. Identification of non-contiguous multiword expressions is another area we need to explore (Barreiro & Batista, 2016). There are several opportunities for future research to extend our assessment of the performance and evaluation. As previous research has pointed out, topic modeling algorithms are sensitive to several characteristics such as text length and the text preprocessing applied, for instance no stemming or lemmatization was applied that could have impact on the results (Stoy, 2021; Rüdiger et al., 2022). Hence, further investigations including parameters and characteristics are necessary.

Limitations

Since the extraction of the dataset content in this paper is based on a rather polarized dataset and from only two sources, future analyses will focus on testing the reliability of this research on other (larger) text collections. Furthermore, the dataset size is rather small; a limitation of the presented work is the search itself which only used a non-exhaustive list of keywords, basically on novel vaccines and vaccination. Moreover, we have no clue on how diverse the socio-demographic backgrounds of the users are, and therefore how commenting could be related to different sociodemographic characteristics of the sample. Finally, the multiword expressions we explored were all *contiguous*, results would probably be more comprehensive and profound if non-contiguous multiword expressions could also be identified and modelled. Similarly, lemmatization could be an important step to further explore since many of the generated clusters included inflected variants of the same word.

Acknowledgments

This work is part of the project Rumour Mining (MXM19-1161:1) financed by the Bank of Sweden Tercentenary Foundation (Riksbankens Jubileumsfond).

References

Edoardo Airoldi and Jonathan M. Bischof. 2016. Improving and Evaluating Topic Models and Other Models of Text. J of the American Statistical Association 111 (516): 1381-1403. DOI: 10.1080/01621459.2015.1051182.

Markus Aldén, Francisko Olofsson Falla, Daowei Yang, Mohammad Barghouth, Cheng Luan, Magnus Rasmussen and Yang De Marinis. 2022. Intracellular Reverse Transcription of Pfizer BioNTech COVID-19 mRNA Vaccine BNT162b2 In Vitro in Human Liver Cell Line. *Curr. Issues Mol. Biol.* 44(4), 1661-1663.

Nikolaos Aletras and Mark Stevenson. 2013. Evaluating topic coherence using distributional semantics. *Proceedings of the 10th International Conference on Computational Semantics (IWCS)*. Pp. 13-22. Potsdam, Germany. Association for Computational Linguistics.

Mohamad Almgerbi, Andrea De Mauro, Adham Kahlawi and Valentina Poggioni. 2021. Improving Topic Modeling Performance through N-gram Removal. In IEEE/WIC/ACM International Conference on Web Intelligence and Intelligent Agent Technology (pp. 162-169).

Anabela Barreiro and Fernando Batista. 2016. Machine Translation of Non-Contiguous Multiword Units. *Proceedings of the Workshop on Discontinuous Structures in Natural Language Processing*. Pp 22-30. 10.18653/v1/W16-0903.

Jonathan M. Bischof and Edoardo M. Airoldi. 2012. Summarizing topical content with word frequency and exclusivity. *Proceedings of the 29th International Conference on Machine Learning. ICML*. Pages 9–16

David M. Blei, Andrew Y. Ng and Michael I. Jordan. 2003. Latent Dirichlet Allocation. *Journal of Machine Learning Research*. 3. 993-1022.

Jordan Boyd-Graber, Yuening Hu and David Mimno. 2017. *Applications of Topic Models*. Foundations and Trends® in Information Retrieval. Vol. 11:2-3, pp 143-296. 10.1561/1500000030.

Jin Cheevaprawatdomrong, Alexandra Schofield and Attapol Rutherford. 2022. More Than Words: Collocation Retokenization for Latent Dirichlet Allocation Models. *Proceedings of the ACL Workshop: Findings of the Association for Computational Linguistics*. Pp 2696-2704. Dublin, Ireland 10.18653/v1/2022.findings-acl.212.

Leong Ching, Jin Lawrence, Kim Dayoung, Kim Jeongbin, Teo Yik Ying and Ho Teck-Hua . 2022. Assessing the impact of novelty and conformity on hesitancy towards COVID-19 vaccines using mRNA technology. *Commun Med.* 2:61.

Samuel Duraivel and Aby Augustine Lavanya. 2021. Understanding vaccine hesitancy with application of latent dirichlet allocation to reddit corpora. *Ind J of Science and Technology*. Vol 15:37, pp. 1868-1875. 10.21203/rs.3.rs-616664/v1.

Michael D. Fetters, Leslie A. Curry and John W. Creswell. 2013. Achieving Integration in Mixed Methods Designs. Health Serv. Res. 48, 2134-2156. 10.1111/1475-6773.12117.

Stefano Guarino and Mario Santoro. 2018. Multi-word Structural Topic Modelling of ToR Drug Marketplaces. *IEEE 12th International Conference on Semantic Computing (ICSC)*. CA, USA, pp. 269-273. 10.1109/ICSC.2018.00048.

Nataliya V. Ivankova, John W. Creswell and Sheldon L. Stick. 2016. Using mixed-methods sequential explanatory design: From theory to practice. *Field methods*. 18(1):3-20. 10.1177/1525822X05282260.

Pooja Kherwa and Poonam Bansal. 2020. Semantic N-gram topic modeling. *EAI Endorsed Transactions on Scalable Information Systems*, 7 (26). 10.4108/eai.13-7-2018.163131.

Ekaterina Kochmar, Sian Gooding, and Matthew Shardlow. 2020. Detecting Multiword Expression Type Helps Lexical Complexity Assessment. *Proceedings of the Twelfth Language Resources and Evaluation Conference* (LREC). Pp 4426–4435, Marseille, France. European Language Resources Association.

Dimitrios Kokkinakis, Jyrki Niemi, Sam Hardwick, Krister Lindén, and Lars Borin. 2014. HFST-SweNER — A New NER Resource for Swedish. In *Proceedings of the Ninth International Conference on Language Resources and Evaluation (LREC'14)*, pages 2537–2543, Reykjavik, Iceland. European Language Resources Association (ELRA).

Theo Lebryk. 2021. Introduction to The Structural Topic Model (STM). A unique way to use topic modelling for social science research. Towards Data Science: https://towardsdatascience.com/introduction-to-the-structural-topic-model-stm-34ec4bd5383

Daniel Maier, A. Waldherr, P. Miltner, G. Wiedemann, A. Niekler, A. Keinert, B. Pfetsch, G. Heyer, U. Reber, T. Häussler, H. Schmid-Petri and S. Adam. 2018. Applying LDA Topic Modeling in Communication Research: Toward a Valid and Reliable Methodology. *Com Methods & Measures*. 12:2-3, 93-118, 10.1080/19312458.2018.1430754.

David Mimno, Hanna M. Wallach, Edmund Talley, Miriam Leenders and Andrew McCallum 2011. Optimizing Semantic Coherence in Topic Models.

Proceedings of the Empirical Methods in NLP. Edinburgh, UK, c Association for Computational Linguistics, p. 262–272.

Michael Nokel and Natalia Loukachevitch. 2016. Accounting ngrams and multi-word terms can improve topic models. In *Proceedings of the 12th Workshop on Multiword Expressions*, pages 44–49, Berlin, Germany, August 7-12, 2016. Association for Computational Linguistics.

Margaret E. Roberts, Brandon M. Stewart and Dustin Tingley. 2019. Stm: An R package for structural topic models. *Journal of Statistical Software*. 91(2), 1–40. 10.18637/jss.v091.i02.

Matthias Rüdiger, David Antons, Amol M. Joshi and Torsten-Oliver Salge. 2022. Topic modeling revisited: New evidence on algorithm performance and quality metrics. *PLoS One*. 17(4):e0266325. 10.1371/journal.pone.0266325.

Denise Scannell, Linda Desens, Marie Guadagno, Yolande Tra, Emily Acker, Kate Sheridan, Margo Rosner, Jennifer Mathieu and Mike Fulk. 2021. COVID-19 Vaccine Discourse on Twitter: A Content Analysis of Persuasion Techniques, Sentiment and Mis/Disinformation. *J Health Com* 3;26(7). 10.1080/10810730.2021.1955050.

Irena Spasic and Kate Button. 2020. Patient Triage by Topic Modeling of Referral Letters: Feasibility Study. *JMIR Med Inform*. 6;8(11):e21252. 10.2196/21252.

Lazarina Stoy. 2021. *8. Limitations of Topic Modelling Algorithms on Short Text*. https://lazarinastoy.com/topic-modelling-limitations-short-text/ (visited 2023-02-11).

Minmei Wang, Bo Zhao, and Yihua Huang. 2016. Ptr: phrase-based topical ranking for automatic keyphrase extraction in scientific publications. *International Conference on Neural Information Processing*. Pp 120–128. Springer. 10.1007/978-3-319-46681-1_15.

Appendix A: Model Diagnostics.

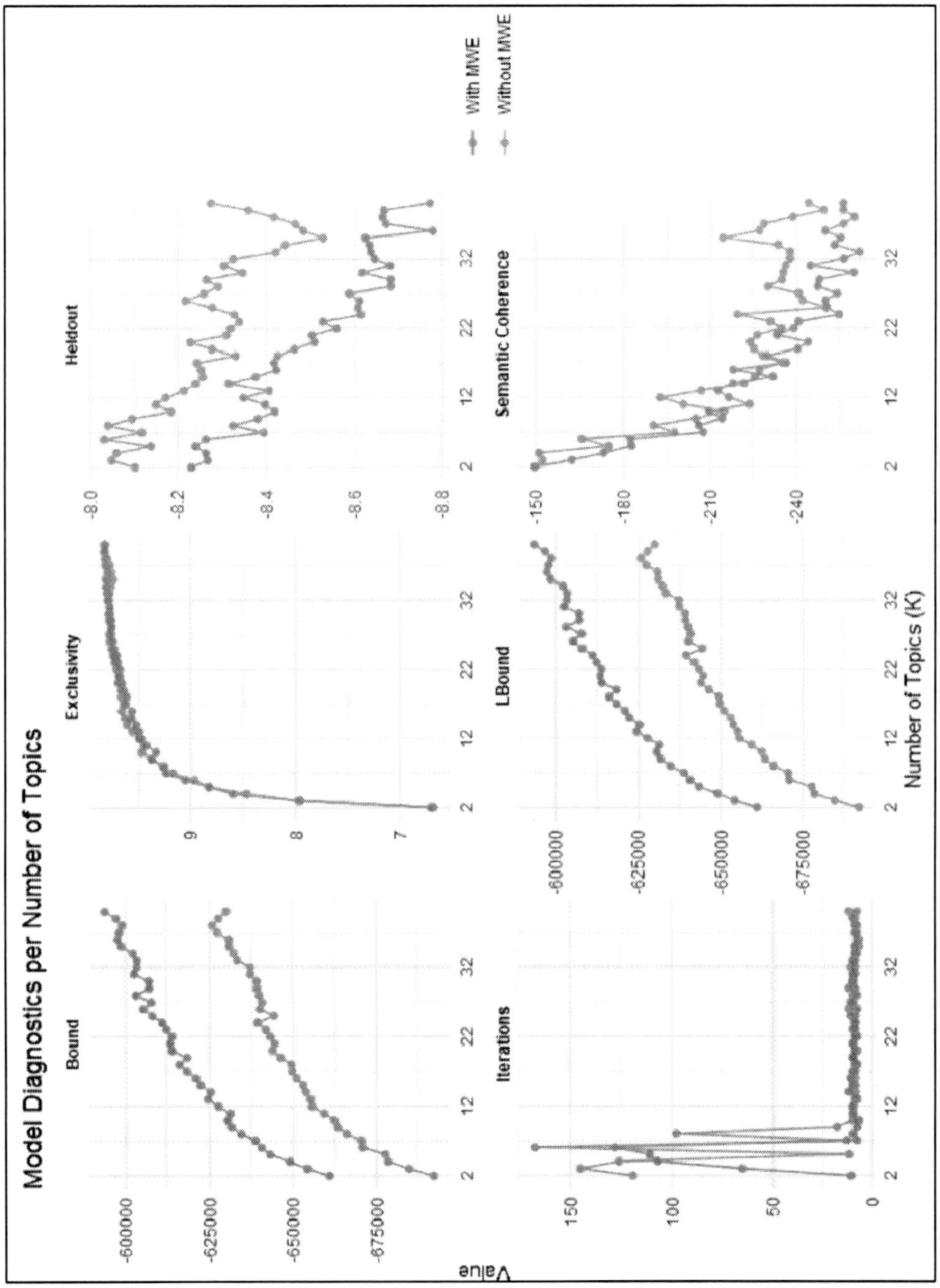

Appendix B: Topic prevalence over time.

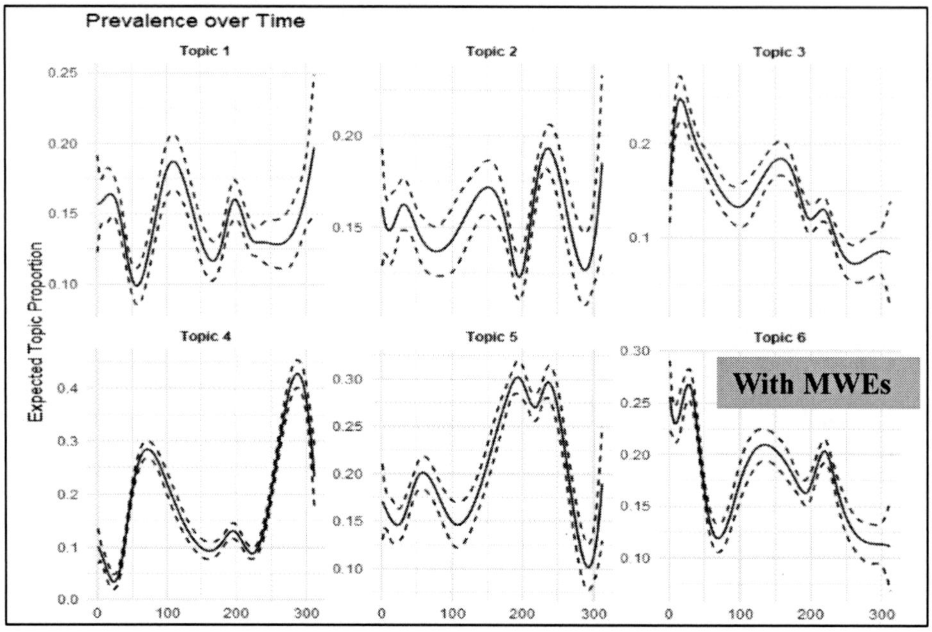

Timeline: February-November 2022

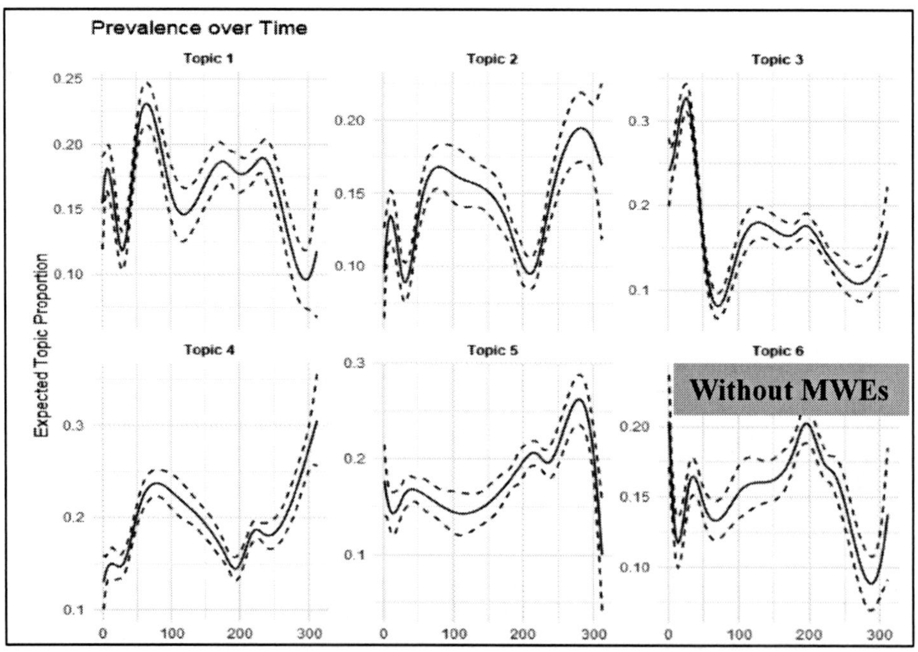

Timeline: February-November 2022

Idioms, Probing and Dangerous Things: Towards Structural Probing for Idiomaticity in Vector Space

Filip Klubička, Vasudevan Nedumpozhimana, John D. Kelleher
ADAPT Centre, Technological University Dublin, Ireland
filip.klubicka@adaptcentre.ie
{vasudevan.nedumpozhimana, john.d.kelleher}@TUDublin.ie

Abstract

The goal of this paper is to learn more about how idiomatic information is structurally encoded in embeddings, using a structural probing method. We repurpose an existing English verbal multi-word expression (MWE) dataset to suit the probing framework and perform a comparative probing study of static (GloVe) and contextual (BERT) embeddings. Our experiments indicate that both encode some idiomatic information to varying degrees, but yield conflicting evidence as to whether idiomaticity is encoded in the vector norm, leaving this an open question. We also identify some limitations of the used dataset and highlight important directions for future work in improving its suitability for a probing analysis.

1 Introduction

In recent years the NLP community has become somewhat enamoured by research on probing vector embeddings (Ettinger et al., 2016; Shi et al., 2016; Veldhoen et al., 2016; Adi et al., 2017) and justifiably so, as the method allows researchers to explore linguistic aspects of text encodings and has broad application potential. To date, however, the majority of impactful probing work focuses on analysing syntactic properties encoded in language representations, and the rich and complex field of semantics is comparably underrepresented (Belinkov and Glass, 2019; Rogers et al., 2020). One semantic problem that has received relatively little attention is the question of how models encode idiomatic meaning.

Laterally, our recently-developed extension of the probing method called *probing with noise* (Klubička and Kelleher, 2022) allows for structural insights into embeddings, highlighting the role of the vector norm in encoding linguistic information and showing that the norm of various embeddings can contain information on various surface-level, syntactic and contextual linguistic properties, as well as taxonomic ones (Klubička and Kelleher, 2023).

We hypothesise that probing idiomatic usage is a relevant task for studying the role of the norm: given there is some agreement that idiomatic phrases are at least partially defined by how strongly they are linked to the cohesive structure of the immediate discourse (Sag et al., 2002; Fazly et al., 2009; Sporleder and Li, 2009; Feldman and Peng, 2013; King and Cook, 2017), our intuition is that an idiomatic usage task should behave similarly to contextual incongruity tasks such as bigram shift and semantic odd-man-out (Conneau et al., 2018), which have been shown to be at least partially stored in BERT's vector norm (Klubička and Kelleher, 2022). For example, the idiomatic usage of a phrase such as *spill the beans* should have a similarly confounding effect on the sentence's word co-occurrence statistics as a semantic odd-man-out. This reasoning aligns with the findings of Nedumpozhimana and Kelleher (2021) who find that BERT can distinguish between sentence disruptions caused by missing words and the incongruity caused by idiomatic usage. Based on this, we are inclined to view an idiomatic usage task as a contextual incongruity task, and would expect to find some information stored in the norm.

To study this we repurpose an existing idiom token identification dataset into a probing task dataset and run it through our *probing with noise* pipeline, using both static GloVe and contextual BERT embeddings. Interestingly, while our experiments show that both GloVe and BERT generally do encode some idiomaticity information, the norm's role in this encoding is inconclusive, and further analysis points to some surprising irregularities in the behaviour of the models, which we trace back to a number of limitations in the dataset.

2 Related Work

Probing in NLP is defined by Conneau et al. (2018) as a classification problem that predicts linguistic properties using dense embeddings as training data.

Proceedings of the 19th Workshop on Multiword Expressions (MWE 2023), pages 45–57
May 6, 2023

The idea is to train a classifier over embeddings produced by some pretrained model, and assess the embedding model's knowledge encoding via the probe's performance. The framework rests on the assumption that the probe's success at a given task indicates that the encoder is storing information on the pertinent linguistic properties.

Given that embeddings are vectors positioned in a shared multidimensional vector space, we are interested in the structural properties of the linguistic information that they encode. Vectors are geometrically defined by two aspects: having both a **direction** and **magnitude**. Direction is the position in the space that the vector points towards (expressed by its dimension values), while magnitude is a vector's length, defined as its distance from the origin (expressed by the vector norm). Information contained in a vector is commonly understood to be encoded in the dimension values, however we have shown that it is also possible for the vector magnitude—the norm—to carry information as well (Klubička and Kelleher, 2022).

This is an important consideration for embedding research as it has been shown that normalising vectors removes information encoded in the norm (Goldberg, 2017; Klubička and Kelleher, 2022). A key step in calculating a cosine similarity measure, which is commonly used as a proxy for word similarity, is to normalise the vectors being compared. This has the side effect of nullifying any distinguishing properties the norms might have and any linguistic information encoded in the norm will be lost when making the comparison, which is an undesirable outcome if one wished to consider it in the comparison. We are thus interested in exploring how idiomaticity is encoded in vector space and whether any of it can be found in the norm.

The term Multi-Word Expression (MWE) frequently encompasses a wide variety of phenomena such as idioms, compound nouns, verb particle constructions, etc. The precise definition sometimes differs depending on the community of interest (Constant et al., 2017), and in this paper we use the terms *MWE*, *idiom* and *idiomatic phrase* somewhat liberally to mean any construction with idiomatic or idiosyncratic properties. This is sufficient for our interest in probing for a general notion of idiomaticity, the difference between idiomatic and literal usage of MWEs and studying how this distinction is encoded by embedding models.

Notably, as probing is a relatively recent framework and idioms are still a difficult phenomenon to model, not much work has been done in this space. Some inspiration can be found in the idiom token identification literature, closely related to word-sense disambiguation, where the goal is to build models that can discriminate idiomatic from literal usage (Hashimoto and Kawahara, 2008, 2009; Fazly et al., 2009; Li and Sporleder, 2010a,b; Peng et al., 2014; Salton et al., 2017; Peng and Feldman, 2017; King and Cook, 2018; Shwartz and Dagan, 2019; Hashempour and Villavicencio, 2020). While they do not overtly apply probing in their work, Salton et al. (2016) were the first to use an idiom token identification pipeline that is comparable to a typical probing framework, where sentence embeddings are used as input to a binary classifier that predicts whether the sentence contains a literal or figurative use of a MWE, indicating that an idiom probing task can be successful.

We have built upon this notion and performed sentence-level probing for idiomaticity in BERT (Nedumpozhimana et al., 2022). We employed the game theory concept of Shapley Values (Shapley, 1953) to rank the usefulness of individual idiomatic expressions for model training, in an effort to identify the types of signal that BERT captures when modelling idiomaticity. This approach has revealed that providing training data that maximises coverage across topics is the most useful form of topic information, and our findings indicate that there is no one dominant property that makes an expression useful, but rather fixedness and topic features are combined contributing factors. This current paper presents a successor study, as we now look for structural traces of idiomaticity at the sentence level. However, recently there have also been some interesting word-level probing studies.

Nedumpozhimana and Kelleher (2021) perform word-level probing experiments on BERT, where they combine probing with input masking to analyse the source of idiomatic information in a sentence, and what form it takes. Results indicate that BERT's idiomatic key is primarily found within an idiomatic expression, but also draws on information from the surrounding context. Meanwhile, Garcia et al. (2021) use probing to assess if some of the expected linguistic properties of idiomatic noun compounds and their dependence on context and sensitivity to lexical choice can be extracted from contextual embeddings. They conclude that idiomaticity is not yet accurately represented by contextual models: while they might be able to detect idiomatic usage, they may not detect that idiomatic noun compounds have a lower degree of substitutability of their individual components.

When it comes to idiomatic probing benchmarks, the Noun Compound Senses Dataset (Garcia et al., 2021) is the only curated idiomaticity probing dataset. Other idiom probing work (Salton et al., 2016; Nedumpozhimana and Kelleher, 2021; Nedumpozhimana et al., 2022) relies on existing MWE and idiom datasets, specifically the VNC-tokens dataset (Cook et al., 2008). Other MWE resources for English include the PARSEME working group's (Savary et al., 2017; Ramisch et al., 2018) VMWE dataset, (Walsh et al., 2018), the STREUSLE corpus (Schneider and Smith, 2015) and a verbal MWE dataset by Kato et al. (2018). However, these are annotated at the word-level, employ a fine-grained taxonomy of labels and only annotate idiomatic usage of MWEs, making it impossible to train models that can differentiate between literal and idiomatic usage. As such, while meticulously crafted and, as we argue in §7.1, of much higher quality than what we use in our work, they are not suited for the type of sentence-level analysis of idiomaticity we are interested in. There are recent datasets that are better suited for this: MAGPIE (Haagsma et al., 2020) and the SemEval-2022 Task 2 dataset (Tayyar Madabushi et al., 2022). Unfortunately we only became aware of the former during the review process, while the latter was not yet freely available at the conception of this research. Instead, to stay consistent with the recent wave of idiom probing work, we repurpose the the VNC-tokens dataset (Cook et al., 2008) to suit our structural probing needs, as presented in §3.

3 Probing Dataset Construction

Our *Idiomatic Usage* (IU) task is based on the VNC-Tokens dataset (Cook et al., 2008), which is a collection of English sentences containing MWEs called Verb-Noun Combinations (VNC), which can be used idiomatically or literally. This includes expressions such as *hit road*, *blow whistle*, *make scene* and *make mark*. The VNC-tokens dataset contains a total of 2,984 sentences with 56 different expressions, with each sentence containing one expression. Each sentence in the dataset is labelled as *Idiomatic*, *Literal*, or *Unknown*. However, the related literature only makes use of a subset of the full dataset. For consistency and comparability with related work (Peng et al., 2014; Salton et al., 2016; Nedumpozhimana and Kelleher, 2021) we apply the same filtering heuristics so the subset used in our experiments contains 1,205 sentences, of which 749 are labelled as *Idiomatic* and 456 are labeled as *Literal*, allowing for straightforward binary classification. A breakdown of each expression in the dataset is displayed in Table 7 in Appendix A.

verb	noun
make	face, pile, hay, scene, mark, hit
pull	leg, weight, plug, punch
blow	whistle, top, trumpet
hit	wall, roof, road
get	wind, sack, nod
lose	head, thread

Table 1: Groups of VNCs based on verb constituent overlap.

3.1 Choosing the right train and test split

In establishing a train and test split we aimed to avoid lexical memorisation (Levy et al., 2015; Santus et al., 2016; Shwartz et al., 2017), as our goal is for the probe to only learn a general, abstract, notion of idiomaticity unrelated to any particular idiomatic phrase, so the train and test sets need to be carefully curated. We tackle this on two fronts:

(a) The probe needs to be tested on a subset of VNCs that it has not seen in training. Having it predict the usage status of only unfamiliar idiomatic phrases forces the model to fall back on its general knowledge of what makes an idiomatic phrase, rather than a memory of any specific VNC.

(b) When training, we also need to ensure that the model attends to general properties of idiomaticity, rather than phrase- or token-specific ones. The surface form of a VNC likely has significant informational value to either the encoder or the probe, so specific VNC constituents might be interpreted as some sort of signal. Upon inspection of the candidate phrases we have found that many of the 28 VNCs in the dataset share the same verb constituent, as shown in Table 1. In fact, the dataset contains only 7 VNCs that contain "unique" verb constituents: *hold fire*, *have word*, *take heart*, *kick heel*, *see star*, *cut figure*, *find foot*.

We attempt to mitigate this by populating the train set exclusively with phrases with overlapping verbs, while placing the phrases with unique verbs in the test set. Thus the importance of individual verbs is reduced as they appear with different nouns. Coincidentally, satisfying condition (b) also satisfies condition (a), so no additional filtering is needed: VNCs from the test set do not appear in the train set, and the usage of verbs in the train set is diverse with different VNCs having the same verb constituent. As such, our test set includes 7 VNCs, while the remaining 21 are used in training. Table 8 in Appendix A shows the final train and test split used in our experiments.

Additionally, to confirm that the chosen train and test split is a viable way to tease out idiomaticity, we also run a parallel set of experiments using a form of bootstrapping where we resample the train and test split multiple times by randomly choosing 7 VNCs to be used in the test set, and using the remaining 21 phrases for training. This violates the above-established principle (b) as verbal constituents might be mixed between train and test sets, but still conforms to principle (a), as the model will always be tested on a set of 7 phrases that were not seen during training. Additionally, as we are not fixing the number of samples in the train and test sets, but rather the number of idiomatic phrases (with a varying number of sentences containing each phrase), there will also be slight differences in the ratio of the train and test sample sizes between different runs. However, we find that when the multitude of runs are averaged the true effect comes to the fore—the bootstrapped results mirror the results of the fixed setting, confirming the chosen split. For transparency and completeness, in Section 5 we report results for both setups: Idiomatic Usage Fixed data split (IU_F) and Idiomatic Usage Resampled data split (IU_R).

4 Experimental Setup

4.1 Chosen Embeddings

Given the prominence of contextual encoders such as BERT (Devlin et al., 2019) and its derivatives, as well as their ability to model in-context meaning and incongruity, they are an obvious choice for our analysis. However, rather than compare different contextual encoders, we prefer to draw a contrastive comparison with a static encoder such as GloVe (Pennington et al., 2014), which is based on a word to word co-occurrence matrix, as this comparison can provide more varied insight.

Given that our idiomatic usage dataset is framed as a classification task at the sentence level, our experiments require sentence representations. We use pretrained versions of BERT and GloVe to generate embeddings for each sentence. The BERT model generates 12 layers of embedding vectors with each layer containing a separate 768-dimensional embedding for each word, so we average the word embeddings in BERT's final layer, resulting in a 768-dimensional sentence embedding. We take the same mean pooling approach with GloVe, which yields a 300-dimensional sentence embedding for each sentence. While BERT uses sub-word tokens to get around out of vocabulary tokens, in the rare instance of encountering an OOV with GloVe, we generate a random word embedding in its stead.

4.2 Probing with Noise

The method is described in detail in Klubička and Kelleher (2022)[1]: in essence it applies targeted noise functions to embeddings that have an ablational effect and remove information encoded either in the norm or dimensions of a vector.

We remove information from the norm (abl.N) by sampling random norm values and scaling the vector dimensions to the new norm. Specifically, we sample the L2 norms uniformly from a range between the minimum and maximum L2 norm values of the respective embeddings in our dataset.[2]

To ablate information encoded in the dimensions (abl.D), we randomly sample dimension values and then scale them to match the original norm of the vector. Specifically, we sample dimension values uniformly from a range between the minimum and maximum dimension values of the respective embeddings in our dataset.[3] We expect this to fully remove all interpretable information encoded in the dimension values, making the norm the only information container available to the probe.

Applying both noise functions to the same vector (abl.D+N) should remove any information encoded in it, meaning the probe has no signal to learn from, a scenario equal to training on random vectors.

Even when an embedding encodes no information, our train set contains class imbalance and the probe can learn the distribution of classes. To account for this, as well as the possibility of a powerful probe detecting an empty signal (Zhang and Bowman, 2018), we establish informative random

[1]Code available here: https://github.com/GreenParachute/probing-with-noise

[2]GloVe: [2.2634,4.2526]
BERT: [7.4844,11.1366]

[3]GloVe: [-1.7866, 2.8668]
BERT: [-5.0826, 1.5604]

baselines against which we compare the probe's performance. We employ two such baselines: (a) we assert a random prediction (*rand.pred*) onto the test set, negating any information that a classifier could have learned, class distributions included; and (b) we train the probe on randomly generated vectors (*rand.vec*), establishing a baseline with access only to class distributions.

Finally, to address the degrees of randomness in the method, we train and evaluate each model 50 times and report the average score of all the runs, essentially bootstrapping over the random seeds (Wendlandt et al., 2018). Additionally, we calculate a confidence interval (CI) to ensure that the reported averages were not obtained by chance, and report it alongside the results to indicate statistical significance when comparing averages.

4.3 Probing Classifier and Evaluation Metric

In our experiments the sentence embeddings are used as input to a Multi-Layered Perceptron (MLP) classifier, which labels them as idiomatic (1) or literal (0). We evaluate the performance of the probe using the micro-average AUC-ROC score,[4] the most appropriate evaluation metric for a dataset with unbalanced labels, as it reflects the classifier's performance on both positive and negative classes. Regarding implementation and parameter details, we used the bert-base-uncased BERT model from the *pytorch_pretrained_bert* library[5] (Paszke et al., 2019), a pre-trained GloVe model[6] and for the MLP probe we used the scikit-learn MLP implementation (Pedregosa et al., 2011) using the default parameters.[7]

5 Experimental Results

Experimental evaluation results for GloVe and BERT on the idiomatic usage (IU) probing task are presented in Tables 2 and 3. The tables include results for both the setting where the VNC's in the hold-out test set are fixed (IU_F) and the setting where they are resampled each time (IU_R), though this is essentially the same probing task. Note that cells shaded light grey belong to the same distribution as random baselines, as there is no statistically significant difference between the different scores; cells shaded dark grey belong to the same distribution as the vanilla baseline; and cells that are not shaded contain a significantly different score than both the random and vanilla baselines, indicating that they belong to different distributions.

GloVe				
Model	**IU_F**		**IU_R**	
	auc	±CI	auc	±CI
rand. pred.	.4994	.0015	.4998	.0013
rand. vec.	.4997	.0015	.5	.0013
vanilla	.7485	.0003	.7717	.0022
abl. N	.7445	.0006	.7687	.0021
abl. D	.5012	.0018	.4993	.0015
abl. D+N	.4991	.0018	.5005	.0015

Table 2: Probing results on GloVe models and baselines, both with fixed (F) and resampled (R) test set. Reporting average AUC-ROC scores and confidence intervals (CI) of the average of all training runs.

BERT				
Model	**IU_F**		**IU_R**	
	auc	±CI	auc	±CI
rand. pred.	.4997	.0015	.4998	.0013
rand. vec.	.4997	.0015	.5013	.0013
vanilla	.8411	.0002	.8524	.0016
abl. N	.8413	.0003	.8532	.0016
abl. D	.4991	.0019	.4978	.0015
abl. D+N	.4999	.0018	.5004	.0015

Table 3: Probing results on BERT models and baselines, both with fixed (F) and resampled (R) test set. Reporting average AUC-ROC scores and confidence intervals (CI) of the average of all training runs.

The results interpretation here is quite straightforward. As the unablated, vanilla baseline significantly outperforms random baselines in both models, this indicates that both GloVe and BERT encode a non-zero amount of idiomatic usage information, which aligns with previous findings.

IU_F vs. IU_R: It important to validate our chosen train and test split (see §3.1) by comparing the respective vanilla performances of IU_F and IU_R. Given that our goal is to nudge the probe to model a representation of idiomaticity that is unrelated to any given phrase, we expect that the IU_F setting

[4] https://scikit-learn.org/stable/modules/generated/sklearn.metrics.roc_auc_score.html

[5] https://pypi.org/project/pytorch-pretrained-bert/

[6] The larger common crawl vectors: https://nlp.stanford.edu/projects/glove/

[7] activation='relu', solver='adam', max_iter=200, hidden_layer_sizes=100, learning_rate_init=0.001, batch_size=min(200,n_samples), early_stopping=False, weight init. $W \sim \mathcal{N}\left(0, \sqrt{6/(fan_{in} + fan_{out})}\right)$ (scikit relu default). See: https://scikit-learn.org/stable/modules/generated/sklearn.neural_network.MLPClassifier.html

should make the task more difficult for the classifier. The results confirm this, showing that in GloVe and BERT vanilla IU_R significantly outperforms vanilla IU_F. Evidently, the curated test split makes prediction on the task more challenging and the lower performance of IU_F indicates that the model is forced to rely on VNC-independent features to make predictions.

GloVe vs. BERT: In terms of differences between encoders, the results show that vanilla BERT significantly outperforms vanilla GloVe in both the IU_F and IU_R scenarios. Evidently, BERT is much better at encoding idiomaticity than GloVe. We suspect this is due to two factors: (a) BERT is a contextual encoder and as such is better suited to modelling the local context necessary to accurately represent idiomaticity in the sentence, and (b) it has a much higher dimensionality, meaning it has the potential to devote more representation space to more complex phenomena.

Idiomaticity and the norm: One of the goals of this experiment was to investigate whether the norm encodes any information relevant to the IU task. Our method states this is most clearly determined in the setting with ablated dimension information (abl.D), where above random performance indicates that the information is stored in the unablated norm container (Klubička and Kelleher, 2022). Our results here show no conclusive indication that the norm encodes idiomaticity information on this task: in all four scenarios ablating only the dimensions already makes the probe's performance comparable to random, which indicates no information is stored in the norm.[8]

As stated in the introduction, given the IU task's similarity with contextual incongruity tasks, we would expect to find some signal in the norm. Our result here is somewhat surprising and motivates further questions, prompting us to perform additional post hoc investigations and analyses that should improve our understanding of the results and help shape our overall findings.

6 Additional Experiments

6.1 Norm Correlation Analysis

For another perspective on the relationship between vector norms and the IU task information, we run a post hoc analysis on the norm container. We investigate both the norms of our embeddings using a Pearson correlation analysis, which can be considered a linear probing study: we test the correlation between each vector norm (L1 and L2) and the sentence labels (*Idiomatic* and *Literal*[9]). The correlation results are presented in Table 4 and seem to be somewhat at odds with our experimental results.

Task	Vectors	GloVe		BERT	
		L1	L2	L1	L2
IU	vanilla	-0.2231	-0.1786	-0.1490	-0.1756
	abl. N	-0.0074	0.0276	-0.0397	-0.0167

Table 4: Pearson correlation coefficients between class labels and L1 and L2 norms for vanilla vectors and vectors with ablated norms. For this analysis the Idiomatic label was mapped to 1 and the Literal label to 0.

The analysis shows that in both vanilla GloVe and BERT both norms have a weak negative correlation with IU labels. While the correlations are weak, they are not zero—we observe a significant drop in the coefficients upon applying the norm ablation function, which seems to fully remove information from both norms, as the correlation coefficients drop to ≈ 0, indicating that relevant information encoded in the norms has been removed.

This difference between vanilla and abl.N points to some slight correlation between the idiomaticity labels and information encoded in the vanilla norm, yet our probing experiments do not align with this finding. What makes this more unusual is that our IU correlations are comparable to the correlations on parse tree depth (0.1908) or semantic odd-man-out (0.2305) tasks which do produce a signal in the *probing with noise* experiments as previously reported Klubička and Kelleher (2022).

It is possible that the correlation is just on the verge of being too weak to be detectable by the method. On the other hand, this could be a sign that other factors are at play—we suspect that the misalignment between the probing and correlation results hints at the imbalanced nature of the IU dataset and its limitations. We run an additional experiment to search for more evidence.

As an aside, it is worth noting that if we were to take the correlation results at face value, they do provide some interesting insight into how idiomatic usage is encoded in vector space. Specifically, a non-zero negative correlation coefficient

[8] We do see a hint of this when ablating the norm in GloVe IU_F, but this is more likely a feature of this particular data split, as the signal is not mirrored in IU_R. Even if it was, without a signal in the abl.D setting, the abl.N setting is insufficient evidence to infer that the norm encodes information.

[9] The Pearson test only works on continuous variables, but it is still possible to calculate with categorical variables if they are binary, by simply converting the categories to 0 and 1.

GloVe				
Model	IU_F		IU_R	
	auc	±CI	auc	±CI
rand. pred.	.4994	.0015	.4998	.0013
rand. vec.	.4997	.0015	.5	.0013
vanilla	.7485	.0003	.7717	.0022
del. 1h	**.7737**	.0005	.7553	.0023
del. 2h	.7043	.0005	.7545	.002

Table 5: Probing results on GloVe dimension deletions both with fixed (F) and randomised (R) test set. Reporting average AUC-ROC scores and confidence intervals (CI) of the average of all training runs.

BERT				
Model	IU_F		IU_R	
	auc	±CI	auc	±CI
rand. pred.	.4997	.0015	.4998	.0013
rand. vec.	.4997	.0015	.5013	.0013
vanilla	.8411	.0002	.8524	.0016
del. 1h	**.8668**	.0002	**.8576**	.0016
del. 2h	.8137	.0003	.8368	.0016

Table 6: Probing results on BERT dimension deletions both with fixed (F) and randomised (R) test set. Reporting average AUC-ROC scores and confidence intervals (CI) of the average of all training runs.

means that sentences containing idiomatic usage are positioned closer to the origin relative to sentences that contain literal usage. In other words, both GloVe and BERT vectors of sentences containing idiomatic usage are slightly shorter, which is an intriguing structural finding.

6.2 Dimension Deletion

We run supplementary experiments to investigate the role of the dimension container as the sole carrier of IU information. To do this we perform a dimension deletion experiment. Partially inspired by the work of Torroba Hennigen et al. (2020) who found that most linguistic properties are reliably encoded by only a handful of dimensions, we attempt to roughly identify the degree of localisation of information in the vector dimensions. In staying consistent with the ablational nature of the method, we simply delete one half of the vector's dimensions and retrain the probe on the truncated vectors, repeating the process for the remaining half.

The dimension deletion results are included in Tables 5 and 6. In these tables the row denoted *del.1h* reports the results for deleting the 1st half of an embedding vector, and *del.2h* reports results for deleting the 2nd half. Given that all relevant IU information seems to be encoded in vector dimensions, we expect that deleting half of the vector would cause a significant drop in performance when compared to vanilla. We would also expect a drop in evaluation scores regardless of which half of the vector is deleted. However, our results reveal some rather surprising effects.

While *del.2h* in GloVe causes the expected performance drop, in IU_F *del.1h* causes a statistically significant *improvement* when compared to the vanilla baseline (marked in bold). We observe quite a large performance spike, though this is not mirrored in the IU_R scenario. We might dismiss this as just a strange artefact of the particular IU_F data split, were it not for the fact that we observe the same behaviour in both IU_F and IU_R in BERT, where *del.2h* causes a significant performance drop, but *del.1h* causes a significant spike.

It seems that both GloVe and BERT exhibit a certain degree of information localisation, with a preference for storing relevant IU information in the first half of dimensions, to the point where the second half reduces the overall information quality of the vector. In principle this interpretation is consistent with the findings of Torroba Hennigen et al. (2020) and Durrani et al. (2020), who showed that certain linguistic properties are localised in dimensions of contextual embeddings. However, we remain skeptical and wonder whether our findings reflect how these embeddings truly encode idiomaticity, or whether this is property of this particular dataset. We consider this in the following section.

7 Discussion and Limitations

While the correlation coefficients between both GloVe's and BERT's norm and the IU labels are non-zero, our probe does not seem to be able to leverage this information from the norm. In isolation, the correlation coefficient would have led us to believe that there may be some idiomaticity information encoded in the norm. However, this has not been confirmed by the *probing with noise* method, which when used in conjunction with the correlation analysis offers conflicting evidence.

The performance spikes exhibited in the deletion experiments are somewhat baffling, especially given the stark differences between the GloVe and BERT architectures. However, if the IU task were truly analogous to a contextual incongruity task, then arguably vanilla GloVe should be much worse at encoding IU than shown in our results—by design, an averaged GloVe sentence embedding cannot be aware of word order or relationships between words in a specific context and should perform much more poorly on such tasks, making even vanilla GloVe's performance a result that raises more questions than it answers.

One pertinent consideration regards the fact that our experiments were performed at the sentence level. It is possible that there is a crisper signal in the norm of individual word embeddings (as shown on a word-level taxonomic probing task (Klubička and Kelleher, 2023)). Averaging word embeddings to obtain sentence representations may have diluted the signal to the point where it is not detectable by the *probing with noise* method. Replicating our experiments at the word-level, or using more direct sentence representation approaches (such as using BERT's CLS token, doc2vec (Le and Mikolov, 2014) or SentenceBERT (Reimers and Gurevych, 2019)) might produce a more salient result.

As it stands, the majority of the results we have observed on the IU dataset behave like surprising outliers that are difficult to explain. This can either be due to strong confounding factors at play that we are not aware of or, perhaps more likely, this is evidence of our suspicion that the dataset is not well-suited for this type of analysis. And while we have learned that vanilla BERT is better at the task than GloVe, the question whether idiomaticity can be encoded in their norms remains an open one.

7.1 Dataset Limitations

While constructing and experimenting with the VNC-tokens dataset we have become aware of some of its shortcomings. Our main concern is that it is two orders of magnitude smaller than more established probing datasets (Conneau et al., 2018). While we addressed this by increasing the number of training runs and resampling the train and test set, its size still limits what the models are able to learn. Unfortunately, in dealing with an intricate phenomenon such as idioms, considerably-sized corpora are few and far between.[10]

The VNC-tokens dataset is also very limited in scope, containing only a single type of verbal MWE, while other datasets include a wider variety of verbal expressions or compounds involving other parts of speech. It is also worth noting that both idiomatic and literal usages of the VMWEs present in the dataset are relatively frequent in English when compared to other more niche idiomatic phrases. This relative frequency is likely also reflected in the pretrained embeddings and could affect a model's ability to model their idiomaticity, raising the question whether relatively rarer phrases might behave differently. Thus the generalisability of our findings to other idiomatic expressions is uncertain.

Furthermore, at this point the VNC-Tokens dataset is a relatively older benchmark and there are indications that it has not been as meticulously crafted as more recent MWE datasets. For example, the dataset does not control for sentence length, which could be a strong confounding factor, it contains some typographical errors, even some seemingly incorrect IU annotations, as well as literary language which contains OOV tokens for the pretrained GloVe model. It is our impression that cleaning up the dataset, aligning it with the PARSEME annotation guidelines[11], and updating it with additional examples of sentences containing VNCs in order to better balance the idiomaticity labels would greatly improve its overall quality.

Overall, in spite of our best efforts at mitigating confounders and constructing the right data split for our task, we still wonder whether the dataset is simply too small and too imbalanced to truly be useful in our probing scenario. Given all the limitations we have become aware of over the course of our experimentation it is difficult to decide whether our results are inconclusive due to the dataset, the type of idioms studied, perhaps some unknown limitation of the approach, or are simply a true observation. This makes our partially inconclusive and partially surprising findings somewhat difficult to reconcile with previous work. We thus emphasise the importance of expanding this work to a wider category of idiomatic phrases and ideally folding in all the datasets mentioned in §2—applying *probing with noise* to the datasets individually as well as an amalgamation of datasets would provide a more comprehensive analysis of general idiomaticity encoding and could provide more salient insights. It might also be beneficial to consider other dimensions of idiomaticity in the experimentation

[10]In fatct, all existing MWE resources are within a comparable size range to the VNC-tokens dataset. Even concatenating them would not nearly approach the size of probing datasets for non-semantic tasks.

[11]`https://parsemefr.lis-lab.fr/parseme-st-guidelines/1.1/?page=010_Definitions_and_scope/020_Verbal_multiword_expressions`

and analysis, such as evaluating MWEs that are differentiated with respect to whether or not they carry a metaphorical mapping to literal usages, and whether or not they are grammatical or extragrammatical (Fillmore et al., 1988).

8 Conclusion and Future Work

In this paper we applied the *probing with noise* method to two different types of word representations—static and contextual—generated by two different embedding algorithms—GloVe and BERT—on a repurposed idiomatic usage probing task, with the aim of obtaining structural insights into the role of the norm encoding idiomatic usage information.

Overall we detect some mixed signals in our findings, which include that **(a)** generally both GloVe and BERT encode idiomatic usage information, but BERT encodes more **(b)** the norm of GloVe and BERT carries no idiomaticity information (or at least this is not recoverable by the probe), even though **(c)** it seems there is a correlation between the norm length and idiomatic usage in a sentence, where sentences containing idiomatic usage are positioned relatively closer to the origin of the vector space. **(d)** Additionally, it seems both GloVe and BERT prefer to store idiomatic usage information in the first half of their vectors, to the point where the second half is detrimental to the vector's overall encoding of idiomaticity. Finally, **(e)** we present these findings with the caveat that they only apply to the VNC-Tokens dataset, which requires a bit of a rework in order to be up to the standard required for a probing framework.

As for our initial research question, we asked whether embeddings models such as BERT might see an idiomatic usage task as being of the same category as a contextual incongruity task.[12] Given that vanilla BERT strongly outperforms vanilla GloVe on the task, this could lend some credence to the interpretation that contextual awareness and the ability to model incongruity, which GloVe lacks but BERT excels at, is what improves its idiomaticity encoding. However, evidence is inconclusive and whether the vector norm of either model plays a role in encoding idiomatic information in the same way that it supplements the encoding of contextual incongruity information remains an open question, which we are committed to further pursue in future work. This would involve cleaning the VNC-Tokens dataset and combining it with other existing MWE datasets in a systematic exploration of the structural encoding of idiomaticity.

[12]This hypothesis inspired the title of the paper, referring to Lakoff (1987) and his work on semantic categories.

Acknowledgements

This research was conducted with the financial support of Science Foundation Ireland under Grant Agreements No. 13/RC/2106 and 13/RC/2106_P2 at the ADAPT SFI Research Centre at Technological University Dublin. ADAPT, the SFI Research Centre for AI-Driven Digital Content Technology, is funded by Science Foundation Ireland through the SFI Research Centres Programme, and is co-funded under the European Regional Development Fund.

References

Yossi Adi, Einat Kermany, Yonatan Belinkov, Ofer Lavi, and Yoav Goldberg. 2017. Fine-grained analysis of sentence embeddings using auxiliary prediction tasks. In *Proceedings of ICLR, 2017.*

Yonatan Belinkov and James Glass. 2019. Analysis methods in neural language processing: A survey. *Transactions of the Association for Computational Linguistics*, 7:49–72.

Alexis Conneau, German Kruszewski, Guillaume Lample, Loïc Barrault, and Marco Baroni. 2018. What you can cram into a single $&!#* vector: Probing sentence embeddings for linguistic properties. In *Proceedings of the 56th Annual Meeting of the Association for Computational Linguistics (Volume 1: Long Papers)*, pages 2126–2136, Melbourne, Australia. Association for Computational Linguistics.

Mathieu Constant, Gülşen Eryiğit, Johanna Monti, Lonneke van der Plas, Carlos Ramisch, Michael Rosner, and Amalia Todirascu. 2017. Survey: Multiword expression processing: A Survey. *Computational Linguistics*, 43(4):837–892.

Paul Cook, Afsaneh Fazly, and Suzanne Stevenson. 2008. The vnc-tokens dataset. In *Proceedings of the LREC Workshop Towards a Shared Task for Multiword Expressions (MWE 2008)*, pages 19–22.

Jacob Devlin, Ming-Wei Chang, Kenton Lee, and Kristina Toutanova. 2019. BERT: Pre-training of deep bidirectional transformers for language understanding. In *Proceedings of the 2019 Conference of the North American Chapter of the Association for Computational Linguistics: Human Language Technologies, Volume 1 (Long and Short Papers)*, pages 4171–4186, Minneapolis, Minnesota. Association for Computational Linguistics.

Nadir Durrani, Hassan Sajjad, Fahim Dalvi, and Yonatan Belinkov. 2020. Analyzing individual neurons in pre-trained language models. In *Proceedings of the 2020 Conference on Empirical Methods in Natural Language Processing (EMNLP)*, pages 4865–4880, Online. Association for Computational Linguistics.

Allyson Ettinger, Ahmed Elgohary, and Philip Resnik. 2016. Probing for semantic evidence of composition by means of simple classification tasks. In *Proceedings of the 1st Workshop on Evaluating Vector-Space Representations for NLP*, pages 134–139, Berlin, Germany. Association for Computational Linguistics.

Afsanesh Fazly, Paul Cook, and Suzanne Stevenson. 2009. Unsupervised type and token identification of idiomatic expressions. In *Computational Linguistics*, volume 35, pages 61–103.

Anna Feldman and Jing Peng. 2013. Automatic detection of idiomatic clauses. In *Computational Linguistics and Intelligent Text Processing*, pages 435–446, Berlin, Heidelberg. Springer Berlin Heidelberg.

Charles J Fillmore, Paul Kay, and Mary Catherine O'connor. 1988. Regularity and idiomaticity in grammatical constructions: The case of let alone. *Language*, pages 501–538.

Marcos Garcia, Tiago Kramer Vieira, Carolina Scarton, Marco Idiart, and Aline Villavicencio. 2021. Probing for idiomaticity in vector space models. In *Proceedings of the 16th Conference of the European Chapter of the Association for Computational Linguistics: Main Volume*, pages 3551–3564, Online. Association for Computational Linguistics.

Yoav Goldberg. 2017. Neural network methods for natural language processing. *Synthesis Lectures on Human Language Technologies*, 10(1):117.

Hessel Haagsma, Johan Bos, and Malvina Nissim. 2020. MAGPIE: A large corpus of potentially idiomatic expressions. In *Proceedings of the 12th Language Resources and Evaluation Conference*, pages 279–287, Marseille, France. European Language Resources Association.

Reyhaneh Hashempour and Aline Villavicencio. 2020. Leveraging contextual embeddings and idiom principle for detecting idiomaticity in potentially idiomatic expressions. In *Proceedings of the Workshop on the Cognitive Aspects of the Lexicon*, pages 72–80, Online. Association for Computational Linguistics.

Chikara Hashimoto and Daisuke Kawahara. 2008. Construction of an idiom corpus and its application to idiom identification based on wsd incorporating idiom-specific features. In *Proceedings of the 2008 Conference on Empirical Methods in Natural Language Processing (EMNLP 2008)*, pages 992–1001.

Chikara Hashimoto and Daisuke Kawahara. 2009. Compilation of an idiom example database for supervised idiom identification. *Language Resources and Evaluation*, 43(4):355–384.

Akihiko Kato, Hiroyuki Shindo, and Yuji Matsumoto. 2018. Construction of large-scale English verbal multiword expression annotated corpus. In *Proceedings of the Eleventh International Conference on Language Resources and Evaluation (LREC 2018)*, Miyazaki, Japan. European Language Resources Association (ELRA).

Milton King and Paul Cook. 2017. Supervised and unsupervised approaches to measuring usage similarity. In *Proceedings of the 1st Workshop on Sense, Concept and Entity Representations and their Applications*, pages 47–52, Valencia, Spain. Association for Computational Linguistics.

Milton King and Paul Cook. 2018. Leveraging distributed representations and lexico-syntactic fixedness for token-level prediction of the idiomaticity of English verb-noun combinations. In *Proceedings of the 56th Annual Meeting of the Association for Computational Linguistics (Volume 2: Short Papers)*, pages 345–350, Melbourne, Australia. Association for Computational Linguistics.

Filip Klubička and John D Kelleher. 2023. Probing taxonomic and thematic embeddings for taxonomic information. In *Proceedings of the 12th International Global Wordnet Conference*.

Filip Klubička and John Kelleher. 2022. Probing with noise: Unpicking the warp and weft of embeddings. In *Proceedings of the Fifth BlackboxNLP Workshop on Analyzing and Interpreting Neural Networks for NLP*, pages 404–417, Abu Dhabi, United Arab Emirates (Hybrid). Association for Computational Linguistics.

George Lakoff. 1987. *Women, fire, and dangerous things: What Categories Reveal about the Mind*, volume 10. University of Chicago press Chicago.

Quoc Le and Tomas Mikolov. 2014. Distributed representations of sentences and documents. In *International conference on machine learning*, pages 1188–1196. PMLR.

Omer Levy, Steffen Remus, Chris Biemann, and Ido Dagan. 2015. Do supervised distributional methods really learn lexical inference relations? In *Proceedings of the 2015 Conference of the North American Chapter of the Association for Computational Linguistics: Human Language Technologies*, pages 970–976, Denver, Colorado. Association for Computational Linguistics.

Linlin Li and Caroline Sporleder. 2010a. Linguistic cues for distinguishing literal and non-literal usages. In *Proceedings of the 23rd International Conference on Computational Linguistics: Posters*, COLING '10, pages 683–691, Stroudsburg, PA, USA. Association for Computational Linguistics.

Linlin Li and Caroline Sporleder. 2010b. Using Gaussian mixture models to detect figurative language in context. In *Human Language Technologies: The*

2010 Annual Conference of the North American Chapter of the Association for Computational Linguistics, pages 297–300, Los Angeles, California. Association for Computational Linguistics.

Vasudevan Nedumpozhimana and John Kelleher. 2021. Finding BERT's idiomatic key. In *Proceedings of the 17th Workshop on Multiword Expressions (MWE 2021)*, pages 57–62, Online. Association for Computational Linguistics.

Vasudevan Nedumpozhimana, Filip Klubička, and John D. Kelleher. 2022. Shapley idioms: Analysing bert sentence embeddings for general idiom token identification. *Frontiers in Artificial Intelligence*, 5.

Adam Paszke, Sam Gross, Francisco Massa, Adam Lerer, James Bradbury, Gregory Chanan, Trevor Killeen, Zeming Lin, Natalia Gimelshein, Luca Antiga, Alban Desmaison, Andreas Kopf, Edward Yang, Zachary DeVito, Martin Raison, Alykhan Tejani, Sasank Chilamkurthy, Benoit Steiner, Lu Fang, Junjie Bai, and Soumith Chintala. 2019. Pytorch: An imperative style, high-performance deep learning library. In H. Wallach, H. Larochelle, A. Beygelzimer, F. d'Alché-Buc, E. Fox, and R. Garnett, editors, *Advances in Neural Information Processing Systems 32*, pages 8024–8035. Curran Associates, Inc.

F. Pedregosa, G. Varoquaux, A. Gramfort, V. Michel, B. Thirion, O. Grisel, M. Blondel, P. Prettenhofer, R. Weiss, V. Dubourg, J. Vanderplas, A. Passos, D. Cournapeau, M. Brucher, M. Perrot, and E. Duchesnay. 2011. Scikit-learn: Machine learning in Python. *Journal of Machine Learning Research*, 12:2825–2830.

Jing Peng and Anna Feldman. 2017. *Automatic Idiom Recognition with Word Embeddings*, pages 17–29. Springer International Publishing, Cham.

Jing Peng, Anna Feldman, and Ekaterina Vylomova. 2014. Classifying idiomatic and literal expressions using topic models and intensity of emotions. In *Proceedings of the 2014 Conference on Empirical Methods in Natural Language Processing (EMNLP)*, pages 2019–2027, Doha, Qatar. Association for Computational Linguistics.

Jeffrey Pennington, Richard Socher, and Christopher Manning. 2014. Glove: Global vectors for word representation. In *Proceedings of the 2014 conference on empirical methods in natural language processing (EMNLP)*, pages 1532–1543.

Carlos Ramisch, Silvio Ricardo Cordeiro, Agata Savary, Veronika Vincze, Verginica Barbu Mititelu, Archna Bhatia, Maja Buljan, Marie Candito, Polona Gantar, Voula Giouli, Tunga Güngör, Abdelati Hawwari, Uxoa Iñurrieta, Jolanta Kovalevskaitė, Simon Krek, Timm Lichte, Chaya Liebeskind, Johanna Monti, Carla Parra Escartín, Behrang QasemiZadeh, Renata Ramisch, Nathan Schneider, Ivelina Stoyanova, Ashwini Vaidya, and Abigail Walsh. 2018. Edition 1.1 of the PARSEME shared task on automatic identification of verbal multiword expressions. In *Proceedings of the Joint Workshop on Linguistic Annotation, Multiword Expressions and Constructions (LAW-MWE-CxG-2018)*, pages 222–240, Santa Fe, New Mexico, USA. Association for Computational Linguistics.

Nils Reimers and Iryna Gurevych. 2019. Sentence-BERT: Sentence embeddings using Siamese BERT-networks. In *Proceedings of the 2019 Conference on Empirical Methods in Natural Language Processing and the 9th International Joint Conference on Natural Language Processing (EMNLP-IJCNLP)*, pages 3982–3992, Hong Kong, China. Association for Computational Linguistics.

Anna Rogers, Olga Kovaleva, and Anna Rumshisky. 2020. A primer in BERTology: What we know about how BERT works. *Transactions of the Association for Computational Linguistics*, 8:842–866.

Ivan A. Sag, Thimothy Baldwin, Francis Bond, Ann Copestake, and Dan Flickinger. 2002. Multiword Expressions: A Pain in the Neck for NLP. In *Computational Linguistics and Intelligent Text Processing: Third International Conference: CICLing-2002, Lecture Notes in Computer Science*, volume 2276, pages 1–15.

Giancarlo Salton, Robert Ross, and John Kelleher. 2016. Idiom token classification using sentential distributed semantics. In *Proceedings of the 54th Annual Meeting of the Association for Computational Linguistics (Volume 1: Long Papers)*, pages 194–204, Berlin, Germany. Association for Computational Linguistics.

Giancarlo Salton, Robert Ross, and John Kelleher. 2017. Idiom type identification with smoothed lexical features and a maximum margin classifier. In *Proceedings of the International Conference Recent Advances in Natural Language Processing, RANLP 2017*, pages 642–651, Varna, Bulgaria. INCOMA Ltd.

Enrico Santus, Alessandro Lenci, Tin-Shing Chiu, Qin Lu, and Chu-Ren Huang. 2016. Nine features in a random forest to learn taxonomical semantic relations. In *Proceedings of the Tenth International Conference on Language Resources and Evaluation (LREC'16)*, pages 4557–4564, Portorož, Slovenia. European Language Resources Association (ELRA).

Agata Savary, Carlos Ramisch, Silvio Cordeiro, Federico Sangati, Veronika Vincze, Behrang QasemiZadeh, Marie Candito, Fabienne Cap, Voula Giouli, Ivelina Stoyanova, and Antoine Doucet. 2017. The PARSEME shared task on automatic identification of verbal multiword expressions. In *Proceedings of the 13th Workshop on Multiword Expressions (MWE 2017)*, pages 31–47, Valencia, Spain. Association for Computational Linguistics.

Nathan Schneider and Noah A. Smith. 2015. A corpus and model integrating multiword expressions and supersenses. In *Proceedings of the 2015 Conference of the North American Chapter of the Association for Computational Linguistics: Human Language Technologies*, pages 1537–1547, Denver, Colorado. Association for Computational Linguistics.

Lloyd S Shapley. 1953. A value for n-person games. *Contributions to the Theory of Games*, 2(28):307–317.

Xing Shi, Inkit Padhi, and Kevin Knight. 2016. Does string-based neural MT learn source syntax? In *Proceedings of the 2016 Conference on Empirical Methods in Natural Language Processing*, pages 1526–1534, Austin, Texas. Association for Computational Linguistics.

Vered Shwartz and Ido Dagan. 2019. Still a pain in the neck: Evaluating text representations on lexical composition. *Transactions of the Association for Computational Linguistics*, 7:403–419.

Vered Shwartz, Enrico Santus, and Dominik Schlechtweg. 2017. Hypernyms under siege: Linguistically-motivated artillery for hypernymy detection. In *Proceedings of the 15th Conference of the European Chapter of the Association for Computational Linguistics: Volume 1, Long Papers*, pages 65–75, Valencia, Spain. Association for Computational Linguistics.

Caroline Sporleder and Linlin Li. 2009. Unsupervised recognition of literal and non-literal use of idiomatic expressions. In *Proceedings of the 12th Conference of the European Chapter of the Association for Computational Linguistics*, pages 754–762.

Harish Tayyar Madabushi, Edward Gow-Smith, Marcos Garcia, Carolina Scarton, Marco Idiart, and Aline Villavicencio. 2022. SemEval-2022 task 2: Multilingual idiomaticity detection and sentence embedding. In *Proceedings of the 16th International Workshop on Semantic Evaluation (SemEval-2022)*, pages 107–121, Seattle, United States. Association for Computational Linguistics.

Lucas Torroba Hennigen, Adina Williams, and Ryan Cotterell. 2020. Intrinsic probing through dimension selection. In *Proceedings of the 2020 Conference on Empirical Methods in Natural Language Processing (EMNLP)*, pages 197–216, Online. Association for Computational Linguistics.

Sara Veldhoen, Dieuwke Hupkes, and Willem H Zuidema. 2016. Diagnostic classifiers revealing how neural networks process hierarchical structure. In *Workshop on Cognitive Computation: Integrating Neural and Symbolic Approaches (at NIPS)*.

Abigail Walsh, Claire Bonial, Kristina Geeraert, John P. McCrae, Nathan Schneider, and Clarissa Somers. 2018. Constructing an annotated corpus of verbal MWEs for English. In *Proceedings of the Joint Workshop on Linguistic Annotation, Multiword Expressions and Constructions (LAW-MWE-CxG-2018)*, pages 193–200, Santa Fe, New Mexico, USA. Association for Computational Linguistics.

Expression	#samples	#idiomatic	ratio
see star	61	5	0.08
hit wall	63	7	0.11
pull leg	51	11	0.22
hold fire	23	7	0.30
make pile	25	8	0.32
blow whistle	78	27	0.35
make hit	14	5	0.36
get wind	28	13	0.46
lose head	40	21	0.53
make hay	17	9	0.53
make scene	50	30	0.60
hit roof	18	11	0.61
blow trumpet	29	19	0.66
make face	41	27	0.66
pull plug	64	44	0.69
take heart	81	61	0.75
hit road	32	25	0.78
kick heel	39	31	0.79
pull punch	22	18	0.82
pull weight	33	27	0.82
blow top	28	23	0.82
cut figure	43	36	0.84
make mark	85	72	0.85
get sack	50	43	0.86
have word	91	80	0.88
get nod	26	23	0.88
lose thread	20	18	0.90
find foot	53	48	0.91
TOTAL:	1205	749	0.62

Table 7: VNCs ordered by % of idiomatic usage: number of samples (#samples), number of idiomatic uses (#idiomatic) % of idiomatic usage (ratio).

Laura Wendlandt, Jonathan K. Kummerfeld, and Rada Mihalcea. 2018. Factors influencing the surprising instability of word embeddings. In *Proceedings of the 2018 Conference of the North American Chapter of the Association for Computational Linguistics: Human Language Technologies, Volume 1 (Long Papers)*, pages 2092–2102, New Orleans, Louisiana. Association for Computational Linguistics.

Kelly Zhang and Samuel Bowman. 2018. Language modeling teaches you more than translation does: Lessons learned through auxiliary syntactic task analysis. In *Proceedings of the 2018 EMNLP Workshop BlackboxNLP: Analyzing and Interpreting Neural Networks for NLP*, pages 359–361, Brussels, Belgium. Association for Computational Linguistics.

VNC	Train set Total	Idiomatic	VNC	Test set Total	Idiomatic
blow top	28	23			
blow trumpet	29	19			
blow whistle	78	27			
get sack	50	43			
get nod	26	23			
get wind	28	13			
hit road	32	25			
hit roof	18	11	cut figure	43	36
hit wall	63	7	find foot	53	48
lose head	40	21	have word	91	80
lose thread	20	18	hold fire	23	7
make face	41	27	kick heel	39	31
make hay	17	9	see star	61	5
make hit	14	5	take heart	81	61
make mark	85	72			
make pile	25	8			
make scene	50	30			
pull leg	51	11			
pull plug	64	44			
pull punch	22	18			
pull weight	33	27			
Total:	814	481		391	268
Ratio:		0.5909			0.6854

Table 8: A breakdown of VNCs and idiomatic instances in the train and test split.

A Appendix A

A.1 Dataset Statistics

In Table 7 the VNC expressions are listed by increasing order of percentage of idiomatic usage: *see star* is the expression with the lowest percentage of idiomatic usage (8.20%) and *find foot* is the expression with the highest percentage of idiomatic usage (90.57%). The overall percentage of idiomatic instances (regardless of the expression) is 62%.

Table 8 displays the final train and test split we used in our experiments, as well as a breakdown of specific expressions and their labels in both sets, sorted according to the verbal constituent. While this split is not focused on the ratio of training instances, but rather subsets of training instances containing the same VNC, this does mirror the 25%/75% data split employed by (Salton et al., 2016). Though the 68% ratio of idiomatic phrases in the test set is somewhat higher than maintained in previous work (≈62%), we expect the specific choices of VNCs will have a positive effect overall in priming the classifier to use its knowledge of idiomaticity to make predictions.

Graph-based multi-layer querying in Parseme Corpora

Bruno Guillaume
Université de Lorraine, CNRS, Inria, LORIA, F-54000 Nancy, France
Bruno.Guillaume@inria.fr

Abstract

We present a graph-based tool which can be used to explore Verbal Multi-Word Expression (VMWE) annotated in the Parseme project. The tool can be used for linguistic exploration on the data, for helping the manual annotation process and to search for errors or inconsistencies in the annotations.

1 Introduction

The Parseme project (Monti et al., 2018) proposes a large set of annotated data with Verbal Multi-Word Expressions (VMWE). In version 1.2 (Ramisch et al., 2020), 14 languages were covered but with older versions and ongoing work[1], there are now data in 26 languages (See Table 4 in appendix for list of languages and the number of sentences for each language). In the last release, Parseme 1.3, only "verbal" Multi-Word Expressions are annotated; the annotation of other categories is planed for future releases.

Parseme data is published with associated morpho-syntactic annotations, in accordance with the Universal Dependencies (de Marneffe et al., 2021) framework. Some parseme annotations are directly built on data available in the UD project. In this case, we have both high-quality morpho-syntactic annotations and VMWE annotations on the same data. Other parts of the Parseme data, which are not built on existing UD data, are accompanied by an automatic morpho-syntactic annotation, obtained with UDPipe (Straka et al., 2016), thus also following the UD annotation framework. This means that all annotated data from the Parseme project can be considered as multi-layer annotated data, with morphosyntactic annotations encoded following UD and VMWE.

In this article, we propose an encoding of the two annotation layers in a common structure, using a graph encoding of both UD and VMWE annotations. With this encoding, it is possible to use graph-based tools to work with the data. In this work, we use our GREW tool (Guillaume, 2021) to make queries on the two layers.

The Parseme 1.3 data will be released on http://hdl.handle.net/11372/LRT-5124. At the time of the final version of the paper, these data are not available. The experiments reported in the paper are done on a preliminary version of the data provided by the Parseme team. We cannot exclude minor differences between the data we used in our observations and the official 1.3 data.

In Section 2, we explain the encoding. The next sections give examples of usage with general observations in Section 3, applications to error mining in Section 4 and some more comprehensive study of the consistency between UD and Parseme annotation layers in Section 5.

2 Graph encoding

The two annotation layers (UD and VMWE) are stored in a common technical format (CUPT)[2], but it is not straightforward to consider both in the same structure. In UD, each sentence is split in a sequence of tokens and each Parseme annotation consists in identifying a subset of the tokens of the sentence which correspond to a VMWE. In addition to the subset, a tag is given to each VMWE.

The Parseme guidelines[3] describes the set of tags and their definitions. The tagset contains three universal tags: LVC.FULL, LVC.CAUSE for light verb constructions and VID for verbal idioms. Three quasi-universal categories are also defined: VPC.FULL, VPC.SEMI for verb-particle constructions and MVC for multi-verb constructions. A few other tags are used in the corpora: the IAV for inherently adpositional verbs, presented

[1] https://gitlab.com/parseme/corpora

[2] http://multiword.sourceforge.net/cupt-format

[3] https://parsemefr.lis-lab.fr/parseme-st-guidelines/1.3/

Proceedings of the 19th Workshop on Multiword Expressions (MWE 2023), pages 58–64
May 6, 2023 ©2023 Association for Computational Linguistics

as experimental in the Parseme guidelines and the tag LS.ICV for inherently clitic verbs (currently only used in Italian data). Some development versions of the data makes also use of the special tag NOTMWE which, as its name indicates, does not encode a VMWE, it is used in the consistency checking mechanism[4].

There are two difficulties in the encoding.

- A VMWE is not always a span of the original text, or in other words it does not always contains a subset of consecutive tokens of the sentence. For instance, in the sentence *Take a look !!!*[5], the subset containing *Take* and *look* is annotated with the tag LVC.FULL the token *a* between the two elements not being part of the VMWE.

- The second problem is that the same token can be included in more than one VMWEs. In the sentence *[...] to get rid of the moral burden [...]*, two subsets are annotated independently: the 3 elements *get*, *rid* and *of* are tagged as IAV (Inherently adpositional verbs) and the 2 elements *get* and *rid* are tagged as MVC (Multi-verb constructions). Such VMWE annotations will be called *overlapping* VMWEs.

In order to take into account theses difficulties, we propose to encode the two layers in a single graph structure. Our graphs contain two kinds of nodes and two kinds of edges:

- UD nodes and UD edges which encode the lexical tokens and the dependency relations between tokens

- Parseme nodes and Parseme edges which encode VMWEs: each VMWE is represented by a new node with a feature named `label` which stores the tag. The node associated with a VMWE is linked with Parseme edges to all the UD token it contains.

Figure 1 shows a simplified picture of the encoding of the two overlapping VMWEs in the sentence *[...] to get rid of the moral burden [...]*. UD nodes and relations are drawn in black whereas Parseme nodes and edges are drawn in blue and below the sentence.

[4]Script `consistencyCheckWebpage.py` available in `https://gitlab.com/parseme/utilities`

[5]English examples come from the English Parseme corpus: `https://gitlab.com/parseme/parseme_corpus_en`

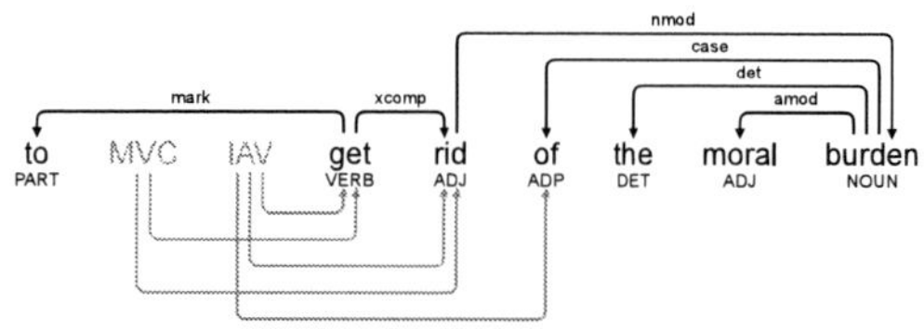

Figure 1: Graph representation (simplified) of two overlapping VMWE annotations

Note that Parseme nodes are not really inserted in the linear structure of the sentence. By convention, these nodes are drawn before the first token of the subset, just to ease the reading of the figures.

3 Multi-layer queries

The benefit of having the two annotation layers in the same structure is that it is possible to make queries which refer to both layers and then to make cross observations. We use the GREW tool which allows to write graph queries that can be executed on the Parseme corpora represented has above. The tool is available in an online web interface: GREW-MATCH[6] on a predefined set of treebanks. A Python library, named GREWPY, is also available to use queries in scripts.

We give a few examples of GREW queries on the Parseme graph encoding.

3.1 VWMEs by types

Using the fact that all Parseme nodes have a feature named `label` (and that UD nodes do not have such a feature), the simple request below returns the set of all annotated VMWEs.

```
1 pattern { MWE [label] }
```

In the request, `MWE` is an node identifier. The query can be rephrased as: "search for any node having a feature named `label` and call this node `MWE`".

GREW proposes a mechanism to cluster the output of a query following some criterion. With the clustering key `MWE.label`, the set of solutions of the previous query is clustered in a partition of subsets according to the value of the feature `label` of the node `MWE`.

In Table 1 in appendix, each line correspond to the size of the clusters obtained for each language in the Parseme data.

[6]`http://parseme.grew.fr`

3.2 VWMEs by sizes

We keep the same basic request used in the previous subsection. In GREW, the clustering key `MWE.__out__` splits the occurrences returned by a request depending on the number of outgoing edges on the node `MWE`. Following the encoding described in Section 2, this corresponds to the number of tokens implied in the VMWE. Table 2 in appendix reports the sizes of the clusters obtained with this clustering for all languages.

According to the notion of Multi-Word Expression, we do not expect to have one-token annotation as VMWE. All languages have a few number of such VMWEs (above 50 occurrences) except for four languages: Hungarian, Chinese, Swedish and German.

In Hungarian data, there are 5745 one-token VMWEs; this is probably linked to the fact that Hungarian is an agglutinative language; among the cases, the same noun with lemma *bekezdés* '*paragraph*' appears 995 times, it is tagged as VPC.FULL and it is built from the verb *bekezd* '*to indent*' and with a noun-forming suffix *-és*[7].

There are 5382 cases in Chinese, but Chinese, not using whitespaces, is well know to be a language in which tokenization is challenging.

In Swedish, there are 1614 occurrences and 1268 occurrences in German. In both languages, the major part of cases are particle verbs. In German, the four most frequent lemmas are: *einsetzen* '*to insert*', *anbieten* '*to offer*', *ankündigen* '*to announce*', *mitteilen* '*to share*'. Unlike English where particles of particle verbs always remain separate words (*put off*, *to put off*), German particles of infinitival forms are fronted and spelled as one word, joining the main verb (*abschrecken* '*to put off*', *abgeschreckt* '*be put off*'). whereas particles of finite verb forms are positioned behind the main verb and spelled as separate words (*schreckt* ab 'put off') just as in English. In Swedish, just as in German, there are many particle verbs that alternate between realizing the particle as a separate word and as a prefix. This shows that the notion of tokenisation is considered quite differently in both projects.

Apart from one-token annotations, the size 2 is the most common setting in all languages. Size 6 and higher are quite rare and the maximum is reached by Hebrew with one VMWE containing 13 tokens.

[7]`https://en.wiktionary.org/wiki/bekezdés`

3.3 Ratio of overlapping VMWEs

With a graph request, we can distinguish VMWE annotations with or without overlapping. The request below corresponds to the "without overlapping" case:

```
1 pattern {
2   MWE1 [label]
3 }
4 without {
5   MWE2 [label];
6   MWE1 -> X; MWE2 -> X
7 }
```

Lines 1-3 is a request for any VWME. Lines 4-7 use the `without` construction of GREW which filters the output of a query: each occurrence of the basic query (line 1-3) which satisfies the constraint expressed in the `without` part is filtered out. In our example, cases where some `MWE2` exists, which shares a token `X` with the one previously found `MWE1` are removed. The result of the full query is then only the non-overlapping VMWEs.

For the "with overlapping" case, the request is the same where the keyword `without` is replaced by the keyword `with` (line 4). Table 3 shows the ratio of overlapping VMWEs for each language.

4 Error mining

One of the common usage of GREW and mainly GREW-MATCH is error mining. By looking at all examples of a given query, we can spot inconsistencies and potential annotation errors. A first example of error mining is to explore the occurrences of one-token VMWEs (see Subsection 3.2) which are unexpected and require manual inspection. Let us see a few other examples.

4.1 VMWEs without any verb

We can test whether each annotation does contain a verb. This is expected as the current version of Parseme focuses on "Verbal" Multi-Word Expressions. The following request searches for Parseme VMWEs without any verb, according to UD annotation (UD uses the two POS tags AUX and VERB for the verbal forms).

```
pattern {
  MWE [label];
}
without {
  MWE -> V;
  V[upos=VERB|AUX]
}
```

Table 4 in appendix gives the numbers of occurrences in each language for this request (column **no_verb**). The median of the number of occurrences in the 26 treebanks is 91.5, with two treebanks above 1000 occurrences. The two exceptions are Hungarian (we have already seen that many nouns are tagged as VMWE because there are built from a verb and a noun-forming affix) and Arabic (where we also observe many cases of noun describing an action, build on a verbal root). This shows that the definition of what is a "verb" in Parseme is not fully aligned with the UD policy.

4.2 Inherently reflexive verbs

Parseme consider the tag IRV for Inherently reflexive verbs. In the meantime in UD, there is the feature `Reflex=Yes` which can be used on reflexive pronouns (but this is not mandatory). We can expect that a VMWE annotated as IRV contains such a reflexive pronoun. The request above allows to search for the exceptions to this rule.

```
pattern {
  MWE [label = "IRV"];
}
without {
  MWE -> P;
  P[upos=PRON, Reflex=Yes]
}
```

Table 4 in appendix gives the numbers of occurrences in each language for this request (column **IRV_no_reflex**). For the three highest numbers are 1144 in Italian, 1021 in Portuguese and 237 in Swedish. This is due to the fact that these three languages does not annotate feature `Reflex` in the UD data. Romanian and French have both annotations IRV in Parseme and `Reflex=Yes` on pronoun in UD, but there are many inconsistencies.

Is is worth noting that Slovenian also appeared in the problematic languages at the submission time. but it was due to a bug in the data which was found thanks to the current work and which was fixed in the mean time.

5 Consistency UD/Parseme

In this section, we give a few examples of requests which can be used in GREW-MATCH to explore how some specific class of VWME is annotated in one treebank.

N1.upos \ N2.upos	217 ADP	199 ADV	3 NOUN	2 VERB
415 VERB	217	198		
6 NOUN		1	3	2

Figure 2: POS of the tokens used in the VPC construction in English

5.1 Verb-particle constructions in English

The example runs on Verb-particle constructions (VPC) and on English data. According to Parseme guidelines, two subtags must be used: VPC.FULL for fully non-compositional VPC and VPC.SEMI for semi-non-compositional.

First, we can have a look at the distribution of this kind of VMWE according to the number of tokens implied[8]. We observed 421 occurrences (368 VPC.FULL and 53 VPC.SEMI)[9] of this label, all of them having exactly two tokens.

Another request[10], specifying the two tokens `N1` and `N2`, can display the distribution of the POS of the tokens in the Figure 2 which shows that two constructions `VERB-ADP` and `VERB-ADV` covers all but 6 cases.

Exploring further[11], we observed in the 217 `VERB-ADP` cases, a large majority (202) of annotation where the `VERB` is linked to the `ADP` with relation `compound:prt`. Other cases are: no direct relation between the two nodes (10 cases), relation `advmod` (3 cases), `compound` (2 cases). Similarly[12], we observed in the 198 `VERB-ADV` cases, a majority (118) of annotation where the `VERB` is linked to the `ADP` with relation `compound:prt`. Other cases are: relation `advmod` (75 cases), no direct relation between the two nodes (2 cases), `compound`, `obl` and `xcomp` (1 case fo each).

These irregularities in the annotation would require a careful inspection by a native English speaker but we can already see a bunch of annotation inconsistencies either in the UD annotation layer or in the Parseme one.

[8] `http://parseme.grew.fr/?custom=63f1ee845234a`

[9] The numbers of this section are based on requests done on 2023/02/19, they may changed when the data is updated. Requests on a stable data from a release will be provided for final version.

[10] `http://parseme.grew.fr/?custom=63f1eeda64fe8`

[11] `http://parseme.grew.fr/?custom=63f1f03dea172`

[12] `http://parseme.grew.fr/?custom=63f1f0d94e4ec`

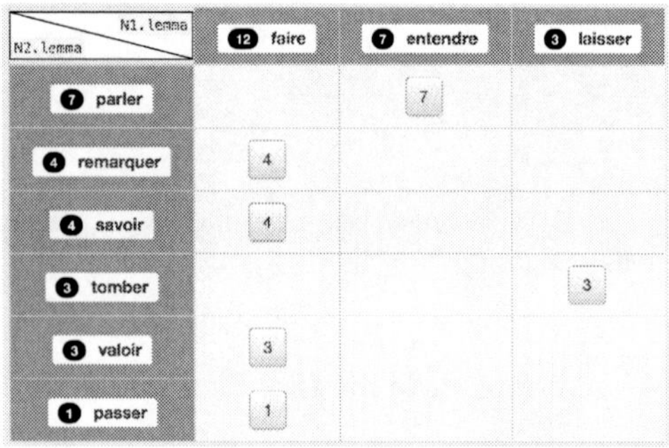

Figure 3: Lemmas used with MVC label in French data. Translations of columns lemmas are '*to do*', '*to hear*' and '*to let*'. Translations of rows lemmas are '*to speak*', '*to remark*', '*to leave*', '*to fall*', '*to be worth*' and '*to pass*'.

5.2 MVC in French

There are 22 occurrences of the MVC in the French data, all having two tokens. All are continuous except one containing a negation *on n'**entendra** plus **parler** de...* '*one will no more hear about...*'. The Figure 3 shows the distribution of lemmas of the two tokens N1 and N2 (following the linear order).

The syntactic annotation is regular with lemma *faire* '*to do*' for N1 as a causative auxiliary of N2 and for the two other lemmas (*entendre* '*to hear*' et *laisser* '*to let*'), an xcomp relation from N1 to N2.

By searching the corresponding lemmas, we found a few annotation errors or annotation inconsistencies.

6 Conclusion

We have shown in this paper that using a graph encoding to represent a multi-layer annotation in a common structure is useful and can be exploited for different purposes, like error mining or linguistic exploration of the data. This methodology opens new perspectives for corpora maintenance and is complementary to existing tools like the UD validation script[13] and the Parseme consistency checking. Using the same idea, it would be possible to encode other annotation layers, like the ones available in a corpus like the GUM corpus[14] (Zeldes, 2017).

[13] https://universaldependencies.org/validation-rules.html

[14] https://gucorpling.org/gum/

Acknowledgments

We would like to thank the reviewers for their helpful comments. Thanks also to Kim, Joakim and Khensa for their help on German, Swedish and Arabic respectively.

References

Marie-Catherine de Marneffe, Christopher D. Manning, Joakim Nivre, and Daniel Zeman. 2021. Universal Dependencies. *Computational Linguistics*, 47(2):255–308.

Bruno Guillaume. 2021. Graph Matching and Graph Rewriting: GREW tools for corpus exploration, maintenance and conversion. In *EACL 2021 - 16th conference of the European Chapter of the Association for Computational Linguistics*, Kiev/Online, Ukraine.

Johanna Monti, Savary Agata, Marie Candito, Verginica Barbu Mititelu, Bejček Eduard, Cap Fabienne, Čéplö Slavomir, Silvio Ricardo Cordeiro, Eryiğit Gülşen, Voula Giouli, Maarten van Gompel, HaCohen-Kerner Yaakov, Kovalevskaitė Jolanta, Krek Simon, Liebeskind Chaya, Carla Parra Escartín, Lonneke van der Plas, Qasemizadeh Behrang, Ramisch Carlos, Federico Sangati, Stoyanova Ivelina, and Vincze Veronika. 2018. Parseme multilingual corpus of verbal multiword expressions.

Carlos Ramisch, Agata Savary, Bruno Guillaume, Jakub Waszczuk, Marie Candito, Ashwini Vaidya, Verginica Barbu Mititelu, Archna Bhatia, Uxoa Iñurrieta, Voula Giouli, Tunga Güngör, Menghan Jiang, Timm Lichte, Chaya Liebeskind, Johanna Monti, Renata Ramisch, Sara Stymne, Abigail Walsh, and Hongzhi Xu. 2020. Edition 1.2 of the PARSEME shared task on semi-supervised identification of verbal multiword expressions. In *Proceedings of the Joint Workshop on Multiword Expressions and Electronic Lexicons*, pages 107–118, online. Association for Computational Linguistics.

Milan Straka, Jan Hajič, and Jana Straková. 2016. UDPipe: Trainable pipeline for processing CoNLL-U files performing tokenization, morphological analysis, POS tagging and parsing. In *Proceedings of the Tenth International Conference on Language Resources and Evaluation (LREC'16)*, pages 4290–4297, Portorož, Slovenia. European Language Resources Association (ELRA).

Amir Zeldes. 2017. The GUM corpus: Creating multilayer resources in the classroom. *Language Resources and Evaluation*, 51(3):581–612.

A Example Appendix

Language	IAV	IRV	LS.ICV	LVC.cause	LVC.full	MVC	VID	VPC.full	VPC.semi
Arabic	581	0	0	303	2678	5	1182	0	0
Basque	0	0	0	214	3152	0	880	0	0
Bulgarian	90	3223	0	222	1909	0	1260	0	0
Croatian	1388	1193	0	147	880	0	293	1	0
Chinese	0	0	0	177	1214	3826	973	0	4629
Czech	0	10000	0	0	2923	0	1613	0	0
English	71	0	0	51	333	51	187	368	53
Farsi	0	1	0	0	3435	0	17	0	0
French	0	1501	0	97	1878	22	2157	0	0
German	0	322	0	33	311	0	1437	1744	194
Greek	0	1	0	179	5293	51	2841	143	0
Hebrew	0	0	0	223	1049	0	1108	153	0
Hindi	0	0	0	26	641	306	61	0	0
Hungarian	0	0	0	401	1143	0	104	5156	956
Irish	187	0	0	118	200	0	106	28	20
Italian	497	1144	37	174	734	33	1484	105	2
Lithuanian	0	0	0	25	479	0	308	0	0
Maltese	0	1	0	1	700	2	518	4	0
Polish	0	3688	0	314	2478	0	833	0	0
Portuguese	0	1021	0	127	3954	18	1306	0	0
Romanian	3340	3826	0	182	516	0	1644	0	0
Serbian	0	564	0	69	402	0	269	0	0
Slovenian	710	1626	0	64	239	0	724	0	0
Spanish	511	714	0	81	392	713	327	1	0
Swedish	0	237	0	10	417	0	441	1461	589
Turkish	0	0	0	0	3583	5	4141	0	0

Table 1: Numbers of occurrences of VMWEs with their labels.

Language	1	2	3	4	5	6	7	8	9	10	11	12	13
Arabic	17	3673	946	91	11	10	0	1	0	0	0	0	0
Basque	0	4164	70	12	0	0	0	0	0	0	0	0	0
Bulgarian	11	5974	604	102	13	0	0	0	0	0	0	0	0
Croatian	0	3182	640	75	3	2	0	0	0	0	0	0	0
Chinese	5382	5224	136	35	15	14	6	5	1	0	1	0	0
Czech	0	11178	2571	664	97	18	8	0	0	0	0	0	0
English	4	1001	73	25	7	3	0	1	0	0	0	0	0
Farsi	1	3004	404	38	4	2	0	0	0	0	0	0	0
French	5	4353	1048	180	34	28	6	1	0	0	0	0	0
German	1268	1976	644	129	15	7	1	0	1	0	0	0	0
Greek	1	6253	1511	523	166	31	9	7	5	1	1	0	0
Hebrew	42	1781	584	87	21	5	8	2	2	0	0	0	1
Hindi	0	961	15	46	9	1	1	0	1	0	0	0	0
Hungarian	5745	2010	5	0	0	0	0	0	0	0	0	0	0
Irish	3	477	152	21	5	1	0	0	0	0	0	0	0
Italian	9	2693	1118	288	64	27	11	0	0	0	0	0	0
Lithuanian	0	683	99	21	7	1	0	1	0	0	0	0	0
Maltese	13	680	391	100	32	3	4	1	1	0	1	0	0
Polish	0	6550	653	88	13	6	0	2	0	0	0	1	0
Portuguese	1	5449	650	263	32	20	6	4	0	1	0	0	0
Romanian	0	8009	1368	74	45	12	0	0	0	0	0	0	0
Serbian	0	1151	128	17	4	3	1	0	0	0	0	0	0
Slovenian	0	2732	531	72	21	4	2	1	0	0	0	0	0
Spanish	2	2089	569	69	10	0	0	0	0	0	0	0	0
Swedish	1614	1336	188	14	3	0	0	0	0	0	0	0	0
Turkish	6	7233	445	41	4	0	0	0	0	0	0	0	0

Table 2: Numbers of tokens of VMWEs.

Language	Yes	No
Bulgarian	0.0%	100.0%
Maltese	0.16%	99.84%
Turkish	0.57%	99.43%
Farsi	0.58%	99.42%
Lithuanian	0.74%	99.26%
Serbian	1.38%	98.62%
Slovenian	1.4%	98.6%
Basque	1.77%	98.23%
Swedish	2.31%	97.69%
Hebrew	2.88%	97.12%
Polish	2.95%	97.05%
French	3.04%	96.96%
Chinese	3.38%	96.62%
Czech	3.78%	96.22%
Portuguese	4.17%	95.83%
Arabic	4.27%	95.73%
English	4.67%	95.33%
Greek	4.82%	95.18%
Irish	4.86%	95.14%
Hungarian	5.54%	94.46%
German	6.9%	93.1%
Italian	12.19%	87.81%
Hindi	12.86%	87.14%
Romanian	18.46%	81.54%
Spanish	22.82%	77.18%
Croatian	28.86%	71.14%

Table 3: Ratio of VMWEs which overlap with another annotation.

Language	# sentences	no_verb	irv_no_reflex
Arabic	7483	1302	0
Basque	11158	4	0
Bulgarian	21599	416	2
Croatian	6133	146	2
Chinese	48929	526	0
Czech	49431	790	0
English	7436	11	0
Farsi	3617	1	1
French	20961	2	107
German	8996	126	3
Greek	26175	26	1
Hebrew	19200	264	0
Hindi	1684	0	0
Hungarian	6159	5901	0
Irish	1705	214	0
Italian	15728	65	1144
Lithuanian	11104	12	0
Maltese	10600	59	1
Polish	23547	836	0
Portuguese	32062	26	1021
Romanian	56664	5	206
Serbian	3586	91	0
Slovenian	27825	0	5
Spanish	5515	23	8
Swedish	6026	92	237
Turkish	22306	330	0

Table 4: Numbers of occurrences of VMWEs without any verbal token (column `no_verb`) and of VMWEs tagged IRV without any reflexive pronoun (column `irv_no_reflex`).

Enriching Multiword Terms in Wiktionary with Pronunciation Information

Lenka Bajčetić
Innovation Center of the School of Electrical Engineering in Belgrade
Bulevar kralja Aleksandra 73
11000 Belgrade, Serbia
lenka.bajcetic@ic.etf.ac.bg.rs

Thierry Declerck
DFKI GmbH, Multilingual Technologies
Saarland Informatics Campus D3 2
Stuhlsatzenhausweg, 3
D-66123 Saarbrücken, Germany
declerck@dfki.de

Gilles Sérasset
Université Grenoble Alpes
CNRS, Grenoble INP*, LIG
38000 Grenoble, France
gilles.serasset@imag.fr

Abstract

We report on work in progress dealing with the automated generation of pronunciation information for English multiword terms (MWTs) in Wiktionary, combining information available for their single components. We describe the issues we were encountering, the building of an evaluation dataset, and our teaming with the DBnary resource maintainer. Our approach shows potential for automatically adding morphosyntactic and semantic information to the components of such MWTs.

1 Introduction

In this paper, we describe our approach to enrich English multiword terms (MWTs) included in Wiktionary by generating pronunciation information using the existing pronunciation(s) of their sub-parts. Results of our work can also be integrated in other lexical resources, like the Open English WordNet (McCrae et al., 2020),[1] where pronunciation information has been added only for single word entries, as described in (Declerck et al., 2020a).

The main focus of our work is on generating pronunciation information for MWTs that contain (at least) one heteronym[2], as for this a specific processing of the Wiktionary data is needed, disambiguating between the different senses of the heteronym for selecting the appropriate pronunciation of this one component to be attached to the overall pronunciation. An example of such a case is given by the Wiktionary entry "acoustic bass", for which our algorithm has to specify that the pronunciation /beɪs/ (and not /bæs/) has to be selected and combined with /əˈkuː.stɪk/. It is important to mention that although Wiktionary often lists several pronunciations for various variants of English, in this work we focus only on the standard, received pronunciation as encoded by the International Phonetic Alphabet (IPA)[3] (more about this in the Limitations Section).

Since we need to semantically disambiguate one or more components of a MWT for generating its pronunciation, our work can lead to the addition of morphosyntactic and semantic information of those components and thus enrich the overall representation of the MWTs entries, a task we have started to work on.

2 Wiktionary

Wiktionary[4] is a freely available web-based multilingual dictionary. Like other Wikimedia[5] supported initiatives, it is a collaborative project. This means that there might be inaccuracies in the resource, but the editing system is helping in mitigating this risk. The fact that Wiktionary is build by a collaborative effort means that the coverage and variety of lexical information is much larger than any single curated resource, while Wiktionary is

[1] See also https://en-word.net/

[2] The online Oxford Dictionary gives this definition: "A heteronym is one of two or more words that have the same spelling but different meanings and pronunciation, for example 'tear' meaning 'rip' and 'tear' meaning 'liquid from the eye'" https://www.oxfordlearnersdictionaries.com/definition/english/heteronym, [accessed 27.03.2023.]

[3] See https://www.internationalphoneticalphabet.org/ipa-sounds/ipa-chart-with-sounds/

[4] https://en.wiktionary.org/

[5] https://www.wikimedia.org/

Proceedings of the 19th Workshop on Multiword Expressions (MWE 2023), pages 65–72
May 6, 2023

integrating information from expert-based dictionary resources, when their licensing conditions allow it. Nastase and Strapparava (2015) discussed already the quality (and quantity) of information included in the English Wiktionary edition, also in comparison with WordNet.[6]

Wiktionary includes, among others, a thesaurus, a rhyme guide, phrase books, language statistics and extensive appendices. Wiktionary's information also (partly) includes etymologies, pronunciations, sample quotations, synonyms, antonyms and translations.[7] Wiktionary has also developed categorization practices which classify an entry along the lines of linguistics (for example "developed terms by language") but also topical information (for example "en:Percoid fish").[8]

It has been shown that the access and use of Wiktionary can be helpful in Natural Language Processing (NLP). Kirov et al. (2016) and McCarthy et al. (2020), for example, describe work to extract and standardize the data in Wiktionary and to make it available for a range of NLP applications, while the authors focus on extracting and normalizing a huge number of inflectional paradigms across a large selection of languages. This effort contributed to the creation of the UniMorph data (http://unimorph.org/). Metheniti and Neumann (2018, 2020) describe a related approach, but making use of a combination of the HTML pages and the underlying XML dump of the English edition of Wiktionary,[9] which is covering also 4,315 other languages, but some of them with a very low number of entries.[10] Segonne et al. (2019) describe the use of Wiktionary data as a resource for word sense disambiguation tasks.

BabelNet[11] is also integrating Wiktionary data,[12] with a focus on sense information, in order to support, among others, word sense disambiguation and tasks dealing with word similarity and sense clustering (Camacho-Collados et al., 2016). The result of our work could be relevant for BabelNet, as the audio files displayed by BabelNet are not based on the reading of pronunciation alphabets but on external text-to-speech systems, which are leading to errors, as can be seen in the case of the heteronym "lead", for which BabelNet offers only one pronunciation.[13]

3 Multiword Terms in Wiktionary

Wiktionary introduces the category "English multiword terms" (MWTs), which is defined as "lemmas that are an idiomatic combination of multiple words,"[14] while Wiktionary has its page "multiword expression", categorized as a MWTs and defined as "lexeme-like unit made up of a sequence of two or more words that has properties that are not predictable from the properties of the individual words or their normal mode of combination".[15] We see these two definitions are interchangeable, since they both focus on the aspect of non-compositionality of a lexeme built from multiple words. We will therefore use in this paper the terms MWE and MWT interchangeably, but stressing that we are dealing with MWEs as they are categorized as MWTs in Wiktionary.

4 Related Work

Wiktionary is often used as a source for various text-to-speech or speech-to-text models, as described in our previous work (Bajčetić and Declerck, 2022). For instance, the work of Schlippe et al. (2010) developed a system which automatically extracts phonetic notations in IPA from Wiktionary to use for automatic speech recognition. A more recent example is the work by Peters et al. (2017) which is aimed at improving grapheme-to-phoneme conversion by utilizing

[6]See (Fellbaum, 1998) and http://wordnetweb.princeton.edu/perl/webwn for the on-line version of Princeton WordNet.

[7]See https://en.wikipedia.org/wiki/Wiktionary for more details.

[8]So that the entry "sea bass" is categorized, among others, both as an instance of "English multiword terms" and of "en:Percoid fish". The categorization system is described at https://en.wiktionary.org/wiki/Wiktionary:Categorization

[9]Wiktionary data dumps are available at https://dumps.wikimedia.org/.

[10]Details on the number of entries in the different languages contained in the English Wiktionary is given here: https://en.wiktionary.org/wiki/Special:Statistics?action=raw.

[11]See (Navigli and Ponzetto, 2010) and https://babelnet.org/.

[12]As far as we are aware of, BabelNet integrates only the English edition of Wiktionary, including all the languages covered by this edition.

[13]See the audio file associated with the two different senses of the entry for "lead": https://babelnet.org/synset?id=bn%3A00006915n&orig=lead&lang=EN and https://babelnet.org/synset?id=bn%3A00050340n&orig=lead&lang=EN.

[14]https://en.wiktionary.org/wiki/Category:English_multiword_terms. This category is an instance of the umbrella category "Multiword terms by language" see https://en.wiktionary.org/wiki/Category:Multiword_terms_by_language.

[15]https://en.wiktionary.org/wiki/multi-word_expression.

Wiktionary. Grapheme-to-phoneme is necessary for text-to-speech and automatic speech recognition systems.

Besides text-to-speech, there are various other applications which rely on extracting pronunciation information from Wiktionary. A recent tool is WikiPron (Lee et al., 2020), which is an open-source command-line tool for extracting pronunciation data from Wiktionary. It stores the extracted word/pronunciation pairs in TSV format.[16] We observe that no Wiktionary multiword terms are included in those lists. Also, no (semantic) disambiguation is provided and, for example, the word "lead" is listed twice, with the different pronunciations, but with no sense information, as WikiPron is providing solely word/pronunciation pairs. Results of our work consisting in generating pronunciation information to multiword terms could thus be included to WikiPron directly or via Wiktionary updates. In the other direction, WikiPron could be re-used for our purposes, as it harmonizes phonemic pronunciation data across various Wiktionary language editions, while the pronunciations are segmented, and stress and syllable boundary markers removed. Especially the latter is relevant for our work, as it will ease future evaluation work (see the issues described in Section 6).

Another related effort, and a very relevant resource for our approach, is DBnary.[17] DBnary extracts different types of information from Wiktionary (covering 23 languages) and represents it in a structured format, which is compliant to the guidelines of the Linguistic Linked Open Data framework.[18] In the DBnary representation of Wiktionary we find lexical entries (including words, MWEs or affixes, but without marking those explicitly, an issue that has been fixed in new release of DBnary, as this is requested for continuing our approach in the context of DBnary), their pronunciation (if available in Wiktionary), their sense(s) (definitions in Wiktionary), example sentences and DBnary glosses, which are offering a kind of "topic" for the (disambiguated) entries, but those glosses are not extracted from the category system of Wiktionary. They are taken from available information used to denote the lexical sense of the source of the translation of an entry from English to other languages.

DBnary does not include categorial information from Wiktionary, and also did not offer support for dealing with MWTs lacking pronunciation information and that contain (at least) one heteronym. Therefore, we still need(ed) to access and consult Wiktionary directly, using methods that are described in Section 5, also for building the Gold Standard for evaluating our work (MWTs in Wiktionary that are carrying pronunciation information). Hence, our results can also be integrated in DBnary, directly or via the updated Wiktionary entries. In fact, our work lead to the adaptation of DBnary, as this is briefly described in Section 5.3

5 Method

We describe in this section the various approaches we implemented and tested, leading finally to a closer cooperation with the maintainer of DBnary, as it became apparent that the release of a new version of this resource is the most efficient way for achieving and widening our goals.

5.1 Data Extraction and an Evaluation Dataset

The current version of the English edition of Wiktionary is listing 157,883 English multiword terms[19], and 75,401 expressions are categorized as "English terms with IPA pronunciation"[20]. This is quite a small number in comparison to the whole English Wiktionary, which has over 8.5 million expressions.

When we are analysing these figures, we need to be aware that they are representing the number of pages categorized as a particular category, and a Wiktionary page can often contain several lexical entries, although this is typically not the case for MWTs. Also, it is important to keep in mind that the English Wiktionary contains a lot of terms which are not English. We can see the exact number of Wiktionary pages classified as English lemmas if we look at the category itself[21]. The actual

[16]As of today, more than 3 million word/pronunciation pairs from more than 165 languages. Corresponding files are available at https://github.com/CUNY-CL/wikipron/tree/master/data.

[17]See (Sérasset and Tchechmedjiev, 2014; Sérasset, 2015) and http://kaiko.getalp.org/about-dbnary/ for the current state of development of DBnary.

[18]See (Declerck et al., 2020b) and http://www.linguistic-lod.org/.

[19]https://en.wiktionary.org/wiki/Category:English_multiword_terms [accessed 27.03.2023.]

[20]https://en.wiktionary.org/wiki/Category:English_terms_with_IPA_pronunciation [accessed 27.03.2023.]

[21]https://en.wiktionary.org/wiki/Category:English_lemmas [accessed 27.03.2023.]

number of 711,641 means that a little over 10% of English lemmas have pronunciation, while approximately 22% of all English lemmas belong in the MWT category. So there is clearly a gap that needs to be filled when it comes to pronunciation information in Wiktionary. While introducing pronunciation for the remaining 90% of lemmas seems like it has to be a manual task (or semi-automatic, using other lexical resources) - we have investigated ways to produce the missing pronunciation for numerous MWTs.

The first approach we have attempted seems to be the most straightforward, but turned out to be inefficient: download and parse the latest Wiktionary XML dump, and check for each page whether it is an English MWT using the Wiktionary API, as the corresponding category information (English multiword terms) is not included in the dump, so that it can not be accessed on the local computer. This would be simple if the size of Wiktionary dump was not so massive: more than 8.5 million entries need to be checked, which means 8.5 million requests sent to Wiktionary API. This approach was quite slow, and we thought there must be a better way for future extraction tasks that have to deal with the Wiktionary category system. Using this approach we have extracted over 98% of MWTs from Wiktionary pages and compiled a list of 153,525 multiword terms without IPA, and a gold standard of 4,979 MWTs with IPA information - we can see that only about 3% of MWTs have pronunciation information in Wiktionary.

The other approach we have followed was using the data that DBnary extracted from Wiktionary, in a structured fashion. Unfortunately, DBnary did not, at that time, encode explicitly Wiktionary MWTs. It encoded all lexical entries included in Wiktionary pages the same way, independently if they were single words, MWEs or affixes. Nevertheless, this approach was much faster, but we could only extract English multiword terms that have a blank space or a hyphen - which is not as precise as using the Wiktionary categories. We could collect 6,767 MWTs equipped with pronunciation information (in contrast to 152,082 MWTs without such information), which, combined with the data extracted with the help of the Wiktionary API, is being used as our Gold Standard for evaluating the generation of pronunciation information for MWTs.

Figure 1: The heteronymous word "bass"

We need to stress, here, that DBnary operates with lexical entries and not just pages, and therefore we had some small differences in the counted set of MWTs with pronunciations.

5.2 Generating Pronunciation Information for MWTs

As a first step, we looked at words which are unambiguous when it comes to their pronunciation. This means that a particular word has one pronunciation, even if the word has several meanings. In this case, we were not concerned with semantic ambiguity, since this is not reflected in the pronunciation, and we can easily create new pronunciation of the MWT using the pronunciations of its components. For example, "river bank" and "bank robber" both have the same sounding word "bank", albeit its meaning is different.

But there are many words that can be included in MWTs which have pronunciation-related ambiguity. As we have previously mentioned, these words are known as heteronyms, and they have different pronunciations connected to their different meanings. Wiktionary lists over 1,000 examples of English heteronyms.[22]

In the case of MWTs that contain heteronyms, it is not straightforward to create their pronunciation by combining pronunciations of their components. Luckily, Wiktionary has other useful features, which we have exploited in this case: "Etymology" and "Derived terms" sections.

Wiktionary organizes its pages in different sections called "Etymology". We can have distinct part-of-speech (PoS) information in one Etymology section, and for each PoS different senses. Pronunciation information is distributed over the distinct Etymology sections. So that the page "bass" has 3 Etymology sections, with a total of 5 word categories. Two distinct pronunciations

[22] Listed here: `https://en.wiktionary.org/wiki/Category:English_heteronyms` [accessed 27.03.2023.]

are listed, whereas one pronunciation is only for the first Etymology section and the second is distributed over the other Etymology sections. We need therefore to identify the right Etymology section for extracting the correct pronunciation for the word "bass" when being a component of a MWT.

The "Derived terms" section(s) are included in the page at the level of the PoS information, and is giving us a decisive hint, as many derived terms are in fact a MWT. The MWT "black bass" is listed as a derived term of the second Etymology category of the entry "bass", and we can thus pick the associated pronunciation information for this component for building the pronunciation information for the whole MWT entry.

Using the "Etymology" and "Derived terms" sections of Wiktionary, we can make sure that we are detecting the correct lexical entry carrying the pronunciation information to produce the pronunciations of all the MWTs that contain it, as a first manual comparison with our evaluation dataset confirms.

In this context, we discovered an even easier approach, which is still to be implemented: if in the list of "Derived terms" we find one MWT with pronunciation information, we can segment this pronunciation information and propagate it to all other MWTs containing the one word of which the MWT is listed as a "Derived term". This approach is currently under evaluation, and seems to be more accurate, as in the "Derived terms" section only one pronunciation type is given, while in the entries of the single words, there are different types of pronunciation information.

To summarize: The access to the "Derived terms", coupled with the "Etymology" classification, is the key that allows us not only to compute the pronunciation information, but also add morphosyntactic and semantic information to the components of a MWT.

5.3 A new Release of DBnary

As we already mentioned, DBnary was not explicitly marking MWEs in its data extracted from Wiktionary. DBnary was also not considering the "Derived terms" sections. The maintainer of DBnary could offer this information in a new update, and therefore we focus in the current and future work on the use of DBnary for achieving our goals.

An additional aspect that motivated our decision is the fact that DBnary is exclusively making use

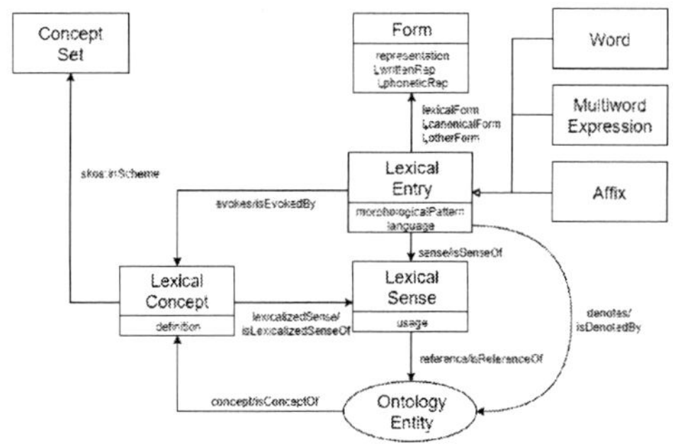

Figure 2: The core module OntoLex-Lemon. Taken from https://www.w3.org/2016/05/ontolex/#core

of accepted specifications and standards for representing its data. Lexical data in DBnary is represented using the Linked Open Data (LOD) principles[23] and as such it is using RDF[24] as its representation model. It is freely available and may be either downloaded or directly queried on the internet. DBnary uses the *ontolex* standard vocabulary (Cimiano et al., 2016),[25] displayed in Figure 2, to represent the lexical entries structures, along with other widely accepted RDF-based vocabularies in the field of language technologies.

As DBnary is making use of the OntoLex-Lemon model, we can take advantage of the existence of the "Decomposition" module of this model.[26] We display in Figure 3 the graphical representation of this module.

We can directly map the data extracted from the "Derived terms" sections in Wiktionary to elements of the Decomposition module of Ontolex, and mark the full lexical description of a single word as a "ontolex:subterm" of a MWE encoded in the Ontolex model.

As a result, the recent adaptations of DBnary allow not only to generate pronunciation informa-

[23] See https://www.w3.org/wiki/LinkedData for more information on those principles

[24] The Resource Description Framework (RDF) model is a graph based model for the representation of data and metadata, using URIs to represent resources (nodes) and properties (edges).

[25] See also the specification document at https://www.w3.org/2016/05/ontolex/.

[26] The specification of OntoLex-Lemon describes "Decomposition" in those terms: "Decomposition is the process of indicating which elements constitute a multiword or compound lexical entry. The simplest way to do this is by means of the subterm property, which indicates that a lexical entry is a part of another entry. This property allows us to specify which lexical entries a certain compound lexical entry is composed of.". Taken from https://www.w3.org/2016/05/ontolex/#decomposition-decomp

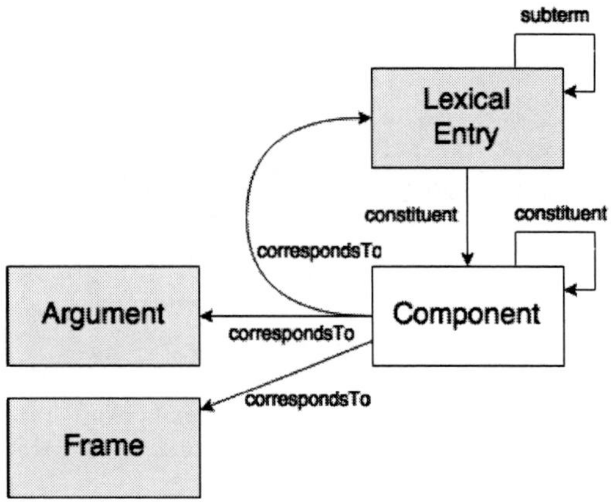

Figure 3: The Decomposition module of OntoLex-Lemon. Taken from https://www.w3.org/2016/05/ontolex/#decomposition-decomp

tion for MWTs contained in the English edition of Wiktionary, but also to add all the lexical information encoded in the lexical description of the components of such MWTs, and to represent this information in such a way that the new data set can be published on the Linguistic Linked Open Data cloud.

6 An initial Evaluation Study

In order to evaluate the newly created pronunciations, we use those MWTs which already carry pronunciation information in Wiktionary. In a first "naive" approach, we just compared the result of combining the extracted pronunciation information from the components of the MWTs with those MWTs which are equipped with pronunciation in Wiktionary. This simple string matching lead to poor results, as it might have been expected. One of the reasons being that in some cases the pronunciation information included in the MWT is containing either space(s), suprasegmental information, or other markers. The combination of pronunciation information extracted from the components do not contain those additional information (at least not in the same way).

Another issue we were confronted with, lies in the fact that in many cases, Wiktionary is listing more than one pronunciation information for a single word. Our algorithm needs to be tuned in order to select only the one pronunciation information that is included in the corresponding MWT.

Some editing of the evaluation set is also needed, towards the creation of an evaluation set that is containing no suprasegmental pronunciation information (and other markers) or spaces. A first analysis of such a cleaned evaluation data set showed already an improved computation of recall and precision. We plan to use for this also the data set generated by the WikiPron initiative (see the description in Section 4.

7 Conclusion and Future Work

We described work in progress consisting in adding automatically generated pronunciation information to MWTs included in the English edition of Wiktionary. The current outputs of our work consist of an evaluation data set for this task, and a set of algorithms for accessing specific information in Wiktionary. We motivated our decision for teaming with the DBnary maintainer, as we can this way widen our goals to the inclusion of morphosyntactic and semantic information to the components of MWTs included in Wiktionary.

Future work includes adding the pronunciations to Wiktionary and enriching other lexical resources, beginning with the Open English WordNet. We will also extend our work to the other language editions of Wiktionary covered by DBnary, at least dealing with the addition of morphosyntactic and semantic information to the components of MSTs, in those languages.

Limitations

While our approach can probably be transferred to other languages, in cases where the Wiktionary structure for those languages is similar, there is one aspect of pronunciation extraction and combination that we have not discussed and this concerns the pronunciation(s) of variants of English, which are included in Wiktionary, like British, General American, Irish, Canadian, Australian and New Zealand English. In our current work we have decided to focus on the non-specific variant, so for now we "overlook" some pronunciation(s) of entries, as we did not want to mix different variants and produce potentially unusable new pronunciations. The standard version is typically considered to be "Received pronunciation", commonly known as "BBC English".[27] However, we would want to include all these variants in our future work. The approach would follow the same

[27] https://en.wiktionary.org/wiki/Received_Pronunciation

principle as explained in the paper, with one extra layer of variant matching.

Another limitation of our work lies in the fact that Wiktionary is ever-changing. So anything done at one point in time needs to be re-done in the future due to changes in the data and also newly added data. The fact that Wiktionary grows quite fast means that the best approach would be incremental or recursive in some way, and automatically check for newly added pronunciations which can create new MWEs pronunciations, while also confirming that the previously created ones have not been altered and need updating. This is a reason why we teamed with the makers of DBnary for this, as DBnary is updated twice a month.

Ethics Statement

We consider our work to have a broad impact because Wiktionary is widely used across the world, and it is free and open-source. Additionally, we plan to include the output of our research into the Open English WordNet and other lexical resources, which are free to use and open-source. We hope that in this way the result of our work can potentially be useful to people all around the world who read or speak English, as well as text-to-speech (and possibly speech-to-text) systems which are gaining popularity and are very important for the visually impaired community, among others.

We do not see any ethical issue related to the generation of additional information to be attached to Wiktionary MWTs and their components.

Acknowledgements

The presented work is pursued in the context of the COST Action NexusLinguarum – European network for Web-centered linguistic data science (CA18209), 731015). The DFKI contribution is also pursued within the LT-BRIDGE project, which has received funding from the European Unions Horizon 2020 Research and Innovation Programme under Grant Agreement No 952194.

References

Lenka Bajčetić and Thierry Declerck. 2022. Using Wiktionary to Create Specialized Lexical Resources and Datasets. In *Proceedings of the Thirteenth Language Resources and Evaluation Conference*, pages 3457–3460, Marseille, France. European Language Resources Association.

José Camacho-Collados, Mohammad Taher Pilehvar, and Roberto Navigli. 2016. Nasari: Integrating explicit knowledge and corpus statistics for a multilingual representation of concepts and entities. *Artif. Intell.*, 240:36–64.

Philipp Cimiano, John McCrae, and Paul Buitelaar. 2016. Lexicon Model for Ontologies: Community Report, 10 May 2016. Technical report, W3C.

Thierry Declerck, Lenka Bajcetic, and Melanie Siegel. 2020a. Adding pronunciation information to wordnets. In *Proceedings of the LREC 2020 Workshop on Multimodal Wordnets (MMW2020)*, pages 39–44, Marseille, France. The European Language Resources Association (ELRA).

Thierry Declerck, John Philip McCrae, Matthias Hartung, Jorge Gracia, Christian Chiarcos, Elena Montiel-Ponsoda, Philipp Cimiano, Artem Revenko, Roser Saurí, Deirdre Lee, Stefania Racioppa, Jamal Abdul Nasir, Matthias Orlikowsk, Marta Lanau-Coronas, Christian Fäth, Mariano Rico, Mohammad Fazleh Elahi, Maria Khvalchik, Meritxell Gonzalez, and Katharine Cooney. 2020b. Recent Developments for the Linguistic Linked Open Data Infrastructure. In *Proceedings of the Twelfth Language Resources and Evaluation Conference*, pages 5660–5667, Marseille, France. European Language Resources Association.

Christiane Fellbaum, editor. 1998. *WordNet: An Electronic Lexical Database*. Language, Speech, and Communication. MIT Press, Cambridge, MA.

Christo Kirov, John Sylak-Glassman, Roger Que, and David Yarowsky. 2016. Very-large scale parsing and normalization of Wiktionary morphological paradigms. In *Proceedings of the Tenth International Conference on Language Resources and Evaluation (LREC'16)*, pages 3121–3126, Portorož, Slovenia. European Language Resources Association (ELRA).

Jackson L. Lee, Lucas F.E. Ashby, M. Elizabeth Garza, Yeonju Lee-Sikka, Sean Miller, Alan Wong, Arya D. McCarthy, and Kyle Gorman. 2020. Massively multilingual pronunciation modeling with WikiPron. In *Proceedings of the 12th Language Resources and Evaluation Conference*, pages 4223–4228, Marseille, France. European Language Resources Association.

Arya D. McCarthy, Christo Kirov, Matteo Grella, Amrit Nidhi, Patrick Xia, Kyle Gorman, Ekaterina Vylomova, Sabrina J. Mielke, Garrett Nicolai, Miikka Silfverberg, Timofey Arkhangelskiy, Nataly Krizhanovsky, Andrew Krizhanovsky, Elena Klyachko, Alexey Sorokin, John Mansfield, Valts Ernštreits, Yuval Pinter, Cassandra L. Jacobs, Ryan Cotterell, Mans Hulden, and David Yarowsky. 2020. UniMorph 3.0: Universal Morphology. In *Proceedings of the Twelfth Language Resources and Evaluation Conference*, pages 3922–3931, Marseille, France. European Language Resources Association.

John Philip McCrae, Alexandre Rademaker, Ewa Rudnicka, and Francis Bond. 2020. English WordNet 2020: Improving and extending a WordNet for English using an open-source methodology. In *Proceedings of the LREC 2020 Workshop on Multimodal Wordnets (MMW2020)*, pages 14–19, Marseille, France. The European Language Resources Association (ELRA).

Eleni Metheniti and Günter Neumann. 2018. Wikinflection: Massive semi-supervised generation of multilingual inflectional corpus from Wiktionary. In *Proceedings of the 17th International Workshop on Treebanks and Linguistic Theories (TLT 2018)*, Linköping Electronic Conference Proceedings. Linköping University Electronic Press, Linköpings universitet.

Eleni Metheniti and Günter Neumann. 2020. Wikinflection corpus: A (better) multilingual, morpheme-annotated inflectional corpus. In *Proceedings of the 12th International Conference on Language Resources and Evaluation (LREC 2020)*. LREC.

Vivi Nastase and Carlo Strapparava. 2015. knoWitiary: A Machine Readable Incarnation of Wiktionary. *Int. J. Comput. Linguistics Appl.*, 6:61–82.

Roberto Navigli and Simone Paolo Ponzetto. 2010. BabelNet: Building a very large multilingual semantic network. In *Proceedings of the 48th Annual Meeting of the Association for Computational Linguistics*, pages 216–225, Uppsala, Sweden. Association for Computational Linguistics.

Ben Peters, Jon Dehdari, and Josef van Genabith. 2017. Massively multilingual neural grapheme-to-phoneme conversion. *CoRR*, abs/1708.01464.

Tim Schlippe, Sebastian Ochs, and Tanja Schultz. 2010. Wiktionary as a source for automatic pronunciation extraction. In *INTERSPEECH 2010, 11th Annual Conference of the International Speech Communication Association, Makuhari, Chiba, Japan, September 26-30, 2010*, pages 2290–2293. ISCA.

Vincent Segonne, Marie Candito, and Benoît Crabbé. 2019. Using Wiktionary as a resource for WSD : the case of French verbs. In *Proceedings of the 13th International Conference on Computational Semantics - Long Papers*, pages 259–270, Gothenburg, Sweden. Association for Computational Linguistics.

Gilles Sérasset. 2015. Dbnary: Wiktionary as a lemon-based multilingual lexical resource in rdf. *Semantic Web*, 6:355–361.

Gilles Sérasset and Andon Tchechmedjiev. 2014. Dbnary : Wiktionary as Linked Data for 12 Language Editions with Enhanced Translation Relations. In *3rd Workshop on Linked Data in Linguistics: Multilingual Knowledge Resources and Natural Language Processing*, Paris, France.

Detecting Idiomatic Multiword Expressions in Clinical Terminology using Definition-Based Representation Learning

François Remy
Ghent University - Imec
francois.remy@ugent.be

Alfiya Khabibullina
University of Malaga
0611289993@uma.es

Thomas Demeester
Ghent University - Imec
thomas.demeester@ugent.be

Abstract

This paper shines a light on the potential of definition-based semantic models for detecting idiomatic and semi-idiomatic multiword expressions (MWEs) in clinical terminology. Our study focuses on biomedical entities defined in the UMLS ontology and aims to help prioritize the translation efforts of these entities. In particular, we develop an effective tool for scoring the idiomaticity of biomedical MWEs based on the degree of similarity between the semantic representations of those MWEs and a weighted average of the representation of their constituents. We achieve this using a biomedical language model trained to produce similar representations for entity names and their definitions, called BioLORD. The importance of this definition-based approach is highlighted by comparing the BioLORD model to two other state-of-the-art biomedical language models based on Transformer: SapBERT and CODER. Our results show that the BioLORD model has a strong ability to identify idiomatic MWEs, not replicated in other models. Our corpus-free idiomaticity estimation helps ontology translators to focus on more challenging MWEs.

1 Introduction

Translation in the biomedical domain remains particularly challenging due to the large number of specific and ad-hoc usage of terminology (Neves et al., 2018, 2022). Some medical ontologies such as UMLS (Bodenreider, 2004) contain more than 4 million entities. Out of these, only a fraction has already been labelled in languages other than English. While large efforts to translate some medical ontologies such as SnomedCT (Schulz and Klein, 2008) can be noted, few if any of these efforts have yet to yield full coverage of the ontology in their target language (Macary, 2020; Auwers, 2020).

Popularity is of course one factor motivating the prioritization of the expert translation of some entity names over others, as translating popular entities makes the ontology usable to a large number of practitioners at a lower cost. But, with the rise of automatic translation tools, another factor worth considering in the prioritization is the translation difficulty of the entities being passed on to medical translation experts. Their efforts should indeed better be directed to cases where automatic translation does not provide good results.

In this context, idiomaticity has a key role to play. Indeed, the automatic translation of idiomatic[1] MWEs poses a significant challenge, as juxtaposing the translation of each individual constituent often results in a loss of meaning that can, in some cases, be catastrophic. This difficulty has been noted by prominent researchers such as Koehn and Knowles (2017) and Evjen (2018). As a result, identifying such idiomatic MWEs would therefore immensely benefit the prioritization of translation efforts of medical ontologies.

While many strategies for identifying MWEs have been presented in the past (Ramisch et al., 2010; Kafando et al., 2021; Zeng and Bhat, 2021), we found that applying them to the medical domain (and especially its clinical counterpart) was challenging due to the extreme corpus size that would be required to produce statistically significant results for the long tail of medical entities.

In this paper, we investigate another approach relying on an ontological representation learning strategy based on definitions, and the empirical properties of semantic latent spaces, described by Nandakumar et al. (2019) and Garcia et al. (2021). In particular, we investigate whether semantic models trained from ontological definitions perform better than other semantic models for the task of identifying idiomatic MWEs without relying on their usage in context, using a novel self-explainability score which will be introduced in Section 2.

[1] MWEs are referred to as idiomatic if their meaning cannot be deduced from the interpretation of their constituents, in line with the definition of "Multiword Terms" presented by Ramisch et al. (2010); examples in the biomedical domain include "Gray Matter" or "Morning Sickness".

Proceedings of the 19th Workshop on Multiword Expressions (MWE 2023), pages 73–80
May 6, 2023 ©2023 Association for Computational Linguistics

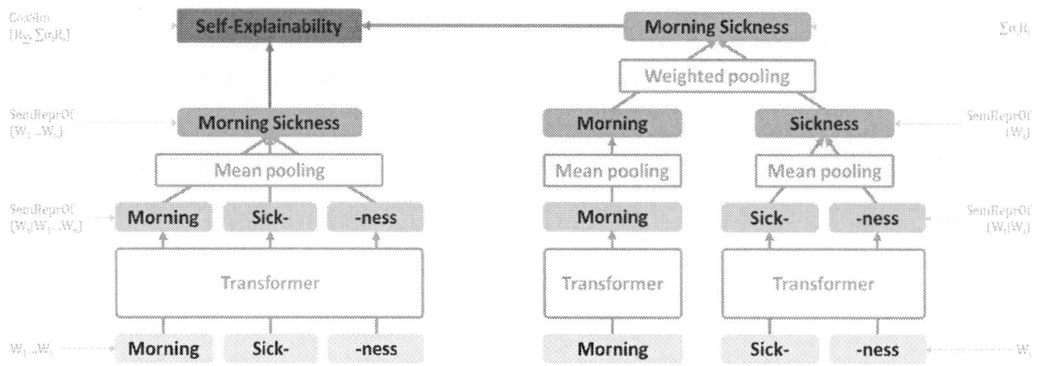

Figure 1: In this paper, we use a cosine similarity metric to compare the representation of a MWE with the weighted average of the representations of its two constituents, after embedding each of these with the same semantic model which is based on a Transformer pipeline. Any difference in representation between these must come from interactions between the constituents within the Transformer when these constituents are combined in the MWE.

2 Methodology

After collecting multiword entity names, a chosen semantic model is used to map the obtained MWEs $(W_1...W_n)$ to their latent representations, either as a whole $(\overline{\mathrm{R}_\Sigma})$ or word-per-word $(\overline{\mathrm{R}_i})$.

$$\begin{aligned}\overline{\mathrm{R}_\Sigma} &:= \mathrm{SemReprOf}(W_1...W_n)\\ \overline{\mathrm{R}_i} &:= \mathrm{SemReprOf}(W_i)\end{aligned}$$

Our semantic model, being based on a Transformer + Mean Pooling pipeline (see Figure 1), produces its representations by averaging the representation of the tokens it is provided as an input (after taking their interactions into account):

$$\overline{\mathrm{R}_\Sigma} = \frac{1}{n}\sum \mathrm{SemReprOf}(W_i|W_1...W_n)$$

To isolate the effect of these interactions, we compute a weighted average of the independent representations of the constituents of the MWE (with weights α_i) as a generalization of the above:

$$\sum \alpha_i \overline{\mathrm{R}_i} = \sum \alpha_i \mathrm{SemReprOf}(W_i)$$

Our novel self-explainability score for MWEs corresponds to the degree of similarity between their latent semantic representation $(\overline{\mathrm{R}_\Sigma})$ and the best[2] weighted average of the independent representations of their constituents $(\sum \alpha_i \overline{\mathrm{R}_i})$.

$$\mathcal{S} := \max_{\alpha_i} \left[\mathrm{CosSim}(\textstyle\sum \alpha_i \overline{\mathrm{R}_i}, \overline{\mathrm{R}_\Sigma})\right]$$

Only strong inter-constituent interactions should be able to explain low self-explainability scores.

[2]We determine the optimal weights α_i in Appendix A.

Based on this insight, we hypothesize that low self-explainability scores identify the MWEs that the semantic model treats as idiomatic. To validate our hypothesis, we will demonstrate that there is indeed a statistically significant difference in self-explainability scores between idiomatic and non-idiomatic MWEs, among a chosen population.

For our analysis, we construct a set of two-words MWEs obtained from UMLS[3], which were then subsequently divided into two groups by our annotators[4]: those which were "perceived as idiomatic or semi-idiomatic" and those which were "perceived as self-explanatory".

We also hypothesize that a definition-based pretraining is essential for this analysis to produce good results. However, as the proposed analysis could be applied to any contextual text representation model, we set out to evaluate the benefits of the definition-based pretraining of the BioLORD model (Remy et al., 2022) by comparing its results with two strong alternatives: SapBERT (Liu et al., 2021) and CODER (Yuan et al., 2022). These two state-of-the-art biomedical language models were also trained using contrastive learning and UMLS, but not using definitions as a semantic anchor.

[3]All two-words entity names from UMLS were included, after filtering out pairs containing words which are either too frequent (>10000 occurences) or too rare (<10 occurences) in the UMLS ontology. This amounts to about 100 thousand two-words MWEs (98.307 to be precise).

[4]The labelling was performed by two annotators: a trained linguist specialized in MWEs who is currently following a course on medical translation, and a NLP practitioner with multiple years of experience in clinical NLP (with an inter-annotator agreement of 82.5% and a kappa score of 0.54).

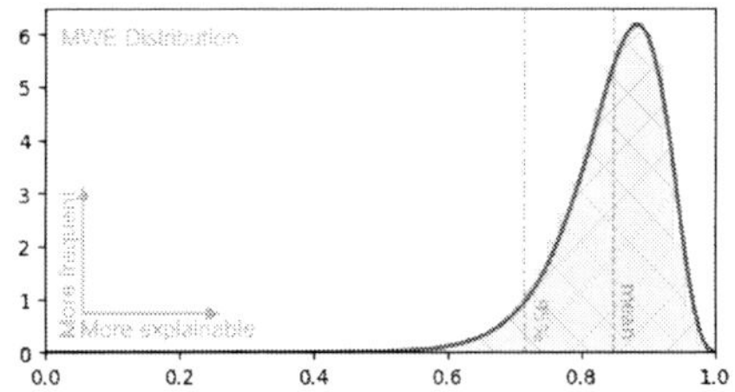

Figure 2: Density of self-explainability scores produced by BioLORD for all the MWEs of our dataset.

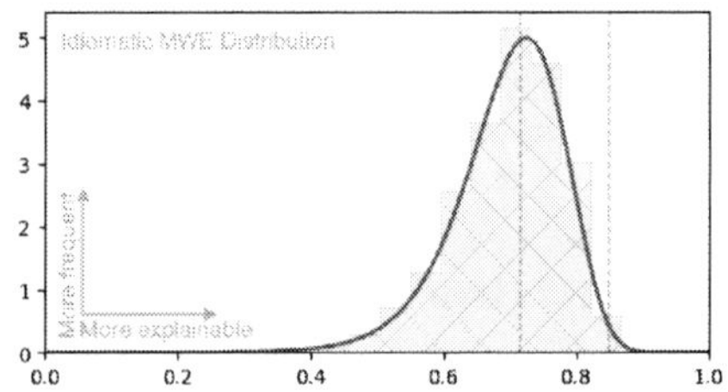

Figure 3: Density of self-explainability scores produced by BioLORD for the idiomatic MWEs of our dataset.

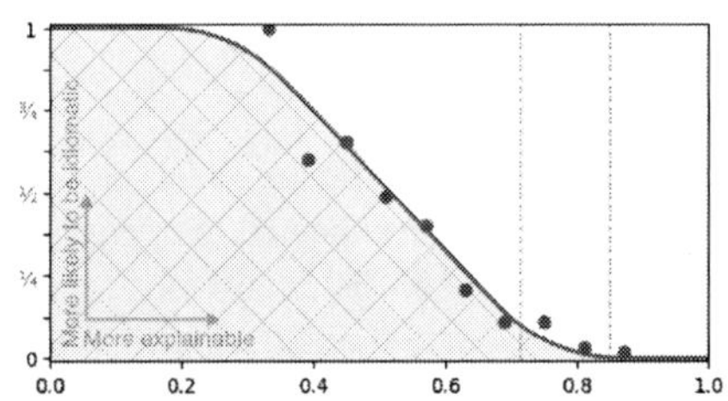

Figure 4: Proportion of MWEs preceived as idiomatic, in function of the self-explainability score produced by BioLORD (bullets represent our annotations).

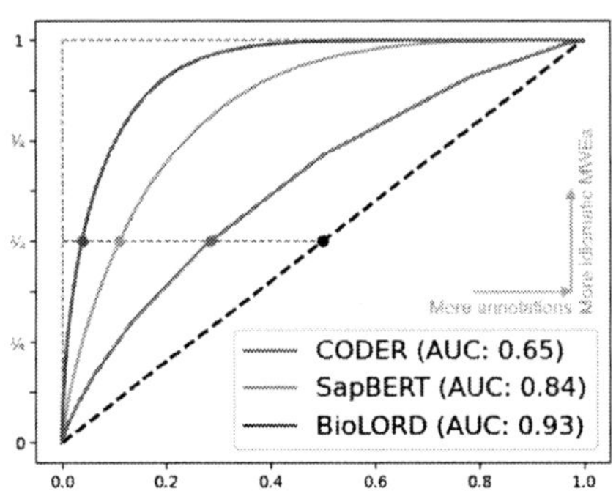

Figure 5: Comparison between the ROC curves of various biomedical models, which shows that BioLORD has a much large area under curve than the other models. The green dot represents the 95th percentile operating point described in the paper; this is the point where about half of the idiomatic MWEs are recalled; achieving the same result with the other models (orange and red dots) or through chance (black dot) requires processing multiple times more MWEs than with BioLORD.

3 Experimental Results

We start our analysis by plotting the empirical distribution of self-explainability scores for all considered UMLS entities. We report this empirical distribution as a histogram in Figure 2.

Interestingly, this distribution is unimodal, which seems to give weight to the hypothesis that MWEs exist on a spectrum of idiomaticity, as described by Cowie (1981), and do not form clearly distinct idiomaticity classes.

Based on our annotations, we evaluate the proportion of idiomatic MWEs present in a subset of 10 bins of self-explainability scores (see Figure 4).

This enables us to estimate the full distribution of idiomatic MWEs by multiplying these ratios with the population counts (see Figure 3).

These two distributions have very different means (0.850 vs 0.697), indicating that our self-explainability score is indeed significantly lower for idiomatic MWEs than for non-idiomatic ones.

We determined based on our annotations that about 2.6% of the MWEs in our dataset appeared idiomatic or semi-idiomatic in nature. To evaluate how effectively our self-explainability score can help identifying idiomatic MWEs, we determined the threshold score enabling a recall of about 50% of idiomatic MWEs in our dataset. This corresponds to about 4000 MWEs featuring a similarity below 0.714, consisting of the outliers at or below the 95% percentile of our self-explainability scores.

To confirm this, we annotated more extensively the MWEs of our dataset falling into these 5 outlier percentiles. We find that about 23% of these MWEs appear idiomatic to our annotators, which is in line with our population-based estimates of 26% (2.6% of idiomatic MWEs * 50% recall = 1.3% of idiomatic MWEs out of these 5% of outliers, yielding an expected precision of 26%).

Of course, a threshold of 0.714 represents only one of the possible operating points of our model. By varying this threshold, we compute the receiver operating characteristic (ROC) of our classifier, and plot it in Figure 5 (green curve). We find that our model shows an area under curve (AUC) of 93%.

Repeating this analysis for other semantic biomedical models demonstrates the importance of BioLORD's definition-based training. Indeed, both SapBERT (orange curve) and CODER (red curve) fail to provide a classifier that is as effective as BioLORD for this task, with AUC scores of 0.84 and 0.65 respectively. See also Figure 6.

To enable a more qualitative appreciation of the results, we also report the MWEs featuring the lowest self-explainability scores, for each of the considered models (see Table 1). Based on this, we note that the outliers of the BioLORD model are not only of higher quality, but also feature a significantly lower self-explainability scores. We interpret this as an indication that, to produce definition-grounded representations for MWEs, the BioLORD model has to devote more of its weights to memorize and specialize idiomatic MWEs than the other models.

We can further this impression by looking at Figure 6. While SapBERT has a distribution of scores similar to BioLORD, the difference between the idiomatic and self-explanatory MWEs is less pronounced, leading to more mixups. Looking further, we also notice that the CODER model seems to feature almost no score variation between MWEs in general, and appears to treat few MWEs as idiomatic (besides a few general-purpose hold-outs from its original pre-training). These findings again comfort the idea that a definition-based pre-training is important to achieve good results.

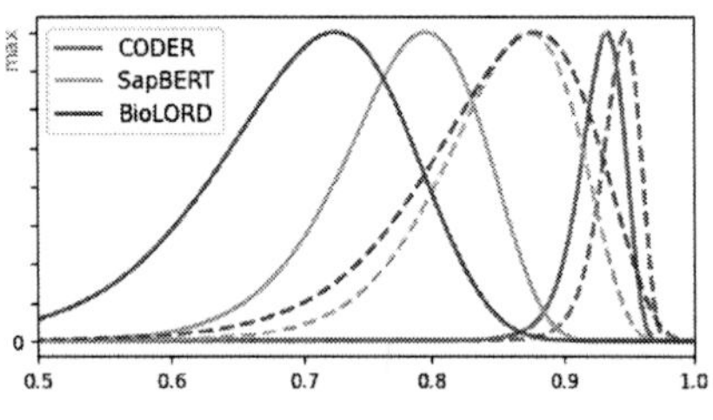

Figure 6: Density of self-explainability scores produced by the compared models for the idiomatic (solid) and self-explainable (dotted) MWEs of our dataset.

Model	MWE	$\mathcal{S}$-score
BioLORD	Gray Matter	0.30
	Neprogenic rest	0.32
	Heyman operation	0.33
SapBERT	Ibuprofen dose	0.49
	Anal Lymphoma	0.53
	Hemoglobin Wood	0.54
CODER	United Kingdom	0.75
	Small Molecule	0.77
	United States	0.78

Table 1: Most extreme self-explainability outliers for the models compared in this study. An extended version of this table can be found in Appendix A.

4 Conclusion

In this paper, we investigated the suitability of definition-based semantic models for detecting idiomatic MWEs in the terminology of a domain. We were able to demonstrate that our proposed self-explainability score can indeed serves as a proxy for idiomaticity, and observed that the BioLORD model indeed displays strong ability to perform this evaluation in the biomedical domain.

The corpus-free idiomaticity estimation thereby developed is powerful enough to help ontology translators to focus on more challenging MWEs, with about half of the idiomatic MWEs contained in the 5% of self-explainability score outliers.

Finally, we were also able to show that biomedical models which were not trained using a definition-based strategy perform significantly worse than our chosen definition-based model, showing the importance of a definition-based pre-training strategy in the development of reliable semantic representations for idiomatic MWEs.

Limitations

It is worth noting that the approach described in this paper can only be expected to operate reliably on entities which can be accurately represented in the latent space by the chosen semantic model (either through its exposure to textual definitions or ontological relationships about the entity during pre-training, or through its generalization abilities).

Unlike past approaches for detecting idiomatic MWEs, our strategy cannot make use of context to recognize idiomatic MWEs from their usage in a corpus. It would be an interesting future work to investigate how to combine examples of uses and ontological knowledge to develop a better in-context idiomaticity evaluation for MWEs.

An additional limitation of our work, is that we limited our analysis to UMLS entities consisting of exactly two words. This is not a limitation of our proposed approach per se, but we acknowledge that further work should probably be carried out to investigate how to best handle longer sequences.

Ethics Statement

The authors of this paper do not report any particular ethical concern regarding its content.

References

Tom Auwers. 2020. Snomed ct translated into dutch and french by belgian national release centre.

Olivier Bodenreider. 2004. The unified medical language system (UMLS): integrating biomedical terminology. *Nucleic Acids Res*, 32(Database issue):D267–70.

A. P. Cowie. 1981. The Treatment of Collocations and Idioms in Learners' Dictionaries. *Applied Linguistics*, II(3):223–235.

John Mervyn Evjen. 2018. Highlighting difficulties in idiomatic translation. *Spectrum*, 2.

Marcos Garcia, Tiago Kramer Vieira, Carolina Scarton, Marco Idiart, and Aline Villavicencio. 2021. Probing for idiomaticity in vector space models. In *Proceedings of the 16th Conference of the European Chapter of the Association for Computational Linguistics: Main Volume*, pages 3551–3564, Online. Association for Computational Linguistics.

Rodrique Kafando, Rémy Decoupes, Sarah Valentin, Lucile Sautot, Maguelonne Teisseire, and Mathieu Roche. 2021. ITEXT-BIO: Intelligent term EXTraction for BIOmedical analysis. *Health Inf. Sci. Syst.*, 9(1):29.

Philipp Koehn and Rebecca Knowles. 2017. Six challenges for neural machine translation. In *Proceedings of the First Workshop on Neural Machine Translation*, pages 28–39, Vancouver. Association for Computational Linguistics.

Fangyu Liu, Ehsan Shareghi, Zaiqiao Meng, Marco Basaldella, and Nigel Collier. 2021. Self-alignment pretraining for biomedical entity representations. In *Proceedings of the 2021 Conference of the North American Chapter of the Association for Computational Linguistics: Human Language Technologies*, pages 4228–4238, Online. Association for Computational Linguistics.

Francois Macary. 2020. An exemplar of collaboration: The first release of the snomed ct common french translation.

Navnita Nandakumar, Timothy Baldwin, and Bahar Salehi. 2019. How well do embedding models capture non-compositionality? a view from multiword expressions. In *Proceedings of the 3rd Workshop on Evaluating Vector Space Representations for NLP*, pages 27–34, Minneapolis, USA. Association for Computational Linguistics.

Mariana Neves, Antonio Jimeno Yepes, Aurélie Névéol, Cristian Grozea, Amy Siu, Madeleine Kittner, and Karin Verspoor. 2018. Findings of the WMT 2018 biomedical translation shared task: Evaluation on Medline test sets. In *Proceedings of the Third Conference on Machine Translation: Shared Task Papers*, pages 324–339, Belgium, Brussels. Association for Computational Linguistics.

Mariana Neves, Antonio Jimeno Yepes, Amy Siu, Roland Roller, Philippe Thomas, Maika Vicente Navarro, Lana Yeganova, Dina Wiemann, Giorgio Maria Di Nunzio, Federica Vezzani, Christel Gerardin, Rachel Bawden, Darryl Johan Estrada, Salvador Lima-lopez, Eulalia Farre-maduel, Martin Krallinger, Cristian Grozea, and Aurelie Neveol. 2022. Findings of the WMT 2022 biomedical translation shared task: Monolingual clinical case reports. In *Proceedings of the Seventh Conference on Machine Translation (WMT)*, pages 694–723, Abu Dhabi, United Arab Emirates (Hybrid). Association for Computational Linguistics.

Carlos Ramisch, Aline Villavicencio, and Christian Boitet. 2010. mwetoolkit: a framework for multiword expression identification. In *Proceedings of the Seventh International Conference on Language Resources and Evaluation (LREC'10)*, Valletta, Malta. European Language Resources Association (ELRA).

François Remy, Kris Demuynck, and Thomas Demeester. 2022. BioLORD: Learning ontological representations from definitions for biomedical concepts and their textual descriptions. In *Findings of the Association for Computational Linguistics: EMNLP 2022*, pages 1454–1465, Abu Dhabi, United Arab Emirates. Association for Computational Linguistics.

Stefan Schulz and Gunnar O. Klein. 2008. Snomed ct – advances in concept mapping, retrieval, and ontological foundations. selected contributions to the semantic mining conference on snomed ct (smcs 2006). *BMC Medical Informatics and Decision Making*, 8(1):S1.

Zheng Yuan, Zhengyun Zhao, Haixia Sun, Jiao Li, Fei Wang, and Sheng Yu. 2022. Coder: Knowledge-infused cross-lingual medical term embedding for term normalization. *Journal of Biomedical Informatics*, 126:103983.

Ziheng Zeng and Suma Bhat. 2021. Idiomatic expression identification using semantic compatibility. *Transactions of the Association for Computational Linguistics*, 9:1546–1562.

A An analytical solution for the optimal vector averaging problem

In this appendix, we derive the analytical solution for the problem of finding the optimal weighted average (of the representation of the constituents of a MWE) given the task of maximizing the cosine similarity between their weighted average and the representation of the MWE itself.

Let $\overline{R_1}$ and $\overline{R_2}$ be two vectors (the representation of the words W_1 and W_2 through the BioLORD model). Let $\overline{R_\Sigma}$ be a vector (the representation of the MWE through the BioLORD model).

... see Figure A.1 ...

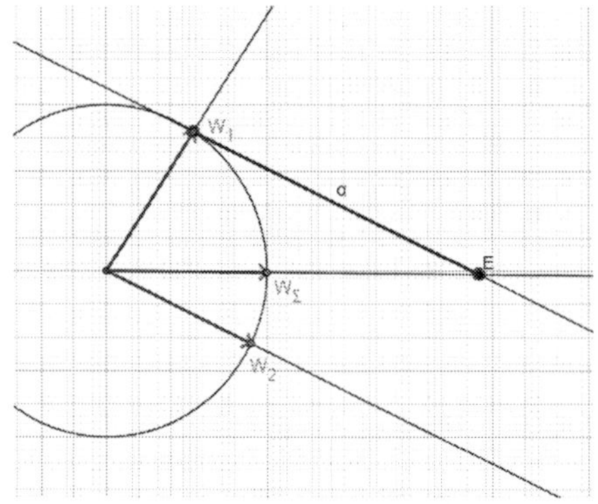

Figure A.1: Representation of the problem

Our objective is to maximize the cosine similarity between $\overline{R_\Sigma}$ and a weighted average of the vectors $\overline{R_i}$ (with weights α_i). Because the cosine similarity between two vectors does not depend on their respective lengths, we can without loss of generality try to maximize the following expression for the mixing parameter $\alpha = \alpha_2/\alpha_1$.

$$CosSim(\overline{R_1} + \alpha\overline{R_2}, \overline{R_\Sigma}) := \frac{(\overline{R_1} + \alpha\overline{R_2}) \cdot (\overline{R_\Sigma})}{|\overline{R_1} + \alpha\overline{R_2}|.|\overline{R_\Sigma}|}$$

Because the maximum cosine similarity will necessarily be positive, we can look for the maximum of its square instead. We will find our optimum by looking at the points where the derivative is equal to 0:

$$\frac{d}{d\alpha}\left[CosSim^2(\overline{R_1} + \alpha\overline{R_2}, \overline{R_\Sigma})\right] = 0$$

... recalling $\frac{d}{dx}\left[\frac{f}{g}\right] = \left[g\frac{df}{dx} - f\frac{dg}{dx}\right]/\left[g^2\right]$ ...

$$(\overline{R_1} + \alpha\overline{R_2})^2\frac{d}{d\alpha}\left[((\overline{R_1} + \alpha\overline{R_2}) \cdot (\overline{R_\Sigma}))^2\right]$$
$$= ((\overline{R_1} + \alpha\overline{R_2}) \cdot (\overline{R_\Sigma}))^2\frac{d}{d\alpha}\left[(\overline{R_1} + \alpha\overline{R_2})^2\right]$$

... computing the inner derivatives ...

$$(\overline{R_1} + \alpha\overline{R_2})^2(2((\overline{R_1} + \alpha\overline{R_2}) \cdot (\overline{R_\Sigma}))(\overline{R_2} \cdot \overline{R_\Sigma}))$$
$$= ((\overline{R_1} + \alpha\overline{R_2}) \cdot (\overline{R_\Sigma}))^2(2(\overline{R_1} + \alpha\overline{R_2})(\overline{R_2}))$$

... dividing both sides by 2 and $(\overline{R_1} + \alpha\overline{R_2})(\overline{R_\Sigma})$ ...

$$(\overline{R_1} + \alpha\overline{R_2})^2(\overline{R_2} \cdot \overline{R_\Sigma})$$
$$= ((\overline{R_1} + \alpha\overline{R_2}) \cdot (\overline{R_\Sigma}))((\overline{R_1} + \alpha\overline{R_2}) \cdot (\overline{R_2}))$$

Let's introduce a more convenient notation for the scalar products ($R_{xy} = \overline{R_x} \cdot \overline{R_y}$). Given we are trying to find scaling coefficients for $\overline{R_i}$ vectors, we can first normalize them to make their norm is equal to one, without loss of generality, such that $R_{11} = R_{22} = R_{\Sigma\Sigma} = 1$.

... expanding the products ...

$$(R_{11} + 2\alpha R_{12} + \alpha^2 R_{22})(R_{2\Sigma})$$
$$= (R_{1\Sigma}R_{12} + \alpha R_{2\Sigma}R_{12} + \alpha R_{1\Sigma}R_{22} + \alpha^2 R_{2\Sigma}R_{22})$$

... isolating α on the left side ...

$$\alpha(R_{12}R_{2\Sigma} - R_{1\Sigma}R_{22}) = (R_{1\Sigma}R_{12} - R_{11}R_{2\Sigma})$$

... giving us the formula of α ...

$$\alpha = \frac{R_{1\Sigma}R_{12} - R_{2\Sigma}R_{11}}{R_{2\Sigma}R_{12} - R_{1\Sigma}R_{22}} = \frac{R_{1\Sigma}R_{12} - R_{2\Sigma}}{R_{2\Sigma}R_{12} - R_{1\Sigma}}$$

... giving us the formula of $\alpha_i > 0$ ...

$$\alpha_1 = R_{1\Sigma} - R_{12}R_{2\Sigma}$$
$$\alpha_2 = R_{2\Sigma} - R_{21}R_{1\Sigma}$$

Intuition: If we assume that the constituents of the entity have orthogonal meanings ($\overline{R_1} \cdot \overline{R_2} = 0$), this gives $\alpha_1 = R_{1\Sigma}$ and $\alpha_2 = R_{2\Sigma}$ which are the cosine similarities of each constituent with respect to the entire MWE.

B Examples of similarity outliers for the considered models

Word1	Word2	Score
Gray	Matter	0.303302
Nephrogenic	rest	0.317366
Heyman	operation	0.328952
Chemical	procedure	0.331814
Morning	sickness	0.359685
Morning	Sickness	0.359685
Green	Card	0.364002
Yellow	Fever	0.365865
Nitrogen	retention	0.372655
molecular	function	0.374572
osseous	survey	0.384946
Refsum	Disease	0.38831
Monteggia's	Fracture	0.392137
Silver	operation	0.393802
Worth	disease	0.395263
Diseases	Component	0.398678
Root	stunting	0.402461
McBride	operation	0.403504
Air	hunger	0.405719
Storage	disease	0.414184
Border	Disease	0.415117
Intersection	syndrome	0.417804
Retinal	correspondence	0.420826
Patch	Testing	0.423289
Dot	haemorrhages	0.423748
Coordination	Complexes	0.4248
White	matter	0.426788
Molar	concentration	0.432153
Book	Syndrome	0.432465
Circulatory	depression	0.4349
German	Syndrome	0.436444
Nissen	Operation	0.438874
Physical	shape	0.440117
External	features	0.442601
Anoxic	neuropathy	0.443183
Compartment	syndromes	0.445978
Visceral	Myopathy	0.447205
Tumour	haemorrhage	0.447391
Mountain	Sickness	0.44767
Growth	Factor	0.451592

Table B.1: Self-explainability outliers for BioLORD

Word1	Word2	Score
ibuprofen	dose	0.488790
Anal	Lymphoma	0.531192
Hemoglobin	Wood	0.542635
Ovarian	injury	0.548922
Ovarian	perforation	0.557121
Ibuprofen	overdose	0.569412
hemoglobin	Aurora	0.575010
miconazole	injection	0.575241
diphenhydramine	Cartridge	0.580044
phenylephrine	Injection	0.584401
Hemoglobin	Mexico	0.585959
Dexamethasone	Powder	0.589987
Hydrocortisone	phosphate	0.592702
Guaifenesin	poisoning	0.592808
hydrocortisone	receptor	0.594878
Vaginal	adenocarcinoma	0.595991
iv	lidocaine	0.598489
Gonadal	Thrombosis	0.598919
Rectal	artery	0.603538
hemoglobin	Cook	0.606404
Ibuprofen	Powder	0.606984
hemoglobin	Thailand	0.608336
Ovarian	vessels	0.609299
Intestinal	hematoma	0.610457
diphenhydramine	Injection	0.611432
hemoglobin	Chicago	0.611646
Ornithine	Ql	0.612263
Aspirin	dose	0.613269
Hydrocortisone	Injection	0.613701
Ovarian	hematoma	0.613911
hemoglobin	Oita	0.614288
Wrist	injection	0.614621
Hemoglobin	Ohio	0.614865
Aspirin	overdose	0.615012
Oral	hemangioma	0.615188
Hemoglobin	Shanghai	0.618727
Sodium	retention	0.619068
Diphenhydramine	overdose	0.619255
hemoglobin	Bristol	0.619368
Gonadal	artery	0.620956

Table B.2: Self-explainability outliers for SapBERT

Word1	Word2	Score
United	Kingdom	0.754104
Small	Molecule	0.772967
United	States	0.775555
Dependent	Variable	0.796870
patch	clamp	0.799848
Index	finger	0.809509
Eggshell	nail	0.810650
single	molecule	0.812445
Data	Administration	0.818826
Alkaline	Phosphatase	0.818921
Brush	Border	0.820135
Czech	Republic	0.821894
CrAsH	compound	0.822972
Nuclear	medicine	0.823420
Nuclear	Medicine	0.823420
Hydrogen	Bonds	0.823888
Replication	Origin	0.825065
Wild	Type	0.825602
Antigen	Presentation	0.826336
outer	membrane	0.827730
Inclusion	Bodies	0.829212
Health	administration	0.829440
Active	Site	0.829467
Focus	Groups	0.830125
Natural	killer	0.830615
Click	Chemistry	0.831714
Strand	breaks	0.832437
proc	gene	0.832669
Lewis	antigen	0.833199
lucifer	yellow	0.833356
Mass	Spectrometry	0.833356
Foreign	Bodies	0.833412
Foreign	body	0.833504
Uvea	language	0.836055
Williams	Syndrome	0.836802
pyridoxine	clofibrate	0.837463
Precision	Medicine	0.838389
Antigen	Switching	0.838619
Public	Domain	0.838712
Data	Acquisition	0.838931

Table B.3: Self-explainability outliers for CODER

Acknowledgements

This work would not have been possible without the joint financial support of the Vlaams Agentschap Innoveren & Ondernemen (VLAIO) and the RADar innovation center of the AZ Delta hospital group.

We also want to thank the SIGLEX-MWE 2023 (19th Workshop on Multiword Expressions) and the ClinicalNLP 2023 Workshop for organizing the joint session to which this paper was submitted, which enabled the blooming of this collaboration between machine learning engineers and linguists thanks to its existence.

Automatic Generation of Vocabulary Lists with Multiword Expressions

John S. Y. Lee and **Adilet Uvaliyev**
Department of Linguistics and Translation
City University of Hong Kong
jsylee@cityu.edu.hk, uvaliyevadilet@gmail.com

Abstract

The importance of multiword expressions (MWEs) for language learning is well established. While MWE research has been evaluated on various downstream tasks such as syntactic parsing and machine translation, its applications in computer-assisted language learning has been less explored. This paper investigates the selection of MWEs for graded vocabulary lists. Widely used by language teachers and students, these lists recommend a language acquisition sequence to optimize learning efficiency. We automatically generate these lists using difficulty-graded corpora and MWEs extracted based on semantic compositionality. We evaluate these lists on their ability to facilitate text comprehension for learners. Experimental results show that our proposed method generates higher-quality lists than baselines using collocation measures.

1 Introduction

Effective processing of multiword expressions (MWEs) is critical for many natural language processing (NLP) applications. In addition to intrinsic evaluation on the quality of extracted MWEs, researchers have conducted extrinsic evaluation to measure their impact on syntactic parsing, machine translation and other tasks (Constant et al., 2017). However, MWE extraction methods have not yet been evaluated in generating vocabulary lists, even though the importance of MWEs, which may require idiosyncratic interpretations, is well established for language learning (Bahns and Eldaw, 1993; Paquot and Granger, 2016).

Graded vocabulary lists recommend a language acquisition sequence for language learners and teachers, in order to optimize learning efficiency of the target language. These lists help prioritize words and expressions that are more likely to be encountered by learners, so that they can understand more texts within a shorter period of study. According to Sag et al (2002), the number of MWEs in a speaker's lexicon has been estimated to be of the same order of magnitude as the number of single words (Jackendoff, 1997). It is no surprise, then, that a significant number of MWEs are included in prominent vocabulary lists such as English Vocabulary Profile (EVP)[1] and the Pearson Global Scale of English (GSE).[2]

We investigate the selection of MWEs for graded vocabulary lists, assuming only a graded corpus for n-gram statistics and large general corpora for MWE extraction. To the best of our knowledge, this is the first evaluation on corpus-based methods for generating vocabulary lists with MWEs. The rest of the paper is organized as follows. After reviewing previous research (Section 2), we present our datasets (Section 3) and evaluation metrics (Section 4). We then describe our approach (Section 5) and report experimental results (Section 6).[3]

2 Previous work

The research most closely related with ours is EFLLex, a vocabulary list for learners of English as a foreign language (Durlich and François, 2018). It contains both single words and MWEs, including compounds and phrasal verbs. A rule-based method identifies the MWEs by considering the dependency labels and verb particles in parse trees of sentences in a large collection of English corpora, followed by manual checking. While CEFRLex resources have been found to be effective in predicting the CEFR levels of the EFLLex entries (Graën et al., 2020), MWEs have not been evaluated. Several other popular vocabulary lists, such as the New General Service List[4] and the Oxford lists[5], do not feature MWEs and therefore are not comparable

[1] https://www.englishprofile.org/wordlists/evp
[2] https://www.english.com/gse/teacher-toolkit/user/lo
[3] Data available at https://github.com/Adilet33709
[4] http://www.newgeneralservicelist.org/
[5] https://www.oxfordlearnersdictionaries.com

Proceedings of the 19th Workshop on Multiword Expressions (MWE 2023), pages 81–86
May 6, 2023 ©2023 Association for Computational Linguistics

List	# single words	# bigram MWEs	# trigram MWEs
EVP	6,749	993	839
GSE	18,391	2,821	1085
EFLLex	10,019	3,745	106

Table 1: Number of single words and MWEs in the graded vocabulary lists in our experiments

with ours.

In addition to EFLLex, we also evaluate a recently proposed MWE extraction method based on unsupervised measurement of semantic compositionality (Pickard, 2020). This method first identifies bigrams and trigrams as MWE candidates using the Poisson collocation measure (Quasthoff and Wolff, 2002). It then ranks these candidates according to the average cosine similarity between the word vector of the MWE candidate and the word vector of each of its constituent words. Experimental results show that the use of `word2vec` embeddings can achieve substantial correlation with human judgment.

3 Data

3.1 Graded corpora

Training set OneStopEnglish (Vajjala and Lučić, 2018) consists of 189 aligned texts, each written at three difficulty levels.[6] WeeBit (Vajjala and Meurers, 2012) consists of 3,125 documents from WeeklyReader and BBC-Bitesize, each labeled at one of five age groups, with 625 documents per group.

Test set The Cambridge corpus (Xia et al., 2016) contains articles for various Cambridge English Exams, labeled at five CEFR levels, A2, B1, B2, C1, and C2.

3.2 Human benchmarks

As human benchmarks, we used two large-scale graded vocabulary lists (Table 1):

English Vocabulary Profile (EVP) EVP is an online vocabulary resource with containing words, phrases, phrasal verbs and idioms (Capel, 2015), all labeled according to the Common European Framework of Reference (CEFR, 2001).[7]

Pearson Global Scale of English (GSE) The GSE Teacher Toolkit is an online database containing English vocabulary items labeled on a proficiency scale from 10 to 90, and also aligned to the CEFR scale based on psychometric research (De Jong et al., 2016).

4 Evaluation methodology

Our evaluation focuses on MWEs up to trigrams only, since longer ones are not available in the dataset from Pickard (2020). Let $S = \{S_1, \ldots, S_k\}$ represent a graded vocabulary list with k grades, where S_i is the set of n-grams ($n \leq 3$) that are recommended for learners at Grade i. All n-grams are in lemma form.

The benchmark vocabulary lists adopt different numbers of grades and lemmas. We transform each list into a single ranked list (Section 4.1) to facilitate a fair evaluation (Section 4.2).

4.1 Transformation to ranked list

To transform a graded vocabulary list into one ranked list, we first rank the n-grams within each set S_i. Let L_i represent the ranked list derived from the set S_i by decreasing order of the n-gram frequency in the test set (Section 3.1). The final list L is then constructed by concatenating L_1, ..., L_n. In other words, *within each grade*, the more frequent n-grams are ranked higher towards the top.

4.2 Evaluation metrics

Suppose user u learns one lemma at a time, following the order prescribed by $L = [w_1, ..., w_l]$. Let u_i represent the user at time unit i, i.e., when s/he has learned all n-grams $w_1, ..., w_i$.

We define a text to be "understood" by user u_i if the percentage of known words exceeds 90%, using the minimum threshold suggested in second language acquisition literature (Laufer, 1989).[8] When a test passage contains a gold MWE (Section 4.3) that has not yet been learned, the MWE is considered unknown even if its constituent words has been learned separately. We evaluate the quality of L in two metrics:

Study Time We define "graduate from grade N" to mean the user understands at least m% of

[6]https://github.com/nishkalavallabhi/

[7]https://www.englishprofile.org/wordlists/evp

[8]The calculation of the percentage of known words in a text excluded tokens tagged as NUM, PROPN, PUNCT, SPACE, SYM, or X by SpaCy (Honnibal and Johnson, 2015); and those consisting of digits and punctuation only. American and British spelling were both accepted.

Gold MWE	# MWEs
In EVP only	1,127
In GSE only	3,386
In both EVP and GSE	697
Added from MWE datasets	626

Table 2: Breakdown of the set of gold MWEs used in our experiments

Training set		Test set	
MWE	freq	MWE	freq
to do so	3,378	go to	150
web browser	1,356	the first	129
to date	1,118	the same	100
go to	1,004	part of	89
the first	891	a lot	87
at the moment	828	come to	71
such as	821	a few	67
the same	767	be so	66
look at	567	out of	61
for example	519	for example	60

Table 3: Top ten most frequent gold MWEs in the training set and test set

the texts included in grades $1, ..., N$ in the test corpus. This metric measures the time required, i.e., the minimum i required for u_i to graduate from level N. We report results for $m = 80$.

Text Comprehension The number of texts that can be understood by u_i, averaged over times $i = 1, ..., j$. We set j to the size of the shortest benchmark vocabulary list, i.e., EVP.

4.3 Gold MWEs

A set of ground-truth MWEs is necessary to apply the automatic metrics defined above. We compiled our gold MWE set from both language learning experts and past MWE research:

- The 5,096 MWEs found in the EVP and/or GSE lists (Section 3.2);
- MWEs that have been assigned an above-average score in the following benchmark MWE datasets: noun compounds (Reddy et al., 2011; Farahmand et al., 2015), adjective-noun compounds (Biemann and Giesbrecht, 2011), verb-particle pairs (McCarthy et al., 2003) and verb-object pairs (McCarthy et al., 2007). These yield an additional 626 MWEs to the gold set.

Method	Text Comp.
Frequency	57.52
Collocation	83.89
Collocation+Disp	87.42
EFLlex+Disp	59.01
Compositionality(50%)+Disp	76.96
Compositionality(75%)+Disp	**90.10**
Compositionality(Gold)+Disp	188.99
EVP	158.95
GSE	135.69
Ceiling	236.28

Table 4: Performance based on the "Text Comprehension" metric: average number of texts understood over the study period

Table 2 shows a breakdown of the 5,722 MWEs in the final set. Table 3 shows the most frequent MWEs in our datasets.

5 Approach

MWEs may include fixed and semi-fixed expressions, syntactically-flexible expressions and institutionalized phrases (Sag et al., 2002). As shown in Table 3, not all entries in vocabulary lists may conform to the standard MWE definition. Nonetheless, their inclusion in these lists by experts suggest that it is useful to treat them as a unit for the purpose of language learning.

Frequency All n-grams ($n \leq 3$) in the training corpora (Section 3.1) are considered as single-word and MWE candidates for the vocabulary list. They are lemmatized and ranked them according to frequency in the training corpora.

Collocation Same as the above, except that the MWE candidates are the top 500,000 n-grams in English Wikipedia based on the Poisson collocation measure (Quasthoff and Wolff, 2002).[9]

Compositionality(N%) Among the 500,000 MWE candidates above, this method retains as candidates only the top $N\%$ according to the semantic compositionality measure (Section 2).[10]

[9] https://github.com/Oddtwang/MWEs
[10] https://github.com/Oddtwang/MWEs

Method	A2	B1	B2	C1	C2
Frequency	7,164	9,054	16,712	58,139	58,139
Collocation	4,980	6,600	10,784	**24,610**	27,045
Collocation+Disp	**4,536**	6,007	**10,323**	25,184	26,326
EFLLex+Disp	/	/	/	/	/
Compositionality(50%)+Disp	8,679	8,679	17,508	/	/
Compositionality(75%)+Disp	4,984	**5,712**	11,253	25,983	**25,983**
Compositionality(Gold)+Disp	2,152	2,853	3,871	7,198	7,198
EVP	2,502	3,610	4,805	/	/
GSE	3,728	3,956	6,165	11,157	11,175
Ceiling	1,685	2,134	2,772	3,915	4,300

Table 5: Performance based on the "Study Time" metric: the number of time units needed for graduation from each level (Shorter time is better; "/" means the learner cannot graduate, as defined in Section 4.2)

EFLLex The MWE candidates are those found in EFLLex (Durlich and François, 2018).

+Disp The raw frequencies are weighted with Juilland's D (Gries, 2020), a dispersion coefficient that measures the degree to which occurrences of the n-gram are distributed evenly in the training set.

In addition, we implemented the following method to gauge the upper limit in performance:

Compositionality(Gold) The MWE candidates are the gold MWEs.

EVP / GSE The expert-crafted lists, transformed into a ranked list using the procedure in Section 4.1.

Ceiling The MWE candidates are the gold MWEs and all n-grams are ranked by frequency in the test set (Section 3.1).

6 Results

Text Comprehension. As shown in Table 4, the Collocation method (83.89) outperformed both the Frequency baseline (57.52) and EFLLex (59.01). The MWE candidates in the Collocation method covered 38% of the gold MWEs; retaining only the best-scoring three-quarters of the MWEs decreased the coverage to 32%, but was compensated by the higher quality among the selected MWEs. This can be seen in the performance of Compositionality(75%)+Disp, which was the best (90.10) of the automatic methods according to the Text Comprehension metric. This result suggests that the semantic compositionality measure was able to reduce the number of superfluous MWEs, and open up the learner's priority for other n-grams that appeared more often in the test set.

Study Time. As shown in Table 5, the learner graduated from the C2 level most quickly with the list generated from the top 75% of the MWEs, a result that is consistent with the Text Comprehension metric. At all lower levels except B1, however, the Compositionality(75%)+Disp method was outperformed by the Collocation method. The collocation statistics appeared to correlate better with the basic gold MWEs (e.g., "a few", "at least", "go out"), but less so with more advanced MWEs, likely because of the more divergent content. At all levels, the best automatic methods still lagged behind the expert-crafted lists, EVP and GSE, by large margins.

7 Conclusion

This paper has presented the first corpus-based evaluation of automatically generated vocabulary lists that incorporate MWEs. Using MWEs extracted by semantic compositionality (Pickard, 2020), we constructed a vocabulary list by ranking both single-word and MWE candidates by frequency and dispersion. Experimental results show that this method outperforms baselines using collocation measures, both in facilitating text comprehension and in shortening the study period. These algorithms can potentially enhance existing human-crafted lists, and compile new ones in resource-poor languages for which no vocabulary list is available.

Limitations

The experiments in this study were limited to MWEs up to three words long, given the dataset provided by Pickard (2020). Future work should explore the effects of longer MWEs on the results. The evaluation can also be made more accurate by considering part-of-speech information. Finally, the gold MWE set could be expanded by harvesting more human-annotated MWEs.

Acknowledgements

This work was partly supported by the Language Fund from the Standing Committee on Language Education and Research (project EDB(LE)/P&R/EL/203/14) and by the General Research Fund (project 11207320).

References

Jens Bahns and Moira Eldaw. 1993. Should we teach efl students collocations? *System*, 21(1):101–114.

Chris Biemann and Eugenie Giesbrecht. 2011. Distributional Semantics and Compositionality 2011: Shared Task Description and Results. In *Proc. Workshop on Distributional Semantics and Compositionality (DiSCo)*.

Anette Capel. 2015. The English Vocabulary Profile. In *English profile in practice*, page 9–27, Cambridge, UK. Cambridge University Press.

CEFR. 2001. *Common European Framework of Reference for Languages: Learning, Teaching, Assessment*. Cambridge University Press, Cambridge.

Mathieu Constant, Gülşen Eryiğit, Johanna Monti, Lonneke van der Plas, Carlos Ramisch, Michael Rosner, and Amalia Todirascu. 2017. Multiword Expression Processing: A Survey. *Computational Linguistics*, 43(4):837–892.

John H. A. L. De Jong, Mike Mayer, and Catherine Hayes. 2016. Developing Global Scale of English Learning Objectives aligned to the Common European Framework. In *Global Scale of English Research Series*. Pearson.

Luise Durlich and Thomas François. 2018. EFLLex: A Graded Lexical Resource for Learners of English as a Foreign Language. In *Proc. 11th International Conference on Language Resources and Evaluation (LREC 2018)*.

Meghdad Farahmand, Aaron Smith, and Joakim Nivre. 2015. A Multiword Expression Data Set: Annotating Non-Compositionality and Conventionalization for English Noun Compounds. In *Proc. 11th Workshop on Multiword Expressions*, page 29–33.

Johannes Graën, David Alfter, and Gerold Schneider. 2020. Using Multilingual Resources to Evaluate CEFRLex for Learner Applications. In *Proc. 12th Conference on Language Resources and Evaluation (LREC)*, pages 346–355, Marseille, France.

Stefan Th. Gries. 2020. Analyzing Dispersion. In *A Practical Handbook of Corpus Linguistics*, pages 99–118.

Matthew Honnibal and Mark Johnson. 2015. An Improved Non-monotonic Transition System for Dependency Parsing. In *Proc. Conference on Empirical Methods in Natural Language Processing (EMNLP)*.

Ray Jackendoff. 1997. *The Architecture of the Language Faculty*. MIT Press, Cambridge, MA.

Batia Laufer. 1989. What percentage of text is essential for comprehension? In *Special Language; from Humans Thinking to Thinking Machines*, pages 316–323, Clevedon. Multilingual Matters Ltd.

Diana McCarthy, Bill Keller, and John Carroll. 2003. Detecting a Continuum of Compositionality in Phrasal Verbs. In *Proc. Workshop on Multiword Expressions: Analysis, Acquisition and Treatment*, page 73–80.

Diana McCarthy, Sriram Venkatapathy, and Aravind Joshi. 2007. Detecting Compositionality of Verb-Object Combinations using Selectional Preferences. In *Proc. Joint Conference on Empirical Methods in Natural Language Processing and Computational Natural Language Learning (EMNLP-CoNLL)*, page 369–379.

Magali Paquot and Sylviane Granger. 2016. Formulaic language in learner corpora. *Annual Review of Applied Linguistics*, 32:130–149.

Thomas Pickard. 2020. Comparing word2vec and GloVe for Automatic Measurement of MWE Compositionality. In *Proc. Joint Workshop on Multiword Expressions and Electronic Lexicons*, page 95–100.

Uwe Quasthoff and Christian Wolff. 2002. The Poisson Collocation Measure and its Applications. In *Proc. 2nd International Workshop on Computational Approaches to Collocations*, Wien. IEEE.

Siva Reddy, Diana McCarthy, and Suresh Manandhar. 2011. An empirical study on compositionality in compound nouns. In *Proceedings of the 5th International Joint Conference on Natural Language Processing*, pages 210–218.

Ivan A. Sag, Timothy Baldwin, Francis Bond, Ann Copestake, and Dan Flickinger. 2002. Multiword Expressions: A Pain in the Neck for NLP. In *Proc. CICLing*, page 1–15.

Sowmya Vajjala and Ivana Lučić. 2018. OneStopEnglish corpus: A new corpus for automatic readability assessment and text simplification. In *Proc. 13th Workshop on Innovative Use of NLP for Building Educational Applications*, pages 297–304.

Sowmya Vajjala and Detmar Meurers. 2012. On Improving the Accuracy of Readability Classification using Insights from Second Language Acquisition. In *Proc. 7th Workshop on Innovative Use of NLP for Building Educational Applications*.

Menglin Xia, Ekaterina Kochmar, and Ted Briscoe. 2016. Text readability assessment for second language learners. In *Proc. 11th Workshop on Innovative Use of NLP for Building Educational Applications*, page 12–22.

Are Frequent Phrases Directly Retrieved like Idioms? An Investigation with Self-paced Reading and Language Models

Giulia Rambelli
University of Bologna
rambelligiulia@gmail.com

Emmanuele Chersoni
The Hong Kong Polytechnic University
emmanuelechersoni@gmail.com

Marco S. G. Senaldi
McGill University
marco.senaldi@mcgill.ca

Philippe Blache
Aix-Marseille University
philippe.blache@univ-amu.fr

Alessandro Lenci
University of Pisa
alessandro.lenci@unipi.it

Abstract

An open question in language comprehension studies is whether non-compositional multiword expressions like idioms and compositional-but-frequent word sequences are processed differently. Are the latter constructed online, or are instead directly retrieved from the lexicon, with a degree of entrenchment depending on their frequency?

In this paper, we address this question with two different methodologies. First, we set up a self-paced reading experiment comparing human reading times for idioms and both high-frequency and low-frequency compositional word sequences. Then, we ran the same experiment using the *Surprisal* metrics computed with *Neural Language Models* (NLMs).

Our results provide evidence that idiomatic and high-frequency compositional expressions are processed similarly by both humans and NLMs. Additional experiments were run to test the possible factors that could affect the NLMs' performance.

1 Introduction

It is a fact that some linguistic forms are stored in the mental lexicon, while some others have to be computed 'on the fly' by composition from smaller parts. However, the debate in linguistics and cognitive science concerns where to put the divide between 'on the fly' construction and direct retrieval (Tremblay, 2012). Theories arguing for a primary role for composition (Chomsky, 1993; Marantz, 1995; Jackendoff, 2002; Szabó, 2004) assume that rules would be responsible for the 'on the fly' computation of regular forms, while the irregular ones have to be stored in the lexicon and retrieved as a whole. On the other hand, usage-based constructionist approaches consider frequency as a crucial factor and claim that frequent forms are stored in the lexicon, while the composition mechanism is reserved to infrequent ones (Goldberg, 2003; Bybee, 2006). Accordingly, the more often a linguistic expression is encountered, the more its representation is entrenched and the easier its retrieval from the mental lexicon is (Bannard and Matthews, 2008).

The usage-based view found some strong supporting evidence in self-paced reading, EEG, and sentence recall experiments (Arnon and Snider, 2010; Tremblay and Baayen, 2010; Tremblay et al., 2011), where the speed at which highly frequent word sequences were processed suggested that they are stored and processed unitarily in the mental lexicon at least to some degree. In this research, considerable attention has been devoted to a class of recurring and conventional phrases denominated *multiword units*, *phraseological units* or *formulaic units* across different theoretical frameworks (Arnon and Snider, 2010; Siyanova-Chanturia et al., 2011; Tremblay and Baayen, 2010; Wulff, 2008; Contreras Kallens and Christiansen, 2022).

Among multiword expressions, the mechanisms underlying idiom comprehension and production have been at the core of extensive research; indeed, idioms (e.g., *break the ice*, *cut the mustard*) convey a figurative interpretation not determined by a compositional syntactic and semantic analysis of their component words (Cacciari and Tabossi, 1988; Libben and Titone, 2008; Senaldi et al., 2022). These expressions have been associated with facilitation effects in reading (Conklin and Schmitt, 2008; Titone et al., 2019) and a more positive electric signal in brain activity (Vespignani et al., 2010). To our knowledge, not many studies have directly compared the processing times of idiomatic multiword expressions and frequent

Proceedings of the 19th Workshop on Multiword Expressions (MWE 2023), pages 87–98

compositional combinations, with the exception of the study by Jolsvai et al. (2020) on three-word phrases (see Section 2.1).

In this paper, we set up a self-paced reading experiment in which we compare human reading times of English verb-determiner-noun constructions in three different conditions: **idiomatic** (*steal my thunder*), **high-frequency compositional** (*steal my wallet*) and **low-frequency compositional** (*steal my trolley*). Additionally, given the success of modern *Neural Language Models* (NLMs) and the increasing interest in using their probabilistic predictions to account for sentence processing phenomena (Futrell et al., 2018; Van Schijndel and Linzen, 2018; Wilcox et al., 2018; Michaelov and Bergen, 2020; Cho et al., 2021; Michaelov and Bergen, 2022a; Michaelov et al., 2023), we repeated the experiment by extracting the *Surprisal* values (Hale, 2001; Levy, 2008) of the words in the stimuli with several RNN- and Transformer-based models, to compare them with the human results. We chose this measure because Surprisal is considered an indicator of the processing load associated with a word; experiments have found a strong correlation between biometric and computational values (Ryu and Lewis, 2021).

Our results show that **humans process idiomatic and high-frequency compositional expressions significantly faster than low-frequency compositional ones** and, in parallel, NLMs assign to them significantly lower Surprisal values. Among the models we tested, we found out that **the smaller version of GPT2 and a 2-layer LSTM obtained the exact same score patterns as human subjects**; we observed no significant difference between the Surprisal scores in the idiomatic and the high-frequency conditions, but the values for the infrequent condition were significantly higher.[1]

2 Related Work

2.1 Direct access of Idiomatic and Frequent Sequences

The idea that frequently-occurring multiword expressions may be stored and processed holistically had been put forth already by Biber et al. (2000). Tremblay et al. (2011) set up a self-paced reading experiment comparing frequent lexical bundles (e.g., *whatever you think about it*) and lower-frequency control sequences (e.g., *whatever you do about it*), and they found that the former were read faster by human subjects across different experimental settings. Arnon and Snider (2010) compared the reaction times in phrasal decision tasks between frequent and infrequent word sequences (e.g., *I don't know why* vs. *I don't know who*), where the subparts of the sequence were matched for frequency, and they reported a clear effect of phrase frequency on recognition times. Tremblay et al. (2011) described a four-word production task in which the participants had to say the word sequences that were shown to them, and their production onset latencies and total durations were measured. The authors found several main effects related to word frequencies, contextual predictability, and mutual information, deemed as indicative of the holistic storage of forms.

Among multiword expressions, it is generally acknowledged that idiomatic constructions play a special role, as they convey a figurative meaning that cannot be accessed by merely combining the semantics of their components (*non-compositionality*; (Jackendoff, 2002)). Converging evidence from online methodologies supports facilitation in processing for idioms with respect to non-idiomatic phrases (Cacciari and Tabossi, 1988; Conklin and Schmitt, 2008; Vespignani et al., 2010; Siyanova-Chanturia et al., 2011; Titone et al., 2019). There is an open debate about how idioms are represented in the mental lexicon and processed during comprehension: while the *non-compositional* view considers idioms as frozen strings directly accessed during comprehension (Swinney and Cutler, 1979; Cacciari and Tabossi, 1988, i.a.), recent evidence suggests that idiom comprehension involves both direct meaning retrieval and compositional analysis at different comprehension stages, thus validating hybrid models of idiom processing (Libben and Titone, 2008; Titone et al., 2019).

In particular, hybrid views predict that an idiom's degree of familiarity or subjective frequency modulates the availability of direct retrieval as a processing strategy. Indeed, prior studies had shown speakers to engage in a more compositional processing strategy when idioms are less frequent or familiar, for example, because they appear in a non-canonical modified form or they are being processed in a second language (Senaldi and Titone, 2022; Senaldi et al., 2022). Vice versa, a question that remains unaddressed is whether frequent but compositional word combinations can benefit

[1] Data and code available at: `https://osf.io/4jg2b/?view_only=e3679a4df4c248fb8819156b392e92ad`.

from some form of direct memory access during processing.

Jolsvai et al. (2020), to our knowledge, is the only study attempting a comparison between three-word idiomatic expressions, frequent compositional phrases, and fragments. A phrasal decision task revealed that the meaningfulness of the chunk sped up reaction times, which were similar for idioms (*play the field*) and frequent phrases (*nothing to wear*), while phrasal fragments (*without the primary*) took considerably more time. However, the stimuli across the three conditions were just matched on sub-components' frequency, without any constraint about the superficial realization of the constructions. Unlike Jolsvai and colleagues, we only focused on English verb constructions. We manipulated frequency and degree of compositionality by changing the direct object while keeping the verb constant. Across experimental conditions, the same verb could appear in an idiom (*spill the beans*), a high-frequency compositional construction (*spill the milk*), and a low-frequency compositional construction (*spill the rice*, see Section 3.1).

2.2 Constructions and Idioms in Transformer Language Models

With the rise to the popularity of Transformer language models in NLP (Vaswani et al., 2017; Devlin et al., 2019), several studies explored the nature of the linguistic representations of Transformers and how they handle compounds and other types of non-compositional expressions (Shwartz and Dagan, 2019; Rambelli et al., 2020; Garcia et al., 2021a,b; Dankers et al., 2022). Interestingly, some studies specifically used the probing paradigm to analyze to what extent Transformers have access to construction knowledge (Weissweiler et al., 2023; Pannitto and Herbelot, 2023), and there is a general agreement that they have some knowledge about the formal/syntactic aspects of constructions (Madabushi et al., 2020; Weissweiler et al., 2022). In contrast, the evidence about the encoding of meaning aspects is mixed, depending on the specific constructions and the type of semantic knowledge being probed (Li et al., 2022; Weissweiler et al., 2022). This literature primarily focused on analyzing idioms and constructions at the level of the Transformer representations.

To our knowledge, there have been no attempts yet to model the effects of such linguistic expressions on human sentence processing, for example, in terms of reading times or eye-tracking fixations. In computational psycholinguistics, it has become common to use NLMs to extract word Surprisals (Hale, 2001; Levy, 2008) and use such values to model human behavioral patterns. For instance, Transformer Surprisal has been shown to accurately predict human reading times from naturalistic reading experiments, outperforming the metrics derived from architectures based on recurrent neural networks (Wilcox et al., 2020; Merkx and Frank, 2021). Evaluating computational models on sentence processing data is, in our view, a necessary complement to the construction probing tasks, as it makes it possible to test the predictions against the cognitively-plausible benchmark represented by human behavior (Rambelli et al., 2019).

3 Experiment 1: Self-paced Reading (SPR)

3.1 Stimuli and SPR Data

Stimuli consisted of 48 English verb-determiner-noun phrases appearing in 3 experimental conditions, namely as idiomatic expressions (ID, *spill the beans*), high-frequency compositional phrases (HF, *spill the milk*) and low-frequency compositional phrases (LF, *spill the rice*). The three conditions shared the same verb. First, we selected all verb-determiner-noun expressions from two normative datasets of American English idioms (Libben and Titone, 2008; Bulkes and Tanner, 2017) and Kyriacou et al. (2020)'s study. To generate matched HF and LF compositional phrases for each of the items, we relied on the enTenTen18 corpus (Jakubíček et al., 2013), a large part-of-speech parsed corpus of English made up of texts collected from the Internet (21.9 billion words). We employed the sketchEngine[2] tools (Kilgarriff et al., 2014) to run our queries. We verified that the HF expression had a comparable log frequency with the corresponding idiom and that the noun-verb association score was similar or larger than the association score in the idiomatic phrase, relying on the LogDice score implemented in SketchEngine (Rychlý, 2008). Moreover, we matched the nouns in all three conditions for log-transformed frequency and character word length. We discarded the idioms for whom finding an appropriate matched HF was impossible. Finally, we ran an *Idiom Familiarity* survey to exclude unfamiliar idioms, and a *Typical Objects Production* study, to verify that the noun in the low-

[2] http://www.sketchengine.eu

Cond.	Context	Precritical region - **Critical region** - Postcritical region
ID	Finn changed his life after his father's death.	All of a sudden he **kicked the habit** and stopped smoking cigarettes.
HF	It was the first match for Finn.	All of a sudden he **kicked the ball** into the net and won the match.
LF	That day, Finn had completely lost his temper.	All of a sudden he **kicked the sister** of his best friend in the head.

Table 1: Example of the stimuli for the self-paced reading experiment.

frequent Condition was not in the list. We collected online judgments from 57 and 74 North American subjects, respectively. Idioms receiving a familiarity score lower than 4 were left out. The final selection led to 48 triplets consisting of a highly familiar idiom and matched frequent and infrequent compositional bigrams.

From the bigram list, we built the experimental stimuli. Specifically, a stimulus consisted of a sentence containing a contextual preamble displayed as a whole and a sentence containing the target phrase[3] presented word-by-word using the moving-window SPR paradigm (see Table 1). Stimuli were split into three counterbalanced lists such that only one condition of the triple was in a list[4], and they were randomized for each participant. The experiment was delivered remotely, and participants were recruited using Prolific [2021].[5] We collected responses from 90 subjects from the United States and Canada, all self-reported L1 speakers of English aged between 18 and 50. We considered the reading times (henceforth RTs) on the object noun, that is, the last word of the target bigram. We removed responses of less than 100 ms (Jegerski, 2013) as well as reading times that were 2.5 standard deviations above each condition's mean, resulting in 7.3% data loss. Then, we ran a linear mixed model in R (v. 3.6.3) with the lme4 package (Bates et al., 2015). We included log-transformed RTs as the dependent variable, while the condition, the noun length, the verb frequency (log-transformed), and the trial number were entered in the models as fixed effects. Finally, the Subject and Item were treated as random effects. Significance was computed using the *lmerTest* package (Kuznetsova et al., 2017), which applies Satterthwaite's method to estimate degrees of freedom and generates *p*-values for mixed models.

[3]Context and target sentences were manually created by the authors and validated by an English teacher.

[4]It is a common methodology in psycholinguistics to prevent possible priming effects.

[5]www.prolific.co

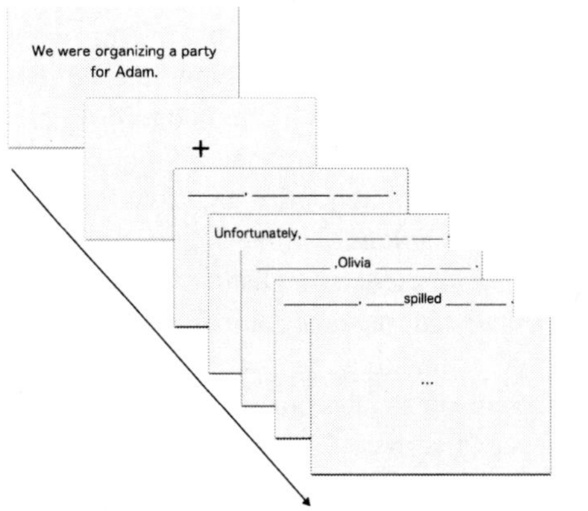

Figure 1: SPR procedure. 1) A context sentence appears in the center of the screen; the participant goes to the next sentence by pressing the space key. 2) The target text is displayed as a series of dashes on the screen, each dash representing a character. The first word appears when the participant presses the space key, replacing the corresponding dashes. Each button presses cause the previous words to be overridden again by dashes during the current word surface.

3.2 Results

The difference in RTs between ID and HF turned out to be not statistically significant (β= .002594, $t = .191$, $p = .85$), while it was significantly different between ID and LF (β = .02982, $t = 2.190$, $p = .0299*$). When mapping the HF condition to the intercept, there was still a statistically significant difference between HF and LF ($\beta = .0272$, $t = 2.007$, $p = .0466*$). To be consistent with common practices in the psycholinguistic literature, we included the trial number as a fixed effect: as expected, RTs at the end of the experiment tended to be shorter than at the beginning.

Analyses revealed no significant differences in reading times between idioms with a non-compositional meaning and high-frequency compositional phrases; there was facilitation in both conditions, compared to low-frequency compositional phrases. Although reading times do not allow to draw conclusions on how these phrases are rep-

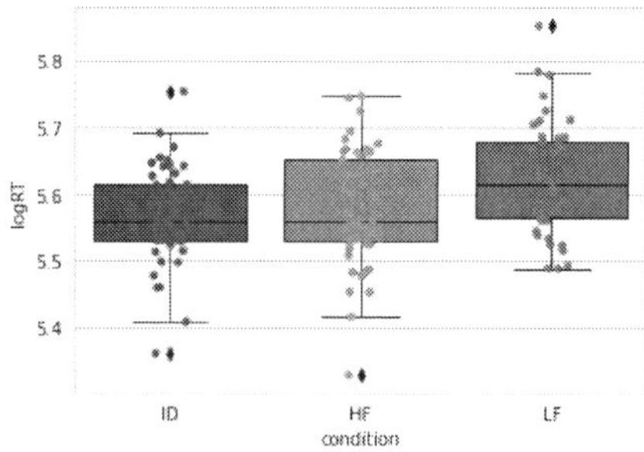

Figure 2: RTs distribution across the conditions.

resented at the brain level, the collected evidence seems in line with the claims of usage-based constructionist models (Goldberg, 2006; Wulff, 2008; Bybee, 2010). Accordingly, frequency of exposure determines the degree of lexical entrenchment of non-compositional and compositional structures alike; thus, even highly frequent compositional structures can end up being represented as wholes in the lexicon without being necessarily composed piecemeal during online processing.

Since our results reveal comparable processing times between HF and ID phrases and there is consistent evidence that idioms are at least to some extent retrieved directly from memory during processing, we can hypothesize a similar processing strategy to be at play for both. Another explanation is that since ID and HF phrases are frequently encountered by speakers, they are read faster because the processing system relies on analogical similarities with a high number of stored exemplars (Ambridge, 2020; Rambelli et al., 2022). Finally, RTs for infrequent phrases were significantly slower, even if the edge on ID and HF was relatively small: we presume that the information introduced in context sentences plays a role in reducing the effort to interpret less predictable expressions.

4 Experiment 2: Modeling Reading Times with Neural Language Models (NLMs)

4.1 NLM Architectures

To investigate which NLM architecture explains SPR data, we chose Transformers and recurrent networks (RNN), which are traditionally ascribed as a cognitively plausible model of human sentence processing (Elman, 1990). RNNs are inherently sequential: a token's representation depends on the previous hidden state to form a new hidden state. In contrast, Transformers have a self-attention layer allowing to 'attend' to parts of previous input directly (Vaswani et al., 2017).

Among the Transformers, we tested both autoregressive models (i.e., GPT), where the probability of the target word is computed based on the left context, and bidirectional models (like BERT (Devlin et al., 2019)) that instead predict a word looking at both the left and right context. **GPT2** (Radford et al., 2019) is a unidirectional Transformer LM pre-trained on WebText for a total of 8 million documents of data (40 GB) and has a vocabulary size of 50.257. We employed all four versions of GPT-2 (small/medium/large/xl) for our experiments to test if the model size has an impact on the results (parameters are reported in Appendix A). Unlike GPT2, **BERT** (Devlin et al., 2019) was the first to adopt the bidirectional training of Transformer for a language modeling task. It is trained both on a masked language modeling task (i.e., the model attempts to predict a masked token based on the surrounding context) and on a next sentence prediction task, as the model receives sentence pairs in input and has to predict whether the second sentence is subsequent to the first one in the training data. BERT has been trained on a concatenation of the BookCorpus and the English Wikipedia for a total of around3300M tokens. We used the `bert-base-uncased` pre-trained version in our experiments. In addition, we selected the Text-To-Text Transfer Transformer (**T5**) (Raffel et al., 2020), an encoder-decoder model pretrained on a multi-task mixture of unsupervised and supervised tasks and for which each task is converted into a text-to-text format. We experimented with the T5-base model (220 million parameters), trained on a 7 TB dataset. All models were loaded through `minicons` (Misra, 2022),[6] a Python library facilitating the probability computations with the LMs that are accessible through the `transformers` package by HuggingFace.

Moreover, we compared Transformers with two kinds of recurrent networks as a baseline. **TinyLSTM** is a two-layer LSTM recurrent neural network trained with a next-word prediction on the Wikitext-2 dataset, a collection of over 100 million tokens (Stephen et al., 2017). **GRNN** is the best-performing model described in the supplementary materials of Gulordava et al. (2018). It was trained on 90 million tokens of English Wikipedia with two hidden layers of 650 hidden units. Both models

[6] `https://github.com/kanishkamisra/minicons`

	ID_{median}	HF_{median}	LF_{median}	ID-HF	ID-LF	HF-LF
GPT2-small	5.36 (IQR 4.82)	6.43 (IQR 3.57)	12.7 (IQR 5.19)	ns	***	***
GPT2-medium	4.59 (IQR 4.60)	6.66 (IQR 5.58)	12.2 (IQR 4.61)	*	***	***
GPT2-large	3.96 (IQR 4.90)	6.71 (IQR 5.93)	12.4 (IQR 4.64)	*	***	***
GPT2-xl	2.41 (IQR 3.98)	4.46 (IQR 3.00)	8.00 (IQR 4.05)	*	***	***
BERT-base-uncased	21.6 (IQR 4.68)	20.1 (IQR 7.12)	21.5 (IQR 4.7)	ns	ns	ns
T5-base	18.5 (IQR 4.32)	17.1 (IQR 5.17)	20.1 (IQR 6.5)	ns	ns	**
TinyLSTM	11.8 (IQR 2.98)	11.7 (IQR 5.28)	14.1 (IQR 3.69)	ns	***	**
GRNN	12.0 (IQR 5.23)	9.60 (IQR 4.02)	14.2 (IQR 4.74)	*	***	***

Table 2: Comparison of Surprisal scores using Wilcoxon Signed-Rank Test (with Bonferroni's correction). *p= < .05, **p= < .01, and ***=p < .001.

were queried with the Language Model Zoo,[7] an open-source repository of state-of-the-art language models, designed to support black-box access to model predictions (Gauthier et al., 2020).

4.2 Methodology

Reading times are a common way to identify readers' facilitation effects in comprehension. For NLMs, we measured the Surprisal of the next word, which is notoriously an important predictor of reading times in humans (Smith and Levy, 2013) and has been largely used to test language models' abilities (cf. Section 2.2).

The Surprisal of a word w (Hale, 2001; Levy, 2008) is defined as the negative log probability of the word conditioned on the sentence context

$$Surprisal(w) = -logP(w|context) \quad (1)$$

where the context can be words on the left (for autoregressive models) or words both on the left and on the right of the target w. We passed the stimuli sentences presented in the previous experiment to all selected NLMs and computed the Surprisal of the object noun in each experimental condition. The Surprisal score should reveal how easy it is to process a target word: the lower the score, the higher the facilitation effect. For out-of-vocabulary words, we computed the sum of the Surprisals of the subtokens.

4.3 Results of Surprisal Analyses

Table 2 summarizes the difference among conditions for each model. We compared the Surprisal distribution in the three conditions by relying on the non-parametric Wilcoxon signed rank test with the Bonferroni correction. We applied the `wilcoxon_test` function from the `rstatix` package in R language. The Wilcoxon test shows a statistical difference between the Surprisals of ID and HF conditions ($p < .05$), differently than in human reading times. Specifically, all the GPT2 models, with the exception of the 'small' version, produce lower scores for ID condition than for HF. This outcome seems to indicate that the idiomatic expression is more expected by the model, even if we controlled the stimuli to have a similar bigram frequency and verb-noun association. Surprisingly, the other Transformer model shows an opposite trend: BERT-base-uncased and T5-base have an average Surprisal of HF lower than those for ID condition, and there is no significant difference not only between ID and HF conditions but also between ID and LF. This outcome, confirmed by the boxplot visualization (Figure 3), reveals that bidirectional models are not sensitive to the difference among the three conditions. Moreover, the scores are consistently higher than GPT2 models, indicating that all the expressions are quite unexpected by the two Transformer architectures.

Considering recurrent networks, GRNN performs similarly to the (larger) T5-base model: the average Surprisal of HF is lower than those for ID condition. However, in this case, HF scores are significantly lower than ID. We could infer that this recurrent neural network prefers the frequent compositional competition, while it is more surprised by the same frequent but figurative expression.

There are only two models whose Surprisals are comparable to human RTs: **GPT2-small** and **tinyLSTM**. The fact that the smaller GPT2 model resembles human performance is interesting and might be further evidence of the *inverse scaling* that has been observed in LMs for several natural language phenomena; that is, the more the model size grows, the less human-like its behavior is (Wei et al., 2022; Michaelov and Bergen, 2022b; Oh and Schuler, 2022; Jang et al., 2023). Oh and Schuler (2022) suggested that this behavior can be explained by the fact that larger LMs have seen many more word sequences than humans; as model size grows, the

[7] `https://github.com/cpllab/lm-zoo`

predictions tend to be more and more accurate for open class words, to the point of underestimating their reading time delays.

We found no statistical correlation between the human RTs with the NLMs' Surprisals, as it is evident from the scatterplots in Figure 5 (analyses were conducted using the Spearman's correlation).

4.4 The Role of Context

The results of the SPR experiment revealed that, while there is a significant difference between ID/HF conditions and infrequent phrases, the advantage is relatively small (in milliseconds). A plausible explanation is that the preceding context has a priming effect on the noun interpretation in the target sentence, regardless of the condition. As an additional investigation, we re-run all models but fed them only with the target sentence without the contextual sentence. A two-way ANOVA was performed to analyze the effect of Condition and Context on Surprisal scores for all models. For a visual comparison, we plotted the Surprisal distribution obtained both with and without the context sentence (Figure 3). This analysis reveals that **recurrent neural networks** (tinyLSTM and GRNN) **and bidirectional models** (BERT and T5) **produce the same Surprisal with or without the context sentence**. Two-way ANOVA revealed no statistically significant interaction between the effects of Condition and Context (BERT: $F = .001, p = .97$; T5: $F = .016, p = .899$; tinyLSTM: $F = .343$, $p = .559$; GRNN: $F = .014, p = .905$). Simple main effects analysis showed that Context did not have a statistically significant effect, while Condition did have a statistically significant effect on Surprisal scores ($p < .001$). This outcome suggests that, for all these models, word prediction is highly localized, and the preceding context has little or no priming effect on the expectation of the next word. This evidence could also explain BERT and T5-base performances: a word's expectancy is not affected by the preceding context, thus the model is highly surprised by all words, regardless of verb associations (frequent or infrequent bigram) and expression type (idiomatic or literal). However, this observation should be further verified with more targeted experiments.

Contrarily, we observe the expected trend for all **GPT2 models: Surprisal scores decrease, giving a context sentence before the stimuli**. The two-way ANOVA revealed that there was not a

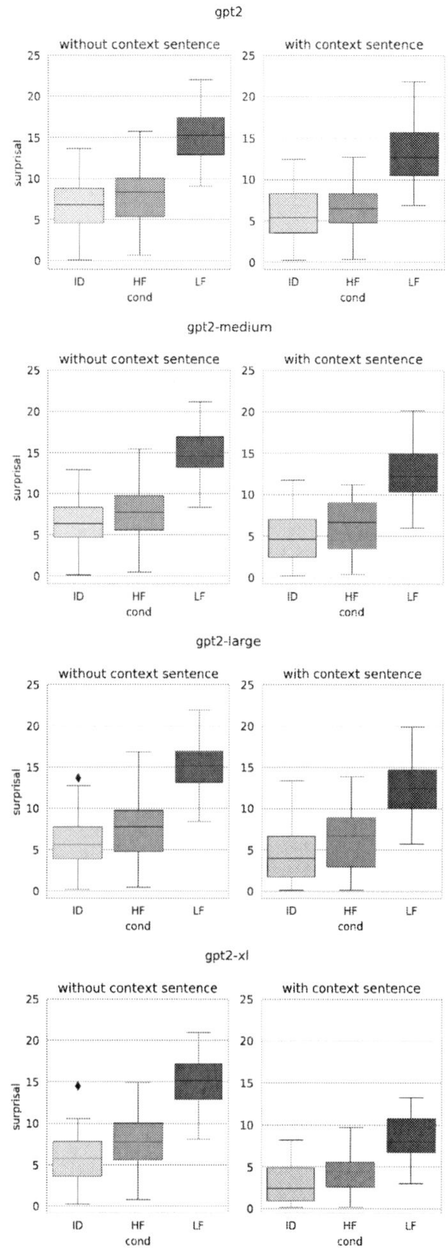

Figure 3: Surprisal distributions per conditions for GPT2 models, with (right) and without (left) the context sentence. The comparison of boxplots reveals that Surprisal scores decrease by giving a context sentence before the stimuli.

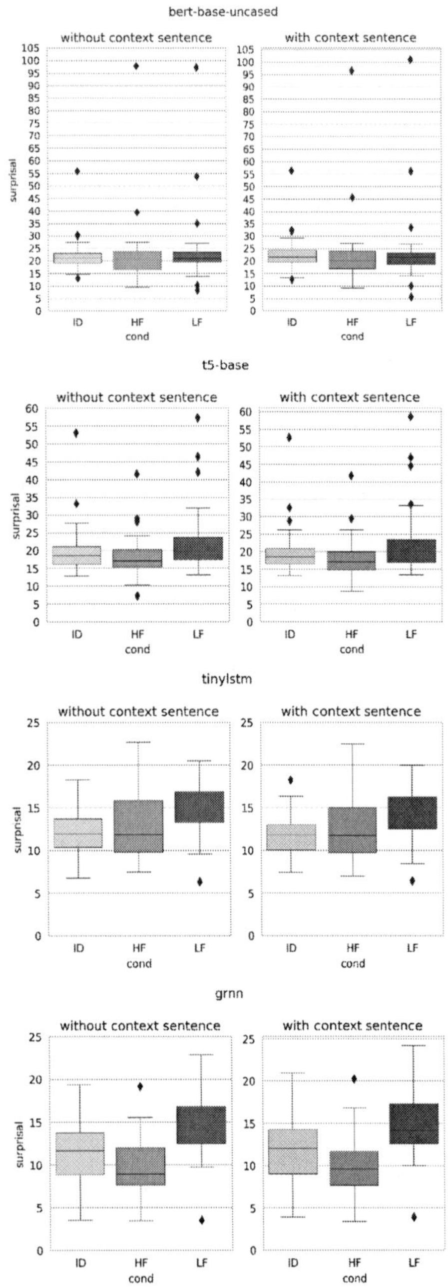

Figure 4: Surprisal distributions per conditions for BERT-base-uncased, T5-base, tinyLSTM, and GRNN, with and without the context sentence. The comparison of boxplots reveals that Surprisal scores are the same regardless the context.

statistically significant interaction between Context and Condition for all variants, with the exception of GPT2-xl (GPT2: $F = .014$, $p = .905$; GPT2-medium: $F = .883$, $p = .348$; GPT2-large: $F = 1.351$, $p = .246$; GPT2-xl: $F = 106.49$, $p < .001***$). However, Context as a simple main effect does have a statistically significant effect in all models (GPT2: $F = 9.559$, $p = .002**$; GPT2-medium: $F = 14.686$, $p < .001***$; GPT2-large: $F = 15.398$, $p < .001***$; GPT2-xl: $F = 8.31$, $p = .004**$). What is important to notice, however, is that the differences among the conditions are kept constant. Accordingly, GPT2 models show LF condition is less expected than the other two, and Surprisal values for idioms and high-frequent expressions are similar independently of the context. This outcome is important because it tells us that, even if the context has a facilitatory effect on LMs' processing, it is not the main cause for Surprisal scores.

5 Discussion

This study is part of a broad research about how people access meaning during language processing and to what extent NLMs replicate human behavior. In our view, comparing idioms to frequent literal expressions may provide novel insights into the influence of phrase frequency on language processing and the integration of compositional and noncompositional mechanisms.

In the SPR experiment, we found that people read idioms and frequent compositional units at comparable speeds. The results of this study require further investigation. For instance, we could analyze the influence of context on comprehension by collecting reading times of the stimuli presented without the contextual sentence; as well, we could present the same stimuli in an eye-tracking paradigm to record more fine-grained measures than mere reading time. Secondly, instead of relying only on corpus frequencies, we could explore the relationship between reading times and other ratings, such as cloze probability, plausibility, or meaningfulness (Jolsvai et al., 2020). Moreover, we restricted this study to N-det-V pattern, but we are planning to apply the experiment to other types of multiword expressions. Finally, we are planning to extend this investigation to other languages to assess the cross-linguistic validity of our findings.

The experimental evidence provided by the computational experiment confirms our behavioral find-

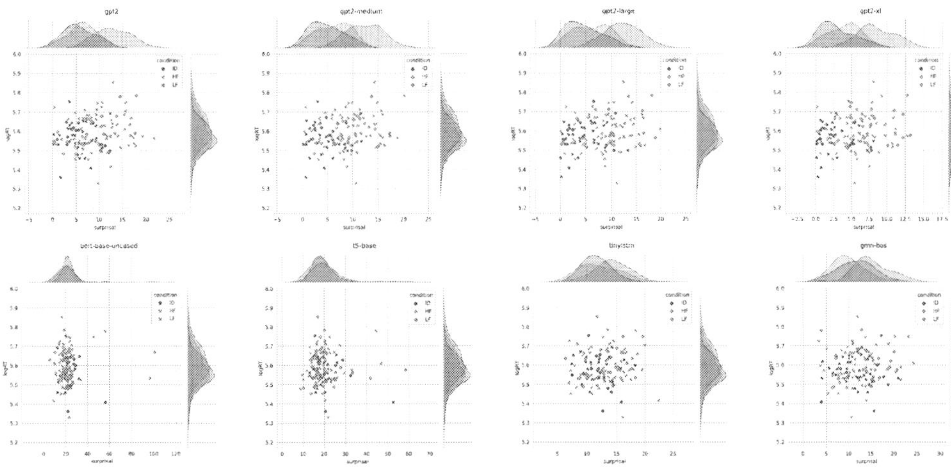

Figure 5: Scatterplot showing the relationship between Surprisal scores (x-axis) and RTs (y-axis).

ings: both idiomatic and frequent expressions are highly expected by GPT2 models. Interestingly, the models that mirrored more closely human reading patterns are the smallest ones, in agreement with the findings recently reported by the literature on *inverse scaling* in NLMs. Future research includes replicating this study with other architectures, including the successor of GPT2, namely GPT3.

A compelling behavior of NLMs regards the role of context: it seems to affect little or not at all the Surprisal scores. This evidence suggests that the Surprisal of a word depends more on the ease of access to a word in the vocabulary than on the semantic integration with previous words. In other words, frequent expressions might be 'memorized' and easily retrieved, and context words do not show relevant priming effects. We plan to investigate this outcome in future experiments and verify how humans react without the contextual sentence. Besides, we can conclude that the converging evidence from humans and LMs suggests that multiword expressions, both idiomatic and compositional ones, are processed more holistically than compositionally.

Our experiment opens up to many possibilities for further analyses and refinements. For example, considering the behavioral experiment, a peculiarity of our design is that the point at which an idiom becomes recognizable is located at the end of the target phrase. Even if reading times on this specific word gives us insight into the facilitation access to construction meaning, the cognitive effort in processing that word is not limited to the word itself but could emerge in the subsequent text (*spillover* effect; Rayner and Duffy (1986); Reichle et al. (2003)). Considering the computational experiment, we just analyzed the probability output of a target word through the Surprisal scores, but in the future, it would be useful to adopt interpretability techniques to get more insights on the hidden representations of the NLMs (Yin and Neubig, 2022; Belrose et al., 2023).

We hope that our findings can contribute to the existing research in multiword expression processing, paving the way for forthcoming studies on how the compositional and noncompositional mechanisms alternate during interpretation.

Limitations

An obvious limitation is that our analysis was limited to English, and we hope to replicate the same experimental design for other languages in the future. Moreover, we limited ourselves to just one type of construction (verb phrases).

Acknowledgements

A special acknowledgment goes to Christelle Zielinski for her support in implementing the online behavioral experiment and data explorations. We would also like to thank the reviewers for their insightful feedback.

This research was supported by grants ANR-16-CONV-0002 (ILCB) and the Excellence Initiative of Aix-Marseille University (A*MIDEX), and by the General Research Fund (B-Q0AH) at the Hong Kong Polytechnic University.

References

Ben Ambridge. 2020. Against Stored Abstractions: A Radical Exemplar Model of Language Acquisition. *First Language*, 40(5-6):509–559.

Inbal Arnon and Neal Snider. 2010. More than Words: Frequency Effects for Multi-word Phrases. *Journal of Memory and Language*, 62(1):67–82.

Colin Bannard and Danielle Matthews. 2008. Stored Word Sequences in Language Learning: The Effect of Familiarity on Children's Repetition of Four-word Combinations. *Psychological Science*, 19(3).

Douglas Bates, Martin Mächler, Ben Bolker, and Steve Walker. 2015. Fitting Linear Mixed-Effects Models Using lme4. *Journal of Statistical Software*, 67(1):1–48.

Nora Belrose, Zach Furman, Logan Smith, Danny Halawi, Igor Ostrovsky, Lev McKinney, Stella Biderman, and Jacob Steinhardt. 2023. Eliciting Latent Predictions from Transformers with the Tuned Lens. *arXiv preprint arXiv:2303.08112*.

Douglas Biber, Stig Johansson, Geoffrey Leech, Susan Conrad, and Edward Finegan. 2000. *Longman Grammar of Spoken and Written English*. Longman London.

Nyssa Z. Bulkes and Darren Tanner. 2017. "Going to town": Large-scale Norming and Statistical Analysis of 870 American English Idioms. *Behavior Research Methods*, 49(2):772–783.

Joan Bybee. 2006. From Usage to Grammar: The Mind's Response to Repetition. *Language*, pages 711–733.

Joan L. Bybee. 2010. *Language, Usage and Cognition*. Cambridge University Press.

Cristina Cacciari and Patrizia Tabossi. 1988. The Comprehension of Idioms. *Journal of Memory and Language*, 27(6):668–683.

Won Ik Cho, Emmanuele Chersoni, Yu-Yin Hsu, and Chu-Ren Huang. 2021. Modeling the Influence of Verb Aspect on the Activation of Typical Event Locations with BERT. In *Findings of ACL-IJCNLP*.

Noam Chomsky. 1993. A Minimalist Program for Linguistic Theory. *The View from Building 20: Essays in Linguistics in Honor of Sylvain Bromberger*.

Kathy Conklin and Norbert Schmitt. 2008. Formulaic Sequences: Are They Processed More Quickly than Nonformulaic Language by Native and Nonnative Speakers? *Applied Linguistics*, 29(1):72–89.

Pablo Contreras Kallens and Morten H Christiansen. 2022. Models of Language and Multiword Expressions. *Frontiers in Artificial Intelligence*, 5:24.

Verna Dankers, Christopher G Lucas, and Ivan Titov. 2022. Can Transformer be too Compositional? Analysing Idiom Processing in Neural Machine Translation. In *Proceedings of ACL*.

Jacob Devlin, Ming-Wei Chang, Kenton Lee, and Kristina Toutanova. 2019. BERT: Pre-training of Deep Bidirectional Transformers for Language Understanding. In *Proceedings of NAACL*.

Jeffrey L Elman. 1990. Finding structure in time. *Cognitive science*, 14(2):179–211.

Richard Futrell, Ethan Wilcox, Takashi Morita, and Roger Levy. 2018. RNNs as Psycholinguistic Subjects: Syntactic State and Grammatical Dependency. *arXiv preprint arXiv:1809.01329*.

Marcos Garcia, Tiago Kramer Vieira, Carolina Scarton, Marco Idiart, and Aline Villavicencio. 2021a. Assessing the Representations of Idiomaticity in Vector Models with a Noun Compound Dataset Labeled at Type and Token Levels. In *Proceedings of ACL*.

Marcos Garcia, Tiago Kramer Vieira, Carolina Scarton, Marco Idiart, and Aline Villavicencio. 2021b. Probing for Idiomaticity in Vector Space Models. In *Proceedings of EACL*.

Jon Gauthier, Jennifer Hu, Ethan Wilcox, Peng Qian, and Roger Levy. 2020. SyntaxGym: An Online Platform for Targeted Evaluation of Language Models. In *Proceedings of ACL: Demo*.

Adele E Goldberg. 2003. Constructions: A New Theoretical Approach to Language. *Trends in Cognitive Sciences*, 7(5):219–224.

Adele E. Goldberg. 2006. *Constructions at Work: The Nature of Generalization in Language*. Oxford University Press on Demand.

Kristina Gulordava, Piotr Bojanowski, Edouard Grave, Tal Linzen, and Marco Baroni. 2018. Colorless Green Recurrent Networks Dream Hierarchically. In *Proceedings of NAACL*.

John Hale. 2001. A Probabilistic Earley Parser as a Psycholinguistic Model. In *Proceedings of NAACL*.

Ray Jackendoff. 2002. *Foundations of Language*. Oxford University Press.

Miloš Jakubíček, Adam Kilgarriff, Vojtěch Kovář, Pavel Rychlý, and Vít Suchomel. 2013. The tenten corpus family. In *7th International Corpus Linguistics Conference CL*, pages 125–127. Lancaster University.

Joel Jang, Seonghyeon Ye, and Minjoon Seo. 2023. Can Large Language Models Truly Understand Prompts? A Case Study with Negated Prompts. In *Transfer Learning for Natural Language Processing Workshop*, pages 52–62. PMLR.

Jill Jegerski. 2013. Self-paced Reading. In *Research Methods in Second Language Psycholinguistics*, pages 36–65. Routledge.

Hajnal Jolsvai, Stewart M McCauley, and Morten H Christiansen. 2020. Meaningfulness Beats Frequency in Multiword Chunk Processing. *Cognitive Science*, 44(10):e12885.

Adam Kilgarriff, Vít Baisa, Jan Bušta, Miloš Jakubíček, Vojtěch Kovář, Jan Michelfeit, Pavel Rychlý, and Vít Suchomel. 2014. The Sketch Engine: Ten Years On. *Lexicography*, 1(1):7–36.

Alexandra Kuznetsova, Per B. Brockhoff, and Rune HB Christensen. 2017. lmerTest Package: Tests in Linear Mixed Effects Models. *Journal of Statistical Software*, 82(1):1–26.

Marianna Kyriacou, Kathy Conklin, and Dominic Thompson. 2020. Passivizability of Idioms: Has the Wrong Tree Been Barked Up? *Language and speech*, 63(2):404–435.

Roger Levy. 2008. Expectation-based Syntactic Comprehension. *Cognition*, 106(3):1126–1177.

Bai Li, Zining Zhu, Guillaume Thomas, Frank Rudzicz, and Yang Xu. 2022. Neural Reality of Argument Structure Constructions. In *Proceedngs of ACL*.

Maya R. Libben and Debra A. Titone. 2008. The Multi-determined Nature of Idiom Processing. *Memory & Cognition*, 36(6):1103–1121.

Harish Tayyar Madabushi, Laurence Romain, Dagmar Divjak, and Petar Milin. 2020. CxGBERT: BERT Meets Construction Grammar. In *Proceedings of COLING*.

Alec Marantz. 1995. The Minimalist Program. In *The Principles and Parameters Approach to Linguistic Theory*, pages 351–382. Blackwell.

Danny Merkx and Stefan L Frank. 2021. Human Sentence Processing: Recurrence or Attention? In *Proceedings of the NAACL Workshop on Cognitive Modeling and Computational Linguistics*.

James A Michaelov and Benjamin K Bergen. 2020. How Well Does Surprisal Explain N400 Amplitude under Different Experimental Conditions? In *Proceedings of CONLL*.

James A Michaelov and Benjamin K Bergen. 2022a. Collateral Facilitation in Humans and Language Models. In *Proceedings of CONLL*.

James A Michaelov and Benjamin K Bergen. 2022b. 'Rarely' a Problem? Language Models Exhibit Inverse Scaling in their Predictions Following 'Few'-type Quantifiers. *arXiv preprint arXiv:2212.08700*.

James A Michaelov, Seana Coulson, and Benjamin K Bergen. 2023. Can Peanuts Fall in Love with Distributional Semantics? *arXiv preprint arXiv:2301.08731*.

Kanishka Misra. 2022. minicons: Enabling Flexible Behavioral and Representational Analyses of Transformer Language Models. *arXiv preprint arXiv:2203.13112*.

Byung-Doh Oh and William Schuler. 2022. Why Does Surprisal From Larger Transformer-Based Language Models Provide a Poorer Fit to Human Reading Times? In *Proceedings of EMNLP*.

Ludovica Pannitto and Aurélie Herbelot. 2023. CALaMo: A Constructionist Assessment of Language Models. *arXiv preprint arXiv:2302.03589*.

Alec Radford, Jeffrey Wu, Rewon Child, David Luan, Dario Amodei, Ilya Sutskever, et al. 2019. Language Models Are Unsupervised Multitask Learners. *OpenAI Blog*, 1(8):9.

Colin Raffel, Noam Shazeer, Adam Roberts, Katherine Lee, Sharan Narang, Michael Matena, Yanqi Zhou, Wei Li, and Peter J Liu. 2020. Exploring the Limits of Transfer Learning with a Unified Text-to-text Transformer. *Journal of Machine Learning Research*, 21(1):5485–5551.

Giulia Rambelli, Emmanuele Chersoni, Philippe Blache, Chu-Ren Huang, and Alessandro Lenci. 2019. Distributional Semantics Meets Construction Grammar. Towards a Unified Usage-based Model of Grammar and Meaning. In *Proceedings of the ACL Workshop on Designing Meaning Representations*.

Giulia Rambelli, Emmanuele Chersoni, Philippe Blache, and Alessandro Lenci. 2022. Compositionality as an Analogical Process: Introducing ANNE. In *Proceedings of the AACL-IJCNLP Workshop on Cognitive Aspects of the Lexicon*.

Giulia Rambelli, Emmanuele Chersoni, Alessandro Lenci, Philippe Blache, and Chu-Ren Huang. 2020. Comparing Probabilistic, Distributional and Transformer-based Models on Logical Metonymy Interpretation. In *Proceedings of AACL-IJCNLP*.

Keith Rayner and Susan A Duffy. 1986. Lexical Complexity and Fixation Times in Reading: Effects of Word Frequency, Verb Complexity, and Lexical Ambiguity. *Memory & Cognition*, 14(3):191–201.

Erik D. Reichle, Keith Rayner, and Alexander Pollatsek. 2003. The EZ Reader Model of Eye-Movement Control in Reading: Comparisons to Other Models. *Behavioral and Brain Sciences*, 26(4):445–476.

Pavel Rychlý. 2008. A Lexicographer-Friendly Association Score. In *RASLAN*, pages 6–9.

Soo Hyun Ryu and Richard L Lewis. 2021. Accounting for Agreement Phenomena in Sentence Comprehension with Transformer Language Models: Effects of Similarity-based Interference on Surprisal and Attention. In *Proceedings of the NAACL Workshop on Cognitive Modeling and Computational Linguistics*.

Marco S. G. Senaldi, Junyan Wei, Jason W Gullifer, and Debra Titone. 2022. Scratching your Tête over Language-switched Idioms: Evidence from Eye-movement Measures of Reading. *Memory & Cognition*, 50(6):1230–1256.

Marco S.G. Senaldi and Debra Titone. 2022. Less Direct, More Analytical: Eye-Movement Measures of L2 Idiom Reading. *Languages*, 7(2):91.

Vered Shwartz and Ido Dagan. 2019. Still a Pain in the Neck: Evaluating Text Representations on Lexical Composition. *Transactions of the Association for Computational Linguistics*, 7:403–419.

Anna Siyanova-Chanturia, Kathy Conklin, and Norbert Schmitt. 2011. Adding More Fuel to the Fire: An Eye-tracking Study of Idiom Processing by Native and Non-native Speakers. *Second Language Research*, 27(2):251–272.

Nathaniel J Smith and Roger Levy. 2013. The Effect of Word Predictability on Reading Time Is Logarithmic. *Cognition*, 128(3):302–319.

Merity Stephen, Xiong Caiming, Bradbury James, and Richard Socher. 2017. Pointer Sentinel Mixture Models. *Proceedings of ICLR*.

David A Swinney and Anne Cutler. 1979. The Access and Processing of Idiomatic Expressions. *Journal of Verbal Learning and Verbal Behavior*, 18(5):523–534.

Zoltán Gendler Szabó. 2004. Compositionality. *Stanford Encyclopedia of Philosophy*.

Debra Titone, Kyle Lovseth, Kristina Kasparian, and Mehrgol Tiv. 2019. Are Figurative Interpretations of Idioms Directly Retrieved, Compositionally Built, or Both? Evidence from Eye Movement Measures of Reading. *Canadian Journal of Experimental Psychology/Revue Canadienne de Psychologie Expérimentale*, 73(4):216.

Antoine Tremblay. 2012. *Empirical Evidence for an Inflationist Lexicon*. De Gruyter.

Antoine Tremblay and R Harald Baayen. 2010. Holistic Processing of Regular Four-word Sequences: A Behavioral and ERP Study of the Effects of Structure, Frequency, and Probability on Immediate Free Recall. *Perspectives on Formulaic Language: Acquisition and Communication*, pages 151–173.

Antoine Tremblay, Bruce Derwing, Gary Libben, and Chris Westbury. 2011. Processing Advantages of Lexical Bundles: Evidence from Self-paced Reading and Sentence Recall Tasks. *Language Learning*, 61(2):569–613.

Marten Van Schijndel and Tal Linzen. 2018. Modeling Garden Path Effects without Explicit Hierarchical Syntax. In *Proceedings of CogSci*.

Ashish Vaswani, Noam Shazeer, Niki Parmar, Jakob Uszkoreit, Llion Jones, Aidan N Gomez, Łukasz Kaiser, and Illia Polosukhin. 2017. Attention Is All You Need. *Advances in Neural Information Processing Systems*, 30.

Francesco Vespignani, Paolo Canal, Nicola Molinaro, Sergio Fonda, and Cristina Cacciari. 2010. Predictive Mechanisms in Idiom Comprehension. *Journal of Cognitive Neuroscience*, 22(8):1682–1700.

Jason Wei, Yi Tay, and Quoc V Le. 2022. Inverse Scaling Can Become U-shaped. *arXiv preprint arXiv:2211.02011*.

Leonie Weissweiler, Taiqi He, Naoki Otani, David R Mortensen, Lori Levin, and Hinrich Schütze. 2023. Construction Grammar Provides Unique Insight into Neural Language Models. *arXiv preprint arXiv:2302.02178*.

Leonie Weissweiler, Valentin Hofmann, Abdullatif Köksal, and Hinrich Schütze. 2022. The Better Your Syntax, the Better Your Semantics? Probing Pretrained Language Models for the English Comparative Correlative. In *Proceedings of EMNLP*.

Ethan Wilcox, Roger Levy, Takashi Morita, and Richard Futrell. 2018. What Do RNN Language Models Learn about Filler-gap Dependencies? *arXiv preprint arXiv:1809.00042*.

Ethan Gotlieb Wilcox, Jon Gauthier, Jennifer Hu, Peng Qian, and Roger Levy. 2020. On the Predictive Power of Neural Language Models for Human Real-Time Comprehension Behavior. *arXiv preprint arXiv:2006.01912*.

Stefanie Wulff. 2008. *Rethinking Idiomaticity: A Usage-based Approach*. A&C Black.

Kayo Yin and Graham Neubig. 2022. Interpreting Language Models with Contrastive Explanations. In *Proceedings of EMNLP*.

Appendix

A GPT2 parameters

	layers	hidden states	heads	parameters
GPT2	12	768	12	110M
GPT2-medium	24	1024	16	345M
GPT2-large	36	1280	20	774M
GPT2-xl	48	1600	25	1558M

Table 3: Details of GPT2 model parameters.

Annotation of lexical bundles with discourse functions in a Spanish academic corpus

Eleonora Guzzi[1], **Margarita Alonso Ramos**[1], **Marcos Garcia**[2], **Marcos Garcia Salido**[1]
[1]CITIC, Universidade da Coruña
[2] CiTIUS Research Center, Universidade de Santiago de Compostela
{eleonora.guzzi,marcos.garcias,margarita.alonso}@udc.es
marcos.garcia.gonzalez@usc.gal

Abstract

This paper describes the process of annotation of 996 lexical bundles (LB) assigned to 39 different discourse functions in a Spanish academic corpus. The purpose of the annotation is to obtain a new Spanish gold-standard corpus of 1,800,000 words useful for training and evaluating computational models that are capable of identifying automatically LBs for each context in new corpora, as well as for linguistic analysis about the role of LBs in academic discourse. The annotation process revealed that correspondence between LBs and discourse functions is not biunivocal and that the degree of ambiguity is high, so linguists' contribution has been essential for improving the automatic assignation of tags.

1 Introduction

Lexical bundles (LB) in academic English have been the object of many studies (Hyland, 2008, Douglas et al., 2004, Simpson-Vlach and Ellis, 2010). Although LBs are strictly defined as recurrent lexical sequences with high frequency and dispersion, their linguistic value comes from the discourse function that they fulfil. It is well known that the mastery of these LBs, such as *it should be noted* ('to emphasize'), *as can be seen* ('to resend'), or *it is clear that* ('to show certainty'), is crucial in academic writing. In English, lexical resources have been proposed (e.g. Granger and Paquot, 2015) in order to offer aid especially to novice writers. However, for academic Spanish few resources are available.

In light of this, the aim of this paper is to discuss the annotation of a Spanish academic corpus with the subset of LBs that have a discursive function, referred here as the umbrella term of *formula*. To the best of our knowledge, it is the first Spanish corpus with this type of annotation. Even though there is an extensive research on Spanish discourse markers, focused on a lexicographic description (Briz et al., 2008) or on its automatic identification and classification (Nazar, 2021), we do not know any Spanish corpus with annotations of academic formulae. Our research is related to Connective-lex (Stede et al., 2019), although it is based on the tagset of Penn Discourse Treebank 3.0 (Webber et al., 2019). Likewise, we must mention da Cunha et al. (2011), the Spanish corpus annotated with the discourse relations used in Rhetorical Structure Theory (Mann and Thompson, 1998).

The purpose of the annotation described here is to obtain a gold-standard corpus to train and evaluate computational models on the automatic identification and classification of academic formulae in new corpora. If generally multiword units have been especially difficult in NLP, formulae have the extra difficulty that they deal with discourse functions that seem more slippery for language models. Although many formulae are compositional, they must be also considered as phraseological units because they work as a whole and cannot be replaced by synonymous expressions that are unnatural; for instance, in English we cannot replace *to put it differently* with *to use some different expressions* or *to say it in a different way*. In our approach (Mel'čuk, 2015) *multiword expressions* (or *phrasemes*) include compositional and non-compositional phrases. Likewise, in the studies developed for academic English such as Simpson-Vlach and Ellis (2010), formulae include compositional and non-compositional expressions but all of them are considered *formulaic sequences*.

In what follows, we describe the process of annotation and human validation, where the main challenge has been to select the proper discourse function to ambiguous formulae.

Proceedings of the 19th Workshop on Multiword Expressions (MWE 2023), pages 99–105
May 6, 2023 ©2023 Association for Computational Linguistics

2 Dataset

This section describes the corpus and the formulae list of academic Spanish used for the present study.

2.1 Corpus

We rely on the HARTA academic corpus (HARTA-Exp) (García-Salido et al., 2019) for the annotation. It contains 2,025,092 word tokens extracted from 413 research articles published in scientific journals in Spanish from different areas. The core of this corpus derives from the Spanish part of SERAC corpus (Pérez-Llantada, 2008). Texts are classified in 4 main areas: (i) Arts and Humanities, (ii) Biology and Health Science, (iii) Physical Science and Engineering, and (iv) Social Sciences and Education. This corpus has been tokenized and lemmatized with LinguaKit (Garcia and Gamallo, 2016) and PoS-tagged with FreeLing (Padró and Stanilovsky, 2012). Lastly, UDPipe (Straka et al., 2016) was used for dependency parsing using universal dependencies (Nivre et al., 2016).

2.2 Academic formulae

The formulae selected for this study are recurrent sequences of words that are relevant for Spanish academic writing. They fulfil a discourse function, namely, they can help writers to reformulate what is said, i.e. *dicho de otro modo* ('in other words'), to indicate opposition, i.e. *no obstante* ('however'), to express certainty, i.e. *es sabido que* ('it is well known that'), and so on.

Initially, the list included 985 formulae that were identified using a semi-automatic method (García-Salido et al., 2018), although it was extended after manual revision, as we show in Section 4. We first automatically extracted from the corpus around 5,772 LBs corresponding to strings from two to six n-grams. A frequency and distribution threshold was set to 10 occurrences per million words and to ≥ 1 occurrence in each of the four areas. Secondly, LBs were exhaustively revised by lexicographers to identify relevant academic formulae. This task consisted of discarding irrelevant structures, such as LBs made up of grammatical elements or LBs that hardly fulfilled textual or interpersonal functions, and to select the candidates that they judged were relevant for academic writing. Once the list was obtained, each formula was assigned to the a discourse function based on García-Salido et al. (2019) classification.

The classification is the result of combining top-down and bottom-up approaches. It consists of 3 main groups which contain 39 discourse functions[1]: (i) bundles related to the research process, such as to 'present the conclusions', e.g. *podemos concluir que* ('we may conclude that'); (ii) text-oriented bundles, e.g. for 'ordering', such as *en primer lugar* ('first'); and (iii) interpersonal bundles, that is, expressions conveying epistemic, deontic and evaluative meanings, such as to 'mitigate', e.g. *tal vez* ('perhaps'). In case of ambiguous formulae with two possible functions, they were assigned to the most frequent function. As a result, we may find formulae such as *de acuerdo con* ('according to'), which can be assigned to two discourse functions depending on the context, or *es más* (lit. 'is more'), which sometimes behaves as a formula that fulfills a function and sometimes does not. The list of academic formulae with their discourse function tags makes the point of departure of the annotation task.

3 Annotation procedure

The procedure followed for annotating academic formulae is summarized in Fig. 1.

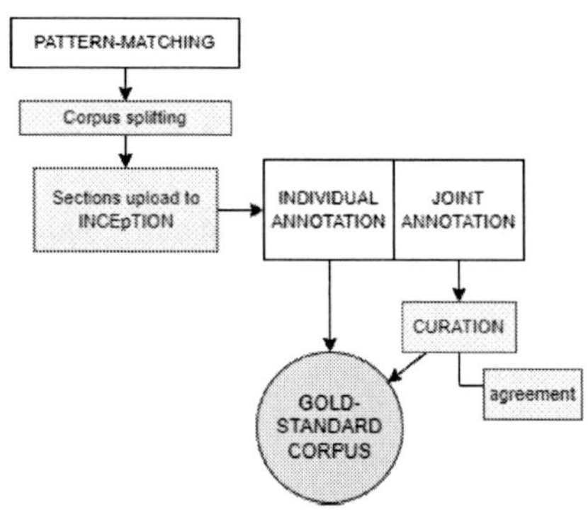

Figure 1: Annotation procedure of LBs.

The first step involved using the academic formulae list with their discourse functions to identify their occurrences in the corpus through a pattern-matching technique. As for the second step, the annotated corpus was split in 15 blocks of ca. 120,000 word tokens each, with the aim of mixing texts from different authors and disciplines. The 15 blocks were uploaded to INCEpTION (Klie et al., 2018), a tool that has been used for the manual

[1]The entire classification is shown in Appendix A, along with the most frequent formula of each discourse function.

evaluation of the automatically annotated corpus to validate the results.

As illustrated by Fig.2, once the corpus is uploaded, the main page for the annotator shows the text, the formula underlined and the discourse function's tag.

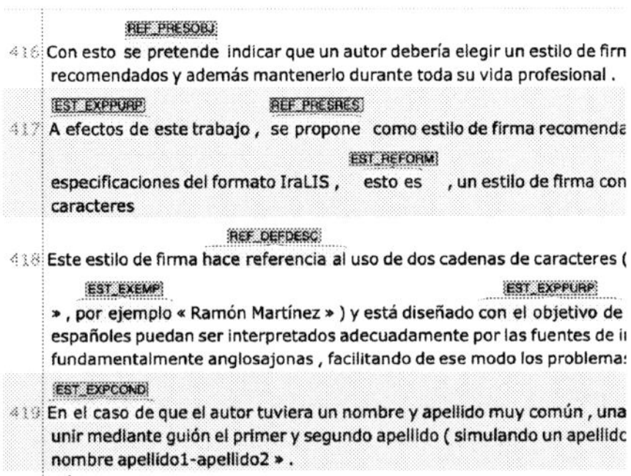

Figure 2: INCEpTION's interface for annotators.

Besides the tagged text, the annotator is provided with a panel with access to the 39 discourse functions. Here, the annotator can change the discourse function, delete it, as well as associate a new discourse function to a formula that needs to be added.

Thus, the main task for annotators has been to validate whether discourse functions were correctly tagged by pattern-matching and to revise whether annotated LBs were proper formulae in all contexts, because different situations could have emerged. A more detailed description of each situation is given in Section 4.

The 15 blocks of texts were distributed among three annotators, in such a way that each annotator had 5 individual annotation blocks, a joint annotation (two annotators who worked on the same block but independently) and, finally, a consensus annotation. The consensus annotation is obtained from applying a curation process to joint annotations. More precisely, the annotator starts a process of "neutralization" of mismatching annotations by changing the discourse function of a formula that was wrongly assigned, by adding a tag in a formula that was not identified, or by removing the formula because it does not behave as such in given contexts. Instead of errors, different annotations might be seen as plausible variations among annotators due to different reasons, as pointed out by Plank (2022).

Once this exhaustive task has been completed, an annotated corpus of ca. 1,800,000 words was obtained (88% of HARTA-Exp), including 360,000 words of consensus annotations. The product obtained from the curation process is a set of peer-reviewed texts that have been used to calculate inter-annotator agreement.

4 Results and Discussion

Manual examination of the automatically annotated corpus has been time consuming and a demanding task for annotators. It lasted around 180 hours only for the individual annotations, at least 12 hours for each block of 120,000 words. In addition to the validation in INCEpTION, we must take into account the previous long and exhaustive linguists' task of identifying formulae and assigning the proper discourse functions. Consequently, we can say that linguists' contribution has been essential to identify academic formulae and their functions in corpora as a first step, as well as to improve a part of the automatic annotation (11%)[2], which ensured the high quality of the data in the gold-standard corpus.

The time invested led to an average of 414 changes per ca. 3,858 tagged formulae in each block that underwent manual examination. Because we wanted to ensure there was coherence among decisions made by annotators, we calculated the agreement for the 3 joint annotations. Results have shown high values for the raw agreement (number of agreed items/nº of total items) of the consensus texts ranging between 89% and 92%, so it provided a positive general overview about the annotation process. Krippendorff α (Krippendorf, 2011) was also performed in order to calculate the amount of agreement that was attained above the level expected by chance or arbitrary coding. Similarly, values for joint annotations revealed a high level of agreement: α=0.885 for block 1; α=0.898 for block 2, and α=0.925 for block 3. Therefore, this agreement was considered as an acceptable reference for annotating the rest of blocks individually.

The main findings provided by the annotation process suggest that annotators dealt with four different types of changes: (i) formulae that annotators judged they do not behave as such in given contexts; (ii) ambiguous formulae associated to two discourse functions; (iii) occurrences of nested formulae where only the longest string was identified;

[2]The 11% is calculated considering that, following annotators judgments, the 89% is correctly annotated by the automatic technique, and the remainder corresponds to manual changes of the automatic annotation.

and (iv) occurrences of new formulae as different morpho-syntactic forms of existing ones.

As we can see in Fig. 3 below, the most faced situations by annotators have been discarding LBs (i), that stands for the 50%, followed by changing the discourse function of ambiguous formulae (ii), that represents the 41% of the total amount of changes. Conversely, nested bundles (iii) and (iv) addition of new morpho-syntactic forms describes only the 4-5%.

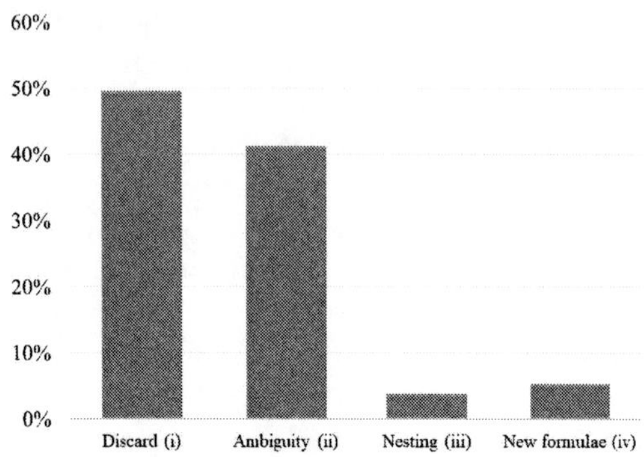

Figure 3: Frequency of each type of annotation change.

Regarding the first type of change (i), it is worth emphasizing that some of the occurrences of 12 formulae, such as *es más* ('in addition'), were discarded because in some specific contexts they were not associated to any discourse function. For instance, *es más* can be used to 'add information' (1), but in contexts such as (2) it is a LB that is not associated to any discourse function, so it must be removed:

(1) **Es más**, la misma alumna emplea este apelativo dirigiéndose a un amigo o amiga.

'**What is more**, the student uses this appellation for addressing to a friend.'

(2) [...] debido a que su fabricación **es más** sencilla.

(lit.)'[...] because its fabrication **is more** simple.'

As for the second type of change (ii), it turned out that the discourse function chosen for 27 [3] ambiguous formulae (two possible functions) was not much more frequent than the other function, so that it involved several changes in annotation. It was especially the case of strings like *en relación con* ('with regard to'), which depending on its position in the sentence is associated to different functions. Thus, *en relación con* and the like, when used sentence-initially normally serve to 'introduce the topic' of a sentence, whereas in sentence-internal distributions they usually head some 'delimiting' modifier. In this regard, the function 'introduce the topic' was substituted for 'delimiting' 499 times, way above other functions, which were modified 30 times on average during the validation process. The difference of switching times from 'delimiting' to other discourse functions in ambiguous formulae is shown in Fig. 4. In this respect, 'delimiting' frequently alternates with 'introduce the topic' (INTOPIC) as well as with 'quoting and reporting' (INDSOURCE), but hardly ever switches to 'compare' (COMP):

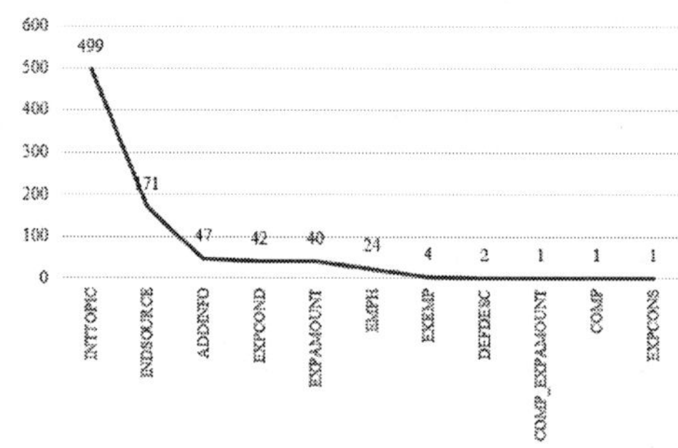

Figure 4: Frequency of changes of 'delimiting' to another discourse function.

Such type of change is reflected also in the formula *de acuerdo con* ('according to'), that is used for 'quoting and reporting' (3) or as a 'delimiting' marker (4):

(3) **De acuerdo con** Takada y Lourenço en 2004, las características generales de esta disciplina [...].

'**According to** Takada and Lourenço in 2004, general features of this discipline [...].'

(4) '[...] tiene que ver con estrategias y prioridades de actuación de cada biblioteca **de acuerdo con** su particular circunstancia local.'

'[...] it has to do with strategies and priorities of action of each library **according to** their particular local circumstance.'

Another example of ambiguity is found within the formula *en torno a* ('around'), that in some contexts it is used for 'delimiting' (5), but in other contexts to 'mitigate' a quantity (6):

(5) Desde el análisis de contenido, hemos normalizado las respuestas **en torno a** cuatro categorías identificativas.

'From the analysis of content, we normalized the responses **around** four identifying categories.'

[3]It should be noted that if we treat ambiguous formulae separately in the final list, the total number of formulae would be 1,023 instead of 996, since 27 formulae have two different entries.

(6) La temperatura media de la capital se sitúa **en torno a** los 15º C.

'The capital's average temperature is **around** 15º C.'

Concerning the third type of change (iii), annotators dealt with some cases where two formulae were nested but only the longest one was automatically tagged by pattern-matching. For instance, in *como podemos observar en la tabla* ('as we can see in the table'), we find *como podemos observar en* (4-gram) and *en la tabla* (3-gram), so the preposition *en* ('in') belongs to both formulae. In those cases, annotators selected the formula they considered the most relevant for each context and assigned them its discourse function.

Finally, the fourth type of change (iv) relates to new formulae that were not identified in the automatic extraction but were of particular interest. New formulae were selected if they met the frequency criterion and were morpho-syntactic variants of already registered ones. For instance, expert writers tend to use the complete and discontinuous formula *por una parte, por otra parte* ('on the one hand, on the other hand'), but we found instances where the abbreviated and grammatically correct counterpart was used (*por otra*; lit. 'on the other') and that were not in our initial list. Thus, 11 different types of morpho-syntactic variants identified during this phase were added to the initial list of 985, that sums up a total amount of 996 formulae.

5 Conclusions

This paper described the annotation process of a new Spanish academic corpus of 1,800,000 words annotated with 996 formulae, that are assigned to 39 different discourse functions. This process is the result of a combination of an automatic annotation and a manual validation. The corpus obtained can be considered a valuable resource because besides of being manually validated, inter-annotator agreement showed high values of coincidence between decisions made by annotators.

Automatic techniques used to identify specific vocabulary from corpus are a good starting point to provide researchers with preliminary data to work with. The same applies for annotating occurrences of formulae in corpora. However, we found that identification and annotation procedures still needed a human validation in order to obtain a gold-standard corpus as a benchmark. Especially in the annotation, ambiguity has demonstrated to be present: many instances with LBs that behaved as a formula in some contexts but not in others were found, as well as different formulae that are associated to two possible discourse functions depending on the context were frequent. Further work aims to use the gold-standard corpus obtained from this study to train and evaluate computational models that are capable of identifying automatically adequate lexical bundles in new corpora, as well as for lexicographic and linguistic studies.

Limitations

This study has two main limitations that are size-related. On the one hand, it is widely accepted the larger the corpora, the better the results, but the annotated corpus used for building the gold-standard is only ca. 1,800,000 words. Therefore, it might be criticized that language models can be trained properly with sufficient amount of data, but in the near future we expect to complete the annotation of the entire corpus. Once completed, we plan to make it available for research purposes. On the other hand, because it was too time-consuming, consensus annotations covered only a part of texts, so we cannot fully ensure the reliability and validity of the entire annotation. However, consensus annotations were made in a triangular way, so that joint annotations from mixed annotators were chosen, and agreements among different annotators were analysed.

Regarding the Inter-Annotator Agreement (IAA), we must also mention some weakness of the manual evaluation since it departs from automatically pre-annotated data and the manual task is only an edition of the result. In this sense, there might be unexpected bias (e.g. the annotator may not read carefully the unannotated part for finding a missing annotation, but focuses only on the pre-annotated part) that can lead to trust and overestimate the IAA. In light of this, a complementary IAA study on a subset of data without pre-annotation is planned for further work.

Acknowledgements

This research was funded by MCIN/AEI (PID2019-109683GB-C21 and PID2021-128811OA-I00), by Xunta de Galicia (ED431C 2020/11 and ED431F 2021/01), and by FEDER GALICIA 2014-2020 (ED431G 2019/01 and ED431G 2019/04). EG is funded by the Programa de Axudas á Etapa predoutoral da Xunta de Galicia, and MG by a Ramón y Cajal grant (RYC2019-028473-I).

References

Antonio Briz, Salvador Pons, and José Portolés. 2008. Diccionario de partículas discursivas del español.

Iria da Cunha, Juan-Manuel Torres-Moreno, and Gerardo Sierra. 2011. On the development of the RST Spanish Treebank. In *Proceedings of the 5th Linguistic Annotation Workshop*, pages 1–10.

Biber Douglas, Susan Conrad, and Viviana Cortes. 2004. If you look at....: lexical bundles in university teaching and textbooks. *Applied Linguistics*, 25(3):371–405.

Marcos Garcia and Pablo Gamallo. 2016. Yet another suite of multilingual NLP tools. In *Communications in Computer and Information Science*, pages 65–75, Cham. Springer.

Marcos García-Salido, Marcos Garcia, and Margarita Alonso-Ramos. 2019. Identifying lexical bundles for an academic writing assistant in spanish. In *Computational and Corpus-Based Phraseology: Third International Conference, Europhras 2019, Malaga, Spain, September 25–27, 2019, Proceedings 3*, pages 144–158. Springer.

Marcos García-Salido, Marcos Garcia, Milka Villayandre-Llamazares, and Margarita A. Ramos. 2018. A lexical tool for academic writing in spanish based on expert and novice corpora. In *Proceedings of the Eleventh International Conference on Language Resources and Evaluation (LREC 2018)*.

Sylviane Granger and Magali Paquot. 2015. Electronic lexicography goes local design and structures of a needs-driven online academic writing aid. *International Annual for Lexicography*, 31(1):118–141.

Ken Hyland. 2008. As can be seen: lexical bundles and disciplinary variation. *English for Specific Purposes*, 27(1):4–21.

Jan-Christoph Klie, Michael Bugert, Beto Boullosa, Richard Eckart de Castilho, and Iryna Gurevych. 2018. The INCEpTION platform: Machine-assisted and knowledge-oriented interactive annotation. In *Proceedings of the 27th International Conference on Computational Linguistics: System Demonstrations*, pages 5–9, Santa Fe, New Mexico. Association for Computational Linguistics.

Klaus Krippendorf. 2011. Computing Krippendorff's alpha-reliability. *Departmental Papers (ASC). University of Pennsylvania.*

William C. Mann and Sandra A. Thompson. 1998. Rhetorical structure theory: Towards a functional theory of text organization. *Text. Interdisciplinary Journal for the Study of Discourse*, 8(3):243–281.

Igor Mel'čuk. 2015. Clichés, an understudied subclass of phrasemes. *Yearbook of Phraseology*, 6(1):55–86.

Rogelio Nazar. 2021. Automatic induction of a multilingual taxonomy of discourse markers. *Electronic lexicography in the 21st century: postediting lexicography*, pages 440–454.

Joakim Nivre, Marie-Catherine Marneffe, Filip Ginter, Yoav Goldberg, Cristopher D. Manning, Ryan Mcdonald, Slav Petrov, Sampo Pyysalo, Natalia Silveira, Reut Tsarfaty, and Daniel Zeman. 2016. Universal dependencies v1: A multilingual treebank collection. In *Proceedings of the 10th International Conference on Language Resources and Evaluation (LREC 2016)*, pages 1659–1666.

Lluís Padró and Evgeny Stanilovsky. 2012. Freeling 3.0: Towards wider multilinguality. In *Proceedings of the 8th International Conference on Language Resources and Evaluation (LREC2012)*, page 2473–2479.

Carmen Pérez-Llantada. 2008. Humans vs. machines? a multiperspective model for esp discourse analysis in intercultural rhetoric research. *ESP Across Cultures*, 5:91–104.

Barbara Plank. 2022. The "problem" of human label variation: On ground truth in data, modeling and evaluation. In *Proceedings of the 2022 Conference on Empirical Methods in Natural Language Processing*, pages 10671–10682, Abu Dhabi, United Arab Emirates. Association for Computational Linguistics.

Rita Simpson-Vlach and Nick C. Ellis. 2010. An academic formulas list: New methods in phraseology research. *Applied linguistics*, 31(4):487–512.

Manfred Stede, Tatjana Scheffler, and Amália Mendes. 2019. Connective-lex: A web-based multilingual lexical resource for connectives. *Discours. Revue de linguistique, psycholinguistique et informatique*, 24.

Milan Straka, Jan Hajic, and Jaja Straková. 2016. UDPipe: Trainable pipeline for processing CoNLL-U files performing tokenization, morphological analysis, pos-tagging and parsing. In *Proceedings of the 10th International Conference on Language Resources and Evaluation (LREC 2016)*, pages 4290–4297.

Bonnie Webber, Rashmi Prasad, Alan Lee, and Aravind Joshi. 2019. The Penn Discourse Treebank 3.0 annotation manual. *Philadelphia, University of Pennsylvania*, 35:108.

A Classification of discourse functions

Discourse Function	NF	Example
Añadir información 'Add information'	49	así como 'as well as'
Comparar 'Compare'	34	igual que 'as'
Delimitar 'Delimiting'	75	respecto a 'regarding to'
Ejemplificar 'Give examples'	25	por ejemplo 'for instance'
Expresar causa 'Express cause'	32	ya que 'because'
Expresar condición 'Express condition'	20	en función de 'depending on'
Expresar consecuencia 'Express consequence'	60	por lo que 'therefore'
Expresar finalidad 'Express purpose'	18	para que 'in order to'
Expresar oposición 'Express opposition'	31	sin embargo 'however'
Expresar concesión 'Express concession'	14	a pesar de 'in spite of'
Hacer referencia al propio trabajo 'Reference to the own work'	16	en este trabajo 'in this work'
Introducir un tema 'Introduce the topic'	9	respecto a 'with respect to'
Introducir una alternativa 'Introduce an alternative'	3	o bien 'or'
Introducir una excepción 'Introduce an exception'	7	a excepción de 'except for'
Ordenar 'Organize'	19	por otro lado 'on the other hand'
Reenviar 'Resend'	30	en la tabla 'in the table'
Reformular 'Reformulate'	19	es decir 'that is'
Resumir 'Summarize'	10	en la práctica 'in practice'
Definir y describir 'Defining and describing'	37	se trata de 'it is about'
Denominar 'Naming'	7	conocido como 'known as'
Establecer grupos 'Listing items'	11	de este tipo 'of this type'
Expresar cantidad 'Express amount'	112	el número de 'the number of'
Expresar frecuencia 'Express frequency'	10	a veces 'sometimes'
Expresar progresión 'Express progression'	3	a medida que 'as'
Expresar correlación 'Express correlation'	1	cuanto más 'the more'
Expresar tiempo 'Express time'	50	después de 'after'
Presentar datos 'Present data'	36	se observa 'it is observed'
Presentar el objeto de estudio 'Present the object of study'	5	se centra en 'focused on'
Presentar la hipótesis 'Present hypothesis'	4	se estima que 'it is estimated that'
Presentar la metodología 'Introduce methodology'	83	a través de 'through'
Presentar las conclusiones 'Introduce conclusions'	24	se encontró 'it was found'
Presentar los objetivos 'Introduce goals'	7	se pretende 'it is intended'
Atenuar 'Mitigate'	21	la mayoría de 'most of'
Expresar necesidad 'Express need'	8	debe ser 'it must be'
Expresar una evaluación 'Evaluate'	4	es importante 'it is important'
Hacer hincapié 'Emphasize'	30	sobre todo 'especially'
Indicar certeza 'Express certainty'	30	de hecho 'in fact'
Indicar la fuente 'Quoting and reporting'	37	de acuerdo con 'according to'
Indicar posibilidad 'Express possibility'	5	puede ser 'it may be'

Table 1: Classification of 39 *Discourse Functions*, number of formulae at type level in each discourse function (*NF*), and the most frequent formulae of each one (*Example*).

A Survey of MWE Identification Experiments: The Devil is in the Details

Carlos Ramisch
Aix Marseille Univ, CNRS,
LIS, Marseille, France
first.last@lis-lab.fr

Abigail Walsh
ADAPT Centre
Dublin City University, Ireland
first.last@adaptcentre.ie

Thomas Blanchard
Centrale Marseille, Aix Marseille Univ,
CNRS, LIS, Marseille, France
first.last@centrale-marseille.fr

Shiva Taslimipoor
ALTA Institute
University of Cambridge, UK
first.last@cl.cam.ac.uk

Abstract

Multiword expression (MWE) identification has been the focus of numerous research papers, especially in the context of the DiMSUM and PARSEME Shared Tasks (STs). This survey analyses 40 MWE identification papers with experiments on data from these STs. We look at corpus selection, pre- and post-processing, MWE encoding, evaluation metrics, statistical significance, and error analyses. We find that these aspects are usually considered minor and/or omitted in the literature. However, they may considerably impact the results and the conclusions drawn from them. Therefore, we advocate for more systematic descriptions of experimental conditions to reduce the risk of misleading conclusions drawn from poorly designed experimental setup.

1 Introduction

The task of identifying Multiword Expressions (MWEs) in texts, as defined by Constant et al. (2017), can be modeled using several paradigms: syntactic parsing (Nagy T. and Vincze, 2014; Constant and Nivre, 2016), compositionality prediction of MWE candidates (Cook et al., 2008; Haagsma et al., 2020; Garcia et al., 2021), or sequence annotation (Constant et al., 2012; Schneider et al., 2014). The *sequence annotation* paradigm has been recently popularised by the DiMSUM shared task (Schneider et al., 2016), and by three editions of the PARSEME shared tasks (Savary et al., 2017; Ramisch et al., 2018a, 2020). Automatic methods designed to solve MWE identification (MWEI) seen as sequence annotation range from more traditional structured sequence tagging (Al Saied et al., 2017) to more free-form recent transformer-based token classification (Taslimipoor et al., 2020).

While the sequence annotation paradigm makes it possible to analyse various idiosyncratic aspects of MWEI in full text, empirical model evaluation is still a challenge. Our survey focuses on experimental design choices that are not always clearly described and discussed in the literature (§ 2).

The *data* used to learn, tune and evaluate MWEI models can influence a study's conclusions. For instance, the PARSEME corpora contain only verbal MWEs; evaluations based on it favour systems that can manage discontinuities (§ 3). Moreover, annotation schemes have different approaches to deal with discontinuity, variability, nesting, and overlaps, which are particular to MWEs. Traditionally, variations of BIO labelling were used to represent some of these aspects (Ramshaw and Marcus, 1995). PARSEME proposes a generic corpus format, taking these above-mentioned phenomena into account. However, the lack of standardisation with the selection and application of labelling schemes leaves the door open for system developers to decide how they want to model MWEs (§ 4).

Another important aspect of evaluation is the choice of the *evaluation metrics* used to assess system performance. While global exact and fuzzy metrics based on precision, recall and F-score are traditionally employed (Green et al., 2013; Constant and Nivre, 2016), they ignore a model's capability to deal with challenging traits like MWE discontinuity, seen/unseen MWEs, and their variability. From edition 1.1, PARSEME designed focused measures to evaluate for these aspects (Ramisch et al., 2018a). We discuss and compare these metrics, and the way systems report and discuss them in papers (§ 5). Furthermore, most related work does not assess whether a superior performance is likely due to chance, that is, whether observed performance differences are statistically significant. Thus, we propose a framework, a free implementation, and report significance analyses on the PARSEME 1.2 shared task results (§ 6). Finally,

Proceedings of the 19th Workshop on Multiword Expressions (MWE 2023), pages 106–120
May 6, 2023 ©2023 Association for Computational Linguistics

we look at whether and how MWEI papers report error analysis (§ 7).

In short, we shed some light on these apparently minor aspects which actually can have a great impact on results and conclusions. We look at corpus constitution and split, pre- and post-processing, MWE tagging, evaluation metrics, statistical significance of system comparison, and error analyses. We compare the experiments of 40 MWEI papers and discuss best practices in designing experimental setup and evaluation.

2 Survey scope

Our survey covers a total of 40 papers selected according to the following criteria:

- Available on the ACL Anthology, and
- Focus on MWEI as per Constant et al. (2017), report experimental results, and:
  - are shared task (ST) or system description papers submitted to DiMSUM (2016) or to one of the 3 editions of the PARSEME STs (2017, 2018, 2020), or
  - are published after the first ST (2016) and report experiments on the DiMSUM or PARSEME corpora.

Our selection is not exhaustive, disregarding influential MWEI articles with experiments on other corpora, e.g. Green et al. (2013); Constant and Nivre (2016), and recent papers on in-context compositionality prediction, e.g. Zeng and Bhat (2021); Tayyar Madabushi et al. (2022). To keep the number of papers manageable, we arbitrarily disregard papers published in venues absent from the ACL Anthology, e.g. Maldonado and QasemiZadeh (2018).[1] Moreover, our sample is certainly biased towards over-represented languages (e.g. English for DiMSUM) and MWE categories (e.g. verbal MWEs for PARSEME). Nonetheless, we believe that it represents a large fraction of work in the MWE annotation paradigm, and could be complemented by a larger survey in the future.

The goal of our survey is to base our discussion on quantitative data extracted from the papers. Thus, intuitions can be confirmed and concrete proposals can be made for clearly identified gray zones. Thus, for each of the surveyed papers, we systematically answered the following questions:

- Languages of the corpora,
- Corpus splits used (train/dev/test),
- MWE categories identified by the models,
- Corpus pre-processing and post-processing,
- MWE encoding and decoding, especially for classification and tagging models,
- Evaluation metrics reported,
- Statistical significance of model comparison,
- Aspects looked at in error analyses.

Hereafter, we distinguish the 27 papers submitted to one of the four recent shared tasks (ST papers) from the 9 standalone papers, not submitted to a shared task (non-ST papers). Moreover, 4 of the papers are overall shared task description papers. For the others, we will use the terms *systems* and *models* interchangeably, as these papers describe experiments using a system that relies on a proposed model or family of models.

3 Corpus constitution and selection

The first aspect that we look at is the corpora used in the MWEI experiments.

Languages The languages of the corpora used mostly depend on the data available for STs. The SEMEVAL DiMSUM ST provided corpora in English (Schneider et al., 2016), whereas PARSEME STs provided corpora for 18 languages in edition 1.0 (Savary et al., 2017), 19 languages in edition 1.1 (Ramisch et al., 2018a), and 14 languages in edition 1.2 (Ramisch et al., 2020). The DiMSUM corpus is based on Streusle (Schneider et al., 2014) and is annotated for most major MWE categories (nominal, verbal, adverbial, functional), but does not include category labels. The PARSEME corpora, on the other hand, contain fine-grained MWE category annotations, but only cover verbal MWEs.

Figure 1 shows the distribution of papers across the 24 languages considered by our paper sample. The reasons that lead to choosing a given corpus and/or set of languages in non-ST works are various: language diversity (Zampieri et al., 2019), corpus domain (Liu et al., 2021), and corpus quality and size (Pasquer et al., 2020b).

Conversely to the number of papers per language, we can also look at the number of languages addressed by each paper. Most papers (26 out of 40) address more than one language, with the following distribution: 1-3 languages: 15 papers; 4-10

[1] One exception was made for the SHOMA system paper, available only on arXiv, but listed in the PARSEME ST 1.1 paper and website (Taslimipoor and Rohanian, 2018).

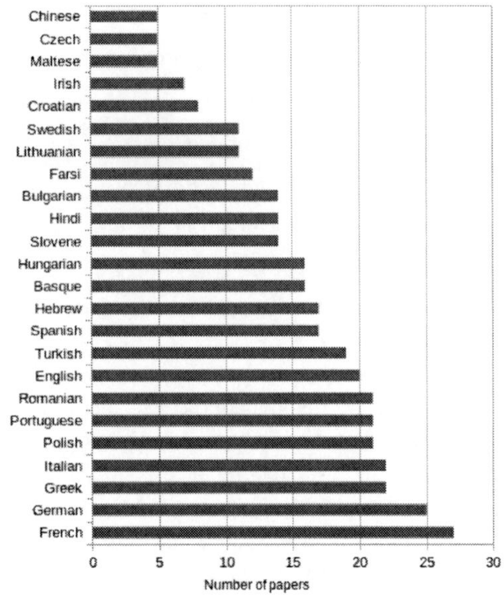

Figure 1: Number of papers per language.

languages: 6 papers, 11 languages or more: 19 papers. Among the 9 non-ST papers, 6 cover only one language, whereas 3 are multilingual.

Only 2 papers reported limiting their predictions to a subset of MWE categories (Foufi et al., 2017; Pasquer et al., 2018), otherwise the target MWE categories are by default all those present in the corpora. The prevalence of multilingual systems is probably due to the large amount of available corpora in the PARSEME collection, and to the use of largely language-independent methods based on these corpora. On the other hand, high cross-lingual variability is observed in most MWEI experiments. This can be due to the heterogeneity in the corpora and/or in the MWEs in each language (and how MWEI methods model them). Language-specific PARSEME corpus description papers not covered here can provide details, e.g. for Basque (Iñurrieta et al., 2018), Chinsese (Jiang et al., 2018), English (Walsh et al., 2018), Irish (Walsh et al., 2020), Italian (Monti and di Buono, 2019), Polish (Savary and Waszczuk, 2020), Portuguese (Ramisch et al., 2018b), Romanian (Barbu Mititelu et al., 2019), Turkish (Berk et al., 2018b; Ozturk et al., 2022), among others.

Domains Corpus domain may play an important role in MWEI. DiMSUM includes texts from 3 domains: web reviews, TED talk transcriptions, and tweets, and the ST paper analyses results per domain. One paper in our sample focuses on tweets, using this corpus (Zampieri et al., 2022b). PARSEME corpora contain mostly newspapers, with a few exceptions (e.g. French contains also Wikipedia, transcripts, and drug notices). One interesting case is that of the PARSEME Hungarian corpus, which contains barely any idioms, due to its highly specialised nature (law texts). Thus, systems using this corpus tend to report good performance, since this difficult category is under-represented (Savary et al., 2018). Liu et al. (2021) report cross-corpus (thus cross-domain) experiments using fine-tuned pre-trained language models with fine MWE+supersense labels.

Corpus and splits The four STs propose a corpus split: DiMSUM and PARSEME 1.0 randomly split the corpora into training and test sets. The PARSEME 1.1 and 1.2 STs add a third part: the development (dev) set (or validation set).[2] In the following discussion, we exclude the 4 general ST description papers, so our total is 36 system papers instead of 40.

External resources, rather than the training corpora, are used in 2 systems (Foufi et al., 2017; Colson, 2020), and 2 papers train models on the Streusle corpus and use PARSEME/DiMSUM only for test (Liu et al., 2021; Zampieri et al., 2022b), while the remaining 32 papers train their models on the PARSEME/DiMSUM training sets.

In DiMSUM, 4 papers mention a fixed train/dev split used to tune the systems, 1 paper mentions tuning on held-out data without further details (Kirilin et al., 2016) and two systems do not mention the issue (Björne and Salakoski, 2016; Scherbakov et al., 2016). For PARSEME 1.0, 3 papers use cross-validation to tune features (Al Saied et al., 2017; Maldonado et al., 2017; Boros et al., 2017), one system used a fixed train/dev split (Klyueva et al., 2017), and one system does not mention the issue (Simkó et al., 2017). For PARSEME 1.1, the languages with no dev set were usually tuned on the dev set of other languages, (Stodden et al., 2018; Taslimipoor and Rohanian, 2018, e.g.).

The use of standard corpus splits is a current practice in the NLP community. It ensures comparability across papers, e.g. to establish leaderboards and define state-of-the-art systems. However, standard splits have been criticised as their use may lead to unreplicable results (Gorman and Bedrick, 2019). Conversely, the use of multiple random splits also presents some disadvantages, leading to

[2] No dev in Hindi, English, and Lithuanian in edition 1.1.

over-estimated performances (Søgaard et al., 2021). As each splitting strategy has advantages and disadvantages, it is crucial to report how splits were obtained and why a given strategy was chosen.

Unseen MWEs The discussion in Ramisch et al. (2020) motivates the adoption of a less naturally distributed split in the PARSEME 1.2 ST corpora. The split is artificially biased to contain at least 100 unseen MWEs in the dev corpus, and 300 unseen MWEs in the test set.[3] While the results of this ST focus on generalisation, their definition of *unseen MWE* may require language-specific adaptations, e.g. Savary et al. (2019) argue that Basque canonical forms should include some morphological features. The use of automatically lemmatised corpora may also induce errors in the definition of unseen MWEs and thus influence the corpus splitting procedure.

The PARSEME 1.2 ST provided raw corpora not annotated for MWEs. However, there is no guarantee that MWEs in the dev and test corpora occur in the raw corpora. Moreover, pre-trained language models now popular in NLP are trained on corpora that are not always known or released, making it tricky to assess whether a given MWE is unseen, i.e. whether it has been observed in pre-training data. Future work on MWEI could propose strategies to address these challenges in assessing the generalisation of models.

Other corpora Finally, we mention corpora not included in our sample and not discussed here. Prior to DiMSUM and PARSEME, treebanks were often used to derive MWE annotations as a by-product. MWEI experiments were reported using the French Treebank (Constant et al., 2016), the Penn Treebank (Shigeto et al., 2013), the Arabic Treebank (Green et al., 2013), and the Szeged treebank (Vincze et al., 2013). For English, Wiki50 was one of the first full-text MWE-annotated corpora (Vincze et al., 2011), followed by the Streusle corpus (Schneider et al., 2014), of which the DiMSUM corpus is an extension.

Quite a few papers explore the task of distinguishing literal from idiomatic occurrences of pre-listed potentially idiomatic expressions. Corpora for this task include the English VNC-tokens corpus (Cook et al., 2008), the German preposition-noun-verb (Fritzinger et al., 2010) and infinitive-verb compounds corpus (Horbach et al., 2016), the English Magpie corpus (Haagsma et al., 2020), and the English, Portuguese and Galician Semeval 2022 task 2 corpora (Tayyar Madabushi et al., 2022). The PARSEME collection could be extended to include literal readings (Savary et al., 2019), and this was explored for German (Ehren et al., 2020).

4 Pre-processing and post-processing

Due to the variety of tagging methods, there is often need for a conversion step between the MWE labelling schemes used in the ST data and that preferred by models. This conversion step is reported to various degrees; omission of reporting can pose a problem for replicability.

BIO-style encoding and sequence tagging BIO-style encoding is frequently preferred for sequence tagging tasks. Common practice for both named-entity recognition (NER) systems and MWEI systems is to label tokens in the input data with one of these three labels, 'B' (begin), 'I' (inside), or 'O' (outside). While tolerably effective for capturing sequences of MWE tokens, it fails to capture discontinuous, nesting, or overlapping MWEs.

Schneider et al. (2014) experimented with 4 different tagging schemes based on BIO-style encoding; the 8 positional tags including BbIiOo_~, where the lower-case counterparts 'o', 'b', and 'i' are additionally introduced for tagging nested MWEs, and '_' and '~' to discriminate among strong (idiomatic) and weak (compositional) MWEs. Example 1 demonstrates how the nested expressions ***leaves*** ***a lot*** ***to be desired*** are annotated with this scheme. This tagset was adopted in DiMSUM (Schneider et al., 2016).

(1)

The	staff	**leaves**	*a*	*lot*	**to**	**be**	**desired**	.
O	O	B	b	i_	I_	I_	I_	0

PARSEME annotation (Ramisch et al., 2018a) took a more generalised approach to annotating verbal MWEs in different languages. In their scheme, each MWE token takes a consecutive numerical index in the sentence and – for the initial token in an MWE – its category. A token can have multiple labels, separated with semicolons, if it belongs to more than one MWEs in the sentence. For example, the overlapping expressions ***did study*** *and* ***research*** would be annotated as in Example 2.

(2)

I	**did**	a	lot	of	**study**	and	**research**	.
*	1:LVC;2:LVC	*	*	*	1	*	2	*

In this paper, we refer to the PARSEME label scheme as "CUPT", which is also the name of the

[3]Unseen MWE: multiset of lemmas not annotated in train.

a tabular data format in which the corpora are released (Ramisch et al., 2018a).[4]

4.1 From ST corpora to system data (pre-processing)

Pre-processing steps can include cleaning the data (e.g. removing long sentences, noisy tokens, or special characters). This step also includes any necessary conversion from ST format to whatever format is required for the prediction of MWEs. Of the 27 ST papers, 12 use some form of IO- or BIO-style encoding, while 7 of the 9 non-ST papers use a similar encoding. Among these 12+9 papers, 12 explicitly account for gaps in the MWE sequences, using a particular token to mark these (e.g. 'G' (gap), 'o').

Nested MWEs are handled with the *gappy 1-level* scheme developed by Schneider et al. (2014) or other variants (i.e. *bigappy-unicrossy* scheme developed by Berk et al. (2019)), however, overlapping MWEs such as the case in Example 2 above are only partially handled by *bigappy-unicrossy* and not handled by *gappy 1-level*. Such cases are rare in the corpora, and as such do not greatly impact the data. One paper (Walsh et al., 2022) attempts to address this problem of overlapping or shared-token expressions by modifying the BIO-style encoding, while another paper (Taslimipoor and Rohanian, 2018) appends multiple categories separated by a semicolon, similar to the CUPT-style encoding.

Other methods employed by systems include the extraction of dependency trees or other sub-graph constructions, or multisets of lemmas.[5] To capture MWE annotations; such methods make use of the tree structure to attend to discontinuities and nesting. Waszczuk (2018) describes a pre-processing step to reattach case dependents to their grandparents, so that MWEs of certain categories (e.g. inherently adpositional verbs) are connected. To handle overlaps, they train one model per MWE category and combine their outputs at post-processing.[6]

Most papers do not explicitly mention their strategy to deal with overlapping MWEs. When mentioned, overlapping MWE annotations are either ignored (Zampieri et al., 2022a), duplicated into separate sentences (Zampieri et al., 2018), or handled by the tagging scheme (Yirmibeşoğlu and Güngör, 2020).

4.2 From system output to ST evaluation (post-processing)

Post-processing steps may require conversion of the labels used during prediction into the ST format to allow for evaluation and comparison with other systems in the ST. 13 ST papers and 5 non-ST papers explicitly describe the post-processing steps taken to perform this conversion. 5 ST papers and 1 non-ST paper did not require this conversion step, with the remaining 9 ST papers and 3 non-ST papers not reporting the methodology applied for this step; this may pose a problem for reproducibility. We explore some of the common methods of label processing below.

Conditional random fields Given their ability to observe relationships between labels in a sequence and consider future relationships when observing a pattern, conditional random fields (CRFs) have seen successful application in sequence-labelling tasks such as named-entity recognition, POS-tagging, and MWEI. One of the advantages of CRFs is that they can be applied to both feature-based (symbolic) and continuous models, as an extra layer on top of standard neural architectures (LSTMs or pre-trained transformers). However, since CRFs in neural models are trained using back-propagation, there is no guarantee that they will generate valid label sequences, potentially requiring heuristics to fix the label sequence in converting BIO-like labels into MWE annotations. In our sample, 8 out of 36 system papers report using CRF to predict labels.

BIO-style conversion Reversing the conversion from BIO-style to ST format requires making decisions regarding the grouping of predicted labels, i.e. to which MWE should each predicted label be assigned? With IO-style or binary encoding, grouping continuous predicted MWE labels together may be straightforward, although this can be more complicated when MWEs directly follow each other, with no gaps in between. A BIO-style scheme for predicting labels addresses this problem, as I-labelled tokens can be assumed to belong with the preceding B-labelled token. However, there remains the issue of how to assign I-labelled tokens that may belong to one of several preceding B-labelled tokens, as is the case with nested or overlapping MWEs. There is also the question of how

[4] `https://multiword.sourceforge.net/cupt-format/`

[5] Multiset: set allowing multiple instances of each element.

[6] This does not handle same-category overlaps, though.

to assign standalone I-labelled tokens. In our sample, a heuristic algorithm is frequently applied (7 of 36 papers), with tokens of the same predicted category grouped together, and standalone I-labelled tokens either filtered out or assigned to a new MWE group. A greedy-matching algorithm can be used to generate deep stacks of nested MWEs with gaps (Scherbakov et al., 2016). Alternatively, Viterbi decoding can be used to prevent invalid BIO sequences from being generated (Liu et al., 2021).

Dependency trees In systems where the MWEs are labelled through predicted dependency trees, conversion to CUPT format is relatively straightforward,[7] with all elements of an MWE assumed to be nodes in the same subtree. Waszczuk (2018) highlights the issue of segmenting MWEs within a dependency tree: their heuristic algorithm groups MWEs of the same category within the subtree. If a group contained two or more verbs, it was divided into the corresponding number of MWEs. Gombert and Bartsch (2020) use dependency trees to group MWEs as a post-processing step.

5 Evaluation metrics

Evaluation strategies for structured tagging tasks are less straightforward than that of classification. System performance is determined based on the correct prediction for sets of labels (e.g. for all tokens in ***raining cats and dogs***). The strict matching between the labels of all components of an MWE in the gold data and its correspondents in the predicted data is measured using MWE-based precision, recall and F1 measures in PARSEME. The same measures are referred to as *exact match* in DiMSUM. Nevertheless, in order to reward systems for partially correct predictions, PARSEME uses token-based precision, recall and F1 measures and DiMSUM (Schneider et al., 2016) introduces link-based measures which are computed based on links (correct use of tags) between consecutive tokens in an expression.[8] 20 out of 21 PARSEME ST papers focused on reporting MWE-based F1 (with the focus of 6 PARSEME 1.2 papers being on unseen expressions only), and only one system (Pasquer et al., 2020a) which was designed for predicting seen MWEs reported MWE-based precision on unseen expressions only.[9]All 6 DiMSUM papers reported linked-based F1, with four of them reporting P and R as well.

Standard machine learning approaches optimize systems towards the best F1-measure. Depending on the target task, precision or recall might be more beneficial. Gombert and Bartsch (2020) boost MWE-based precision by modifying the output of their transformer-based system by filtering out the predictions that involve tokens that are not connected in dependency trees.

Focused measures Introducing focused measures in PARSEME 1.0, 1.1, 1.2 developed over time, motivated by related work. For example, Al Saied et al. (2018) showed the negative correlation between system performance and the number of unseen MWEs.

Seen/Unseen Identifying unseen expressions became the focus of PARSEME 1.2, resulting in interesting insights. Word embeddings trained on extra unannotated data (Yirmibeşoğlu and Güngör, 2020) proved successful in detecting unseen expressions and not surprisingly pre-trained language models (Taslimipoor et al., 2020; Kurfalı, 2020) were the best. While rule-based syntactic pattern-matching based on association measures (Pasquer et al., 2020a) failed at capturing unseen expressions, it showed promising results in detecting various forms of a seen MWE. All 6 PARSEME edition 1.2 papers and 3 papers from previous editions focused on reporting performance on unseen expressions

Diversity Evaluating a system's capability to identify variants of existent MWEs is possible thanks to one of PARSEME's additional focused measures. Only two PARSEME papers reported these focused measures. A more recent study by Lion-Bouton et al. (2022) expanded on the above analysis, and proposed two new measures, namely richness and evenness, for evaluating diversity in models' predictions. In the experiments on MWE identification with PARSEME datasets, they showed that F1-measure performance roughly correlates with the richness of models' predictions but not with their evenness.

[7]No DiMSUM ST paper applied this method.

[8]The linked-based measures only work for DiMSUM data, where the MWE tags exactly follow their tagging scheme in which there is no big O label in between MWE components and no single-token MWE. Single-token MWEs are allowed in PARSEME to account for tokenisation problems, e.g. Spanish ***abstenerse*** (lit. 'abstain oneself'), which occurs as such although ideally it should be tokenised as ***abstener_se***.

[9]4 PARSEME papers did not report precision and recall, but the reports of all PARSEME evaluation measures for all systems are available on the corresponding websites.

Discontinuity MWEs pose a unique challenge to NLP due to the discontinuity that often occurs between the words that make up the expression. This challenge distinguishes MWEs from other similar phrasal structures, such as keyphrases or multiword named entities, making their processing more difficult. PARSEME's STs introduce additional evaluation measures focused on discontinuity. Five out of 27 studies on PARSEME datasets reported results on discontinuous MWEs separately. Most of them use dependency parse grammatical structure to identify the relationships between constituents of an MWE (Waszczuk, 2018; Moreau et al., 2018). Rohanian et al. (2019) propose a model which benefits from combining attention mechanism with graph convolutional network to improve identifying discontinuous MWEs. We believe that these focused measures can be generalized to other NLP tasks to alleviate more thorough evaluation.

6 Hypothesis testing and significance

System (or model) comparison has been one of the most important methodological tools, driving progress in NLP for the last 30 years. In this paradigm, we conclude that system A is superior to system B if it obtains a better evaluation score than system B on some given test set(s). The previous sections discussed data (§ 3) and evaluation metrics (§ 5) usually employed in the context of MWE identification. However, several papers throughout the decades have shown that there is a probability that this conclusion is false in general, because the test set is a limited-size sample of the actual language (text) on which the systems will be applied in production (Yeh, 2000; Berg-Kirkpatrick et al., 2012; Dror et al., 2018). Fortunately, statistic tools can estimate this probability given the characteristics of the test set, and in particular its size.

In a nutshell, *hypothesis testing* can be used to assume no difference between two systems as the null hypothesis to reject. Then, a statistical method can be used to estimate the *p-value*, that is, the probability of type-I error.[10] In other words, a p-value estimates the probability of wrongly rejecting the null hypothesis (i.e. concluding that the systems are indeed different) when there is actually no difference between the systems. One can consider that the difference between the systems is *statistically significant* if the p-value is lower than a confidence threshold (usually set to 0.05).Then, if we claim that system A is superior to B, there is a probability of at most 5% that this conclusion is wrong.

In MWE identification, comparison is based on precision, recall, and F-score, which prevents the use of simple parametric tests like Student's t-test (Yeh, 2000). Thus, non-parametric tests such as the bootstrap (Berg-Kirkpatrick et al., 2012) should be employed. However, our survey showed that p-values were reported for only 2 papers. The DiMSUM ST paper compares system predictions using the non-parametric McNemar's test. The official ST ranking shows three systems tied in first position since their results are not significantly different from each other. However, as discussed by Dror et al. (2018), this test is not very powerful, and this result may fall into type-II error, that is, not being able to reject the null hypothesis when it is actually true. Then, Hosseini et al. (2016) report significance using randomized approximation, which is a more appropriate test in this case since it is both non-parametric and powerful.

Significance analysis Given the lack of systematic significance analysis in our paper sample, we propose a new tool and a first analysis of the system predictions of the PARSEME ST 1.2.

We have re-implemented the ST evaluation script using the `cupt` library.[11] On top of it, we have added an option to compare two systems, estimating the p-value of their difference for all calculated metrics (global and phenomenon specific). P-values are estimated using the bootstrap method which resamples k=10,000 new test sets with replacement from the original test set.[12] The p-value is estimated as the relative frequency of extreme results, that is, the proportion of samples for which the difference between the system scores is at least twice as large as the difference observed on the whole test set. Our tool is available at `https://gitlab.com/parseme/significance`.

In practice, significance is more relevant when the differences between systems are small and/or test sets are small. This is the case for many languages and system pairs in the 1.2 edition of the PARSEME ST.[13] Our analyses were performed on each language individually, running the signifi-

[10] Confidence intervals are an alternative, but p-value seems to be preferred in the NLP literature.

[11] `https://gitlab.com/parseme/cupt-lib`

[12] Our implementation is based on the pseudo-code provided in Berg-Kirkpatrick et al. (2012). We resample test sizes with the same number of sentences as the original one.

[13] `https://gitlab.com/parseme/sharedtask-data/-/tree/master/1.2/system-results`

Systems		Open track					Closed track
		MTLB-STRUCT	TRAVIS-multi	HMSid	Seen2Unseen	FipsCo	Seen2Seen
	F1	**0.4309**	**0.3776**	**0.3739**	**0.2483**	**0.1883**	**0.0354**
TRAVIS-mono	**0.4837**	0.03	0.0	0.0	0.0	0.0	-
MTLB-STRUCT	**0.4309**		0.012	0.015	0.0	0.0	-
TRAVIS-multi	**0.3776**			<u>0.447</u>	0.0	0.0	-
HMSid	**0.3739**				0.0	0.0	-
Seen2Unseen	**0.2483**					0.01	-
ERMI	**0.252**	-	-	-	-	-	0.0

Table 1: p-value of the *MWE-based F1* score for results on *Unseen-in-train* MWEs in French. Non-significant results for $\alpha = 0.05$ are underlined.

Systems		Open track			Closed track
		TRAVIS-multi	Seen2Unseen	TRAVIS-mono	ERMI
	F1	**0.6911**	**0.6892**	**0.6709**	**0.6308**
MTLB-STRUCT	**0.7158**	0.025	0.038	0.0	-
TRAVIS-multi	**0.6911**		<u>0.464</u>	<u>0.081</u>	-
Seen2Unseen	**0.6892**			<u>0.103</u>	-
Seen2Seen	**0.7068**	-	-	-	0.0

Table 2: p-value of the the *MWE-based F1* score for results on *global* MWEs in Swedish. Non-significant results for $\alpha = 0.05$ are underlined.

cance tool on all possible system pairs submitted to the same track (open, closed). For each of these pairs, we calculated the 3 p-values (precision, recall, F-score) for each of the evaluation metrics (MWE-based, Unseen-in-train, etc.)

The results table contains 2,728 p-values in total, which we cannot exhaustively present here. Thus, only a sample of the results is gathered here, trying to cover test sets of different sizes, since sample size is known to influence the significance of results. In Table 1, we observe the behavior of the p-value between the unseen-in-train F-scores of systems, and on a language that had a large dataset, that is, French (1,359 MWEs). Results show that on the represented metric, (here, global MWE-based F-score), most systems are significantly different, with a p-value lower than the 0.05 threshold. However, the difference between Travis-multi and HMSid is not deemed significant, so we cannot conclude that the former is better than the latter.

In Table 2, we look at the global MWE score for another language, Swedish, which test set is much smaller (969 MWEs). Here, we observe that Seen2Unseen, Travis-multi and Travis-mono are not significantly different from each other, although some absolute differences in F-scores are larger than for French. Out of all comparisons made, 783 p-values fall above the 0.05 threshold, so potentially up to 29% of the system predictions are not significantly different from each other. Appendix A presents further examples of significance values.

Our analysis is not exhaustive, and other MWE identification papers did report significance in the past, e.g. Constant et al. (2016). Nonetheless, our analyses show that this methodological precaution is mostly neglected in the field. We hope that our survey can contribute to raising awareness on this issue for future publications.

7 Error analysis

Error analysis, when conducted properly, can help to identify particularly challenging cases for MWEI, whether because of intrinsic properties of the MWEs, the dataset, or the language, or because of weaknesses in the model, as demonstrated by the survey. 33 out of 40 papers carried out some degree of error analysis; certain properties of MWEs, languages, or corpus phenomena are investigated in particular. Comparisons of model performance across languages (sometimes including examination of the linguistic features or MWE categories particular to that language) are carried out in 11 papers (Simkó et al., 2017; Boros et al., 2017), while reporting the model results across the focused measures highlighted in § 5 are carried out in 15 papers. The PARSEME 1.1 and 1.2 papers usually report and discuss focused metrics, as these metrics were implemented in the ST evaluation scripts (Waszczuk, 2018; Berk et al., 2018a).

Analyses tended to take one of two forms: example-based analysis reporting individual instances where the model performed better or worse than usual (Klyueva et al., 2017; Walsh et al., 2022), and automatic metrics aggregated across particular properties or phenomena. Among the focused metrics, some papers pay special attention to discontinuities (Björne and Salakoski, 2016; Moreau et al., 2018; Berk et al., 2018a; Rohanian et al., 2019) and seen/unseen MWEs (Maldonado et al., 2017; Zampieri et al., 2018; Taslimipoor and Rohanian, 2018). Some studies analyse the model's features and modules via ablation experiments (Scherbakov et al., 2016; Tang et al., 2016; Stodden et al., 2018; Pasquer et al., 2020a). Cross-language performance was also discussed, especially in the first editions of PARSEME (Simkó et al., 2017; Boros et al., 2017). More original aspects discussed less often include POS sequence patterns (Cordeiro et al., 2016; Tang et al., 2016), the use of external lexicons (Kirilin et al., 2016), syntactic dependencies between components (Pasquer et al., 2018; Moreau et al., 2018), pre-trained embedding representations (Zampieri et al., 2019), and tagging schemes, as discussed in § 4 (Zampieri et al., 2022b).

In short, although quite heterogeneous, error analyses are usually present in MWEI papers, and tend to uncover interesting research questions for future work.

8 Conclusions and open issues

This paper provides a survey on experimental conditions reported and discussed in recent works on identifying MWEs. Analysis of the details of methodological choices by authors helps researchers and practitioners understand the performance of different models and identify areas for improvement. While STs help benchmark many of such experimental designs and evaluation criteria, tight schedules and less attention to task description papers cause many such details still to be neglected.

This survey focuses on two shared tasks on identifying MWEs and consequent systems designed based on their task definitions, datasets, and evaluations. As common-sense best practices, we advocate reporting on experimental choices such as corpus constitutions and selections, pre- and post-processing, evaluation metrics and significance testing of performance, and some error analysis performed in related work. We encourage the introduction of focused measures that facilitate error analysis, as is done in the later PARSEME editions. For statistical significance testing, we propose a tool that can automatically run such analyses on standard PARSEME-formatted predictions.

However, our analyses are not exhaustive and there are other methodological details to be discussed in the papers. One aspect that we only skim over in our discussion of the use of dev sets is hyper-parameter tuning. Which hyper-parameters were tuned, on which selection of the datasets, and what strategy (if any) was taken (e.g. grid search, random, etc.) are aspects that only very few of the papers clearly reported, and future work should encourage authors to report these.

Currently, most evaluation techniques are automatic. One open issue is whether there is a place in which manual evaluation of detected MWEs should be performed, (e.g. in the context of downstream tasks). New evaluation protocols can be considered in the future, towards answering other questions, e.g. whether some categories of MWEs are more important than others. We expect that our survey can contribute to the gradual adoption of methodological standards and best practices, both for shared tasks and independent research work in our community.

Acknowledgements

This work has been funded by the French Agence Nationale pour la Recherche, through the SELEXINI project (ANR-21-CE23-0033-01), and by the Irish Research Council and CampusFrance, via an Ulysses PHC grant (45358QD). We thank Marius Thorre and Silvio Cordeiro for their contribution to the development of the significance software, Agata Savary for her feedback on an initial version of this paper, and the anonymous reviewers for their valuable suggestions.

References

Hazem Al Saied, Marie Candito, and Matthieu Constant. 2018. A transition-based verbal multiword expression analyzer. In Stella Markantonatou, Carlos Ramisch, Agata Savary, and Veronika Vincze, editors, *Multiword expressions at length and in depth: Extended papers from the MWE 2017 workshop*. Language Science Press., Berlin.

Hazem Al Saied, Matthieu Constant, and Marie Candito. 2017. The ATILF-LLF system for parseme shared task: a transition-based verbal multiword expression tagger. In *Proceedings of the 13th Workshop on Multiword Expressions (MWE 2017)*, pages 127–132, Valencia, Spain. Association for Computational Linguistics.

Verginica Barbu Mititelu, Mihaela Cristescu, and Mihaela Onofrei. 2019. The Romanian corpus annotated with verbal multiword expressions. In *Proceedings of the Joint Workshop on Multiword Expressions and WordNet (MWE-WN 2019)*, pages 13–21, Florence, Italy. Association for Computational Linguistics.

Taylor Berg-Kirkpatrick, David Burkett, and Dan Klein. 2012. An empirical investigation of statistical significance in NLP. In *Proceedings of the 2012 Joint Conference on Empirical Methods in Natural Language Processing and Computational Natural Language Learning*, pages 995–1005, Jeju Island, Korea. Association for Computational Linguistics.

Gözde Berk, Berna Erden, and Tunga Güngör. 2018a. Deep-BGT at PARSEME shared task 2018: Bidirectional LSTM-CRF model for verbal multiword expression identification. In *Proceedings of the Joint Workshop on Linguistic Annotation, Multiword Expressions and Constructions (LAW-MWE-CxG-2018)*, pages 248–253, Santa Fe, New Mexico, USA. Association for Computational Linguistics.

Gözde Berk, Berna Erden, and Tunga Güngör. 2019. Representing overlaps in sequence labeling tasks with a novel tagging scheme: bigappy-unicrossy. In *Computational Linguistics and Intelligent Text Processing*, pages 622–635. Springer International Publishing.

Gözde Berk, Berna Erden, and Tunga Güngör. 2018b. Turkish verbal multiword expressions corpus. In *2018 26th Signal Processing and Communications Applications Conference (SIU)*, pages 1–4.

Jari Björne and Tapio Salakoski. 2016. UTU at SemEval-2016 task 10: Binary classification for expression detection (BCED). In *Proceedings of the 10th International Workshop on Semantic Evaluation (SemEval-2016)*, pages 925–930, San Diego, California. Association for Computational Linguistics.

Tiberiu Boros, Sonia Pipa, Verginica Barbu Mititelu, and Dan Tufis. 2017. A data-driven approach to verbal multiword expression detection. PARSEME shared task system description paper. In *Proceedings of the 13th Workshop on Multiword Expressions (MWE 2017)*, pages 121–126, Valencia, Spain. Association for Computational Linguistics.

Jean-Pierre Colson. 2020. HMSid and HMSid2 at PARSEME shared task 2020: Computational corpus linguistics and unseen-in-training MWEs. In *Proceedings of the Joint Workshop on Multiword Expressions and Electronic Lexicons*, pages 119–123, online. Association for Computational Linguistics.

Mathieu Constant, Gülşen Eryiğit, Johanna Monti, Lonneke van der Plas, Carlos Ramisch, Michael Rosner, and Amalia Todirascu. 2017. Survey: Multiword expression processing: A Survey. *Computational Linguistics*, 43(4):837–892.

Matthieu Constant, Joseph Le Roux, and Nadi Tomeh. 2016. Deep lexical segmentation and syntactic parsing in the easy-first dependency framework. In *Proceedings of the 2016 Conference of the North American Chapter of the Association for Computational Linguistics: Human Language Technologies*, pages 1095–1101, San Diego, California. Association for Computational Linguistics.

Matthieu Constant and Joakim Nivre. 2016. A transition-based system for joint lexical and syntactic analysis. In *Proceedings of the 54th Annual Meeting of the Association for Computational Linguistics (Volume 1: Long Papers)*, pages 161–171, Berlin, Germany. Association for Computational Linguistics.

Matthieu Constant, Anthony Sigogne, and Patrick Watrin. 2012. Discriminative strategies to integrate multiword expression recognition and parsing. In *Proceedings of the 50th Annual Meeting of the Association for Computational Linguistics (Volume 1: Long Papers)*, pages 204–212, Jeju Island, Korea. Association for Computational Linguistics.

Paul Cook, Afsaneh Fazly, and Suzanne Stevenson. 2008. The vnc-tokens dataset. In *Proceedings of the LREC Workshop on Towards a Shared Task for Multiword Expressions (MWE 2008)*, pages 19–22.

Silvio Cordeiro, Carlos Ramisch, and Aline Villavicencio. 2016. UFRGS&LIF at SemEval-2016 task 10: Rule-based MWE identification and predominant-supersense tagging. In *Proceedings of the 10th International Workshop on Semantic Evaluation (SemEval-2016)*, pages 910–917, San Diego, California. Association for Computational Linguistics.

Rotem Dror, Gili Baumer, Segev Shlomov, and Roi Reichart. 2018. The hitchhiker's guide to testing statistical significance in natural language processing. In *Proceedings of the 56th Annual Meeting of the Association for Computational Linguistics (Volume 1: Long Papers)*, pages 1383–1392, Melbourne, Australia. Association for Computational Linguistics.

Rafael Ehren, Timm Lichte, Laura Kallmeyer, and Jakub Waszczuk. 2020. Supervised disambiguation of German verbal idioms with a BiLSTM architecture. In *Proceedings of the Second Workshop on Figurative Language Processing*, pages 211–220, Online. Association for Computational Linguistics.

Vasiliki Foufi, Luka Nerima, and Éric Wehrli. 2017. Parsing and MWE detection: Fips at the PARSEME shared task. In *Proceedings of the 13th Workshop on Multiword Expressions (MWE 2017)*, pages 54–59, Valencia, Spain. Association for Computational Linguistics.

Fabienne Fritzinger, Marion Weller, and Ulrich Heid. 2010. A survey of idiomatic preposition-noun-verb triples on token level. In *Proceedings of the Seventh International Conference on Language Resources and Evaluation (LREC'10)*, Valletta, Malta. European Language Resources Association (ELRA).

Marcos Garcia, Tiago Kramer Vieira, Carolina Scarton, Marco Idiart, and Aline Villavicencio. 2021. Probing for idiomaticity in vector space models. In *Proceedings of the 16th Conference of the European Chapter of the Association for Computational Linguistics: Main Volume*, pages 3551–3564, Online. Association for Computational Linguistics.

Sebastian Gombert and Sabine Bartsch. 2020. MultiVitaminBooster at PARSEME shared task 2020: Combining window- and dependency-based features with multilingual contextualised word embeddings for VMWE detection. In *Proceedings of the Joint Workshop on Multiword Expressions and Electronic Lexicons*, pages 149–155, online. Association for Computational Linguistics.

Kyle Gorman and Steven Bedrick. 2019. We need to talk about standard splits. In *Proceedings of the 57th Annual Meeting of the Association for Computational Linguistics*, pages 2786–2791, Florence, Italy. Association for Computational Linguistics.

Spence Green, Marie-Catherine de Marneffe, and Christopher D. Manning. 2013. Parsing models for identifying multiword expressions. *Computational Linguistics*, 39(1):195–227.

Hessel Haagsma, Johan Bos, and Malvina Nissim. 2020. MAGPIE: A large corpus of potentially idiomatic expressions. In *Proceedings of the Twelfth Language Resources and Evaluation Conference*, pages 279–287, Marseille, France. European Language Resources Association.

Andrea Horbach, Andrea Hensler, Sabine Krome, Jakob Prange, Werner Scholze-Stubenrecht, Diana Steffen, Stefan Thater, Christian Wellner, and Manfred Pinkal. 2016. A corpus of literal and idiomatic uses of German infinitive-verb compounds. In *Proceedings of the Tenth International Conference on Language Resources and Evaluation (LREC'16)*, pages 836–841, Portorož, Slovenia. European Language Resources Association (ELRA).

Mohammad Javad Hosseini, Noah A. Smith, and Su-In Lee. 2016. UW-CSE at SemEval-2016 task 10: Detecting multiword expressions and supersenses using double-chained conditional random fields. In *Proceedings of the 10th International Workshop on Semantic Evaluation (SemEval-2016)*, pages 931–936, San Diego, California. Association for Computational Linguistics.

Uxoa Iñurrieta, Itziar Aduriz, Ainara Estarrona, Itziar Gonzalez-Dios, Antton Gurrutxaga, Ruben Urizar, and Iñaki Alegria. 2018. Verbal multiword expressions in Basque corpora. In *Proceedings of the Joint Workshop on Linguistic Annotation, Multiword Expressions and Constructions (LAW-MWE-CxG-2018)*, pages 86–95, Santa Fe, New Mexico, USA. Association for Computational Linguistics.

Menghan Jiang, Natalia Klyueva, Hongzhi Xu, and Chu-Ren Huang. 2018. Annotating Chinese light verb constructions according to PARSEME guidelines. In *Proceedings of the Eleventh International Conference on Language Resources and Evaluation (LREC 2018)*, Miyazaki, Japan. European Language Resources Association (ELRA).

Angelika Kirilin, Felix Krauss, and Yannick Versley. 2016. ICL-HD at SemEval-2016 task 10: Improving the detection of minimal semantic units and their meanings with an ontology and word embeddings. In *Proceedings of the 10th International Workshop on Semantic Evaluation (SemEval-2016)*, pages 937–945, San Diego, California. Association for Computational Linguistics.

Natalia Klyueva, Antoine Doucet, and Milan Straka. 2017. Neural networks for multi-word expression detection. In *Proceedings of the 13th Workshop on Multiword Expressions (MWE 2017)*, pages 60–65, Valencia, Spain. Association for Computational Linguistics.

Murathan Kurfalı. 2020. TRAVIS at PARSEME shared task 2020: How good is (m)BERT at seeing the unseen? In *Proceedings of the Joint Workshop on Multiword Expressions and Electronic Lexicons*, pages 136–141, online. Association for Computational Linguistics.

Adam Lion-Bouton, Yagmur Ozturk, Agata Savary, and Jean-Yves Antoine. 2022. Evaluating diversity of multiword expressions in annotated text. In *Proceedings of the 29th International Conference on Computational Linguistics*, pages 3285–3295, Gyeongju, Republic of Korea. International Committee on Computational Linguistics.

Nelson F. Liu, Daniel Hershcovich, Michael Kranzlein, and Nathan Schneider. 2021. Lexical semantic recognition. In *Proceedings of the 17th Workshop on Multiword Expressions (MWE 2021)*, pages 49–56, Online. Association for Computational Linguistics.

Alfredo Maldonado, Lifeng Han, Erwan Moreau, Ashjan Alsulaimani, Koel Dutta Chowdhury, Carl Vogel, and Qun Liu. 2017. Detection of verbal multi-word expressions via conditional random fields with syntactic dependency features and semantic re-ranking. In *Proceedings of the 13th Workshop on Multiword Expressions (MWE 2017)*, pages 114–120, Valencia, Spain. Association for Computational Linguistics.

Alfredo Maldonado and Behrang QasemiZadeh. 2018. Analysis and Insights from the PARSEME Shared Task dataset. In Stella Markantonatou, Carlos Ramisch, Agata Savary, and Veronika Vincze, editors, *Multiword expressions at length and in depth: Extended papers from the MWE 2017 workshop*, pages 149–175. Language Science Press., Berlin.

Johanna Monti and Maria Pia di Buono. 2019. PARSEME-It: an Italian corpus annotated with verbal multiword expressions. *IJCoL*, 5:61–93.

Erwan Moreau, Ashjan Alsulaimani, Alfredo Maldonado, and Carl Vogel. 2018. CRF-seq and CRF-DepTree at PARSEME shared task 2018: Detecting verbal MWEs using sequential and dependency-based approaches. In *Proceedings of the Joint Workshop on Linguistic Annotation, Multiword Expressions and Constructions (LAW-MWE-CxG-2018)*, pages 241–247, Santa Fe, New Mexico, USA. Association for Computational Linguistics.

István Nagy T. and Veronika Vincze. 2014. VPCTagger: Detecting verb-particle constructions with syntax-based methods. In *Proceedings of the 10th Workshop on Multiword Expressions (MWE)*, pages 17–25, Gothenburg, Sweden. Association for Computational Linguistics.

Yagmur Ozturk, Najet Hadj Mohamed, Adam Lion-Bouton, and Agata Savary. 2022. Enhancing the PARSEME Turkish corpus of verbal multiword expressions. In *Proceedings of the 18th Workshop on Multiword Expressions @LREC2022*, pages 100–104, Marseille, France. European Language Resources Association.

Caroline Pasquer, Agata Savary, Carlos Ramisch, and Jean-Yves Antoine. 2018. If you've seen some, you've seen them all: Identifying variants of multiword expressions. In *Proceedings of the 27th International Conference on Computational Linguistics*, pages 2582–2594, Santa Fe, New Mexico, USA. Association for Computational Linguistics.

Caroline Pasquer, Agata Savary, Carlos Ramisch, and Jean-Yves Antoine. 2020a. Seen2Unseen at PARSEME shared task 2020: All roads do not lead to unseen verb-noun VMWEs. In *Proceedings of the Joint Workshop on Multiword Expressions and Electronic Lexicons*, pages 124–129, online. Association for Computational Linguistics.

Caroline Pasquer, Agata Savary, Carlos Ramisch, and Jean-Yves Antoine. 2020b. Verbal multiword expression identification: Do we need a sledgehammer to crack a nut? In *Proceedings of the 28th International Conference on Computational Linguistics*, pages 3333–3345, Barcelona, Spain (Online). International Committee on Computational Linguistics.

Carlos Ramisch, Silvio Ricardo Cordeiro, Agata Savary, Veronika Vincze, Verginica Barbu Mititelu, Archna Bhatia, Maja Buljan, Marie Candito, Polona Gantar, Voula Giouli, Tunga Güngör, Abdelati Hawwari, Uxoa Iñurrieta, Jolanta Kovalevskaitė, Simon Krek, Timm Lichte, Chaya Liebeskind, Johanna Monti, Carla Parra Escartín, Behrang QasemiZadeh, Renata Ramisch, Nathan Schneider, Ivelina Stoyanova, Ashwini Vaidya, and Abigail Walsh. 2018a. Edition 1.1 of the PARSEME shared task on automatic identification of verbal multiword expressions. In *Proceedings of the Joint Workshop on Linguistic Annotation, Multiword Expressions and Constructions (LAW-MWE-CxG-2018)*, pages 222–240, Santa Fe, New Mexico, USA. Association for Computational Linguistics.

Carlos Ramisch, Renata Ramisch, Leonardo Zilio, Aline Villavicencio, and Silvio Cordeiro. 2018b. A corpus study of verbal multiword expressions in Brazilian Portuguese. In *Computational Processing of the Portuguese Language 13th International Conference, PROPOR 2018, Canela, Brazil, September 24–26, 2018, Proceedings*, Lecture Notes in Artificial Intelligence, Cham, Switzerland. Springer International Publishing. `https://link.springer.com/chapter/10.1007/978-3-319-99722-3_3`.

Carlos Ramisch, Agata Savary, Bruno Guillaume, Jakub Waszczuk, Marie Candito, Ashwini Vaidya, Verginica Barbu Mititelu, Archna Bhatia, Uxoa Iñurrieta, Voula Giouli, Tunga Güngör, Menghan Jiang, Timm Lichte, Chaya Liebeskind, Johanna Monti, Renata Ramisch, Sara Stymne, Abigail Walsh, and Hongzhi Xu. 2020. Edition 1.2 of the PARSEME shared task on semi-supervised identification of verbal multiword expressions. In *Proceedings of the Joint Workshop on Multiword Expressions and Electronic Lexicons*, pages 107–118, online. Association for Computational Linguistics.

Lance Ramshaw and Mitch Marcus. 1995. Text chunking using transformation-based learning. In *Third Workshop on Very Large Corpora*.

Omid Rohanian, Shiva Taslimipoor, Samaneh Kouchaki, Le An Ha, and Ruslan Mitkov. 2019. Bridging the gap: Attending to discontinuity in identification of multiword expressions. In *Proceedings of the 2019 Conference of the North American Chapter of the Association for Computational Linguistics: Human Language Technologies, Volume 1 (Long and Short Papers)*, pages 2692–2698, Minneapolis, Minnesota. Association for Computational Linguistics.

Agata Savary, Marie Candito, Verginica Barbu Mititelu, Eduard Bejček, Fabienne Cap, Slavomír Čéplö, Silvio Ricardo Cordeiro, Gülşen Eryiğit, Voula Giouli, Maarten van Gompel, Yaakov HaCohen-Kerner, Jolanta Kovalevskaitė, Simon Krek, Chaya Liebeskind, Johanna Monti, Carla Parra Escartín, Lonneke van der Plas, Behrang QasemiZadeh, Carlos Ramisch, Federico Sangati, Ivelina Stoyanova, and Veronika Vincze. 2018. PARSEME multilingual corpus of verbal multiword expressions. In Stella Markantonatou, Carlos Ramisch, Agata Savary, and Veronika Vincze, editors, *Multiword expressions at length and in depth: Extended papers from the MWE 2017 workshop*, pages 87–147. Language Science Press., Berlin.

Agata Savary, Silvio Cordeiro, Timm Lichte, Carlos Ramisch, Uxoa Iñurrieta, and Voula Giouli. 2019. Literal Occurrences of Multiword Expressions: Rare Birds That Cause a Stir. *The Prague Bulletin of Mathematical Linguistics*.

Agata Savary, Carlos Ramisch, Silvio Cordeiro, Federico Sangati, Veronika Vincze, Behrang QasemiZadeh, Marie Candito, Fabienne Cap, Voula Giouli, Ivelina Stoyanova, and Antoine Doucet. 2017. The PARSEME shared task on automatic identification of verbal multiword expressions. In *Proceedings of the 13th Workshop on Multiword Expressions (MWE 2017)*, pages 31–47, Valencia, Spain. Association for Computational Linguistics.

Agata Savary and Jakub Waszczuk. 2020. Polish corpus of verbal multiword expressions. In *Proceedings of the Joint Workshop on Multiword Expressions and Electronic Lexicons*, pages 32–43, online. Association for Computational Linguistics.

Andreas Scherbakov, Ekaterina Vylomova, Fei Liu, and Timothy Baldwin. 2016. VectorWeavers at SemEval-2016 task 10: From incremental meaning to semantic unit (phrase by phrase). In *Proceedings of the 10th International Workshop on Semantic Evaluation (SemEval-2016)*, pages 946–952, San Diego, California. Association for Computational Linguistics.

Nathan Schneider, Emily Danchik, Chris Dyer, and Noah A. Smith. 2014. Discriminative lexical semantic segmentation with gaps: Running the MWE gamut. *Transactions of the Association for Computational Linguistics*, 2:193–206.

Nathan Schneider, Dirk Hovy, Anders Johannsen, and Marine Carpuat. 2016. SemEval-2016 task 10: Detecting minimal semantic units and their meanings (DiMSUM). In *Proceedings of the 10th International Workshop on Semantic Evaluation (SemEval-2016)*, pages 546–559, San Diego, California. Association for Computational Linguistics.

Yutaro Shigeto, Ai Azuma, Sorami Hisamoto, Shuhei Kondo, Tomoya Kose, Keisuke Sakaguchi, Akifumi Yoshimoto, Frances Yung, and Yuji Matsumoto. 2013. Construction of English MWE dictionary and its application to POS tagging. In *Proceedings of the 9th Workshop on Multiword Expressions*, pages 139–144, Atlanta, Georgia, USA. Association for Computational Linguistics.

Katalin Ilona Simkó, Viktória Kovács, and Veronika Vincze. 2017. USzeged: Identifying verbal multiword expressions with POS tagging and parsing techniques. In *Proceedings of the 13th Workshop on Multiword Expressions (MWE 2017)*, pages 48–53, Valencia, Spain. Association for Computational Linguistics.

Anders Søgaard, Sebastian Ebert, Jasmijn Bastings, and Katja Filippova. 2021. We need to talk about random splits. In *Proceedings of the 16th Conference of the European Chapter of the Association for Computational Linguistics: Main Volume*, pages 1823–1832, Online. Association for Computational Linguistics.

Regina Stodden, Behrang QasemiZadeh, and Laura Kallmeyer. 2018. TRAPACC and TRAPACCS at PARSEME shared task 2018: Neural transition tagging of verbal multiword expressions. In *Proceedings of the Joint Workshop on Linguistic Annotation, Multiword Expressions and Constructions (LAW-MWE-CxG-2018)*, pages 268–274, Santa Fe, New Mexico, USA. Association for Computational Linguistics.

Xin Tang, Fei Li, and Donghong Ji. 2016. WHUNlp at SemEval-2016 task DiMSUM: A pilot study in detecting minimal semantic units and their meanings using supervised models. In *Proceedings of the 10th International Workshop on Semantic Evaluation (SemEval-2016)*, pages 918–924, San Diego, California. Association for Computational Linguistics.

Shiva Taslimipoor, Sara Bahaadini, and Ekaterina Kochmar. 2020. MTLB-STRUCT @parseme 2020: Capturing unseen multiword expressions using multitask learning and pre-trained masked language models. In *Proceedings of the Joint Workshop on Multiword Expressions and Electronic Lexicons*, pages 142–148, online. Association for Computational Linguistics.

Shiva Taslimipoor and Omid Rohanian. 2018. SHOMA at Parseme shared task on automatic identification of VMWEs: Neural multiword expression tagging with high generalisation. *arXiv preprint arXiv:1809.03056*.

Harish Tayyar Madabushi, Edward Gow-Smith, Marcos Garcia, Carolina Scarton, Marco Idiart, and Aline Villavicencio. 2022. SemEval-2022 task 2: Multilingual idiomaticity detection and sentence embedding. In *Proceedings of the 16th International Workshop on Semantic Evaluation (SemEval-2022)*, pages 107–121, Seattle, United States. Association for Computational Linguistics.

Veronika Vincze, István Nagy T., and Gábor Berend. 2011. Multiword expressions and named entities in the wiki50 corpus. In *Proceedings of the International Conference Recent Advances in Natural Language Processing 2011*, pages 289–295, Hissar, Bulgaria. Association for Computational Linguistics.

Veronika Vincze, István Nagy T., and Richárd Farkas. 2013. Identifying English and Hungarian light verb constructions: A contrastive approach. In *Proceedings of the 51st Annual Meeting of the Association for Computational Linguistics (Volume 2: Short Papers)*, pages 255–261, Sofia, Bulgaria. Association for Computational Linguistics.

Abigail Walsh, Claire Bonial, Kristina Geeraert, John P. McCrae, Nathan Schneider, and Clarissa Somers. 2018. Constructing an annotated corpus of verbal MWEs for English. In *Proceedings of the Joint Workshop on Linguistic Annotation, Multiword Expressions and Constructions (LAW-MWE-CxG-2018)*, pages 193–200, Santa Fe, New Mexico, USA. Association for Computational Linguistics.

Abigail Walsh, Teresa Lynn, and Jennifer Foster. 2020. Annotating verbal MWEs in Irish for the PARSEME shared task 1.2. In *Proceedings of the Joint Workshop on Multiword Expressions and Electronic Lexicons*, pages 58–65, online. Association for Computational Linguistics.

Abigail Walsh, Teresa Lynn, and Jennifer Foster. 2022. A BERT's eye view: Identification of Irish multiword expressions using pre-trained language models.

In *Proceedings of the 18th Workshop on Multiword Expressions @LREC2022*, pages 89–99, Marseille, France. European Language Resources Association.

Jakub Waszczuk. 2018. TRAVERSAL at PARSEME shared task 2018: Identification of verbal multiword expressions using a discriminative tree-structured model. In *Proceedings of the Joint Workshop on Linguistic Annotation, Multiword Expressions and Constructions (LAW-MWE-CxG-2018)*, pages 275–282, Santa Fe, New Mexico, USA. Association for Computational Linguistics.

Alexander Yeh. 2000. More accurate tests for the statistical significance of result differences. In *COLING 2000 Volume 2: The 18th International Conference on Computational Linguistics*.

Zeynep Yirmibeşoğlu and Tunga Güngör. 2020. ERMI at PARSEME shared task 2020: Embedding-rich multiword expression identification. In *Proceedings of the Joint Workshop on Multiword Expressions and Electronic Lexicons*, pages 130–135, online. Association for Computational Linguistics.

Nicolas Zampieri, Carlos Ramisch, and Geraldine Damnati. 2019. The impact of word representations on sequential neural MWE identification. In *Proceedings of the Joint Workshop on Multiword Expressions and WordNet (MWE-WN 2019)*, pages 169–175, Florence, Italy. Association for Computational Linguistics.

Nicolas Zampieri, Carlos Ramisch, Irina Illina, and Dominique Fohr. 2022a. Identification des expressions polylexicales dans les tweets (identification of multiword expressions in tweets). In *Actes de la 29e Conférence sur le Traitement Automatique des Langues Naturelles. Volume 1 : conférence principale*, pages 365–373, Avignon, France. ATALA.

Nicolas Zampieri, Carlos Ramisch, Irina Illina, and Dominique Fohr. 2022b. Identification of multiword expressions in tweets for hate speech detection. In *Proceedings of the Thirteenth Language Resources and Evaluation Conference*, pages 202–210, Marseille, France. European Language Resources Association.

Nicolas Zampieri, Manon Scholivet, Carlos Ramisch, and Benoit Favre. 2018. Veyn at PARSEME shared task 2018: Recurrent neural networks for VMWE identification. In *Proceedings of the Joint Workshop on Linguistic Annotation, Multiword Expressions and Constructions (LAW-MWE-CxG-2018)*, pages 290–296, Santa Fe, New Mexico, USA. Association for Computational Linguistics.

Ziheng Zeng and Suma Bhat. 2021. Idiomatic expression identification using semantic compatibility. *Transactions of the Association for Computational Linguistics*, 9:1546–1562.

A Further significance analyses

Here, we present two further samples of our significance tool output for the results of the PARSEME 1.2 shared task. Table 3 shows the p-values for French considering the global MWE score (the main paper text shows the analysis for *Unseen-in-train* MWEs in Table 1). In Table 4 we show the analysis for a language with a very small test set, Irish, containing 436 annotated MWEs. In both cases, we observe small F-score variations between systems that are not deemed significant. Thus, one cannot say that Travis-multi (F1=0.7689) is better than Seen2Unseen (F1=0.7677) for the French global MWE measure. The same applies for the difference between Seen2Unseen (F1=0.3058) and MTLB-struct (F1=0.3007) for the Irish global MWE-based score.

Systems		Open track					Closed track
		MTLB-STRUCT	TRAVIS-multi	Seen2Unseen	HMSid	FipsCo	ERMI
	F1	**0.7942**	**0.7689**	**0.7677**	**0.6579**	**0.5067**	**0.6141**
TRAVIS-mono	**0.826**	0.0	0.0	0.0	0.0	0.0	-
MTLB-STRUCT	**0.7942**		0.003	0.009	0.0	0.0	-
TRAVIS-multi	**0.7689**			0.47	0.0	0.0	-
Seen2Unseen	**0.7677**				0.0	0.0	-
HMSid	**0.6579**					0.0	-
Seen2Seen	**0.7863**	-	-	-	-	-	0.0

Table 3: P-value of the the *MWE-based F1* score for results on *global* MWEs in French. Non-significant results for $\alpha = 0.05$ are underlined.

Systems		Open track		Closed track
		MTLB-STRUCT	TRAVIS-multi	ERMI
	F1	**0.3007**	**0.0717**	**0.1958**
Seen2Unseen	**0.3058**	0.423	0.0	-
MTLB-STRUCT	**0.3007**		0.0	-
Seen2Seen	**0.2689**	-	-	0.004

Table 4: P-values of the *MWE-based F1* score for results on *global* MWEs in Irish. Non-significant results for $\alpha = 0.05$ are underlined.

A Multiword Expression Lexicon Formalism Optimised for Observational Adequacy

Adam Lion-Bouton[1], Agata Savary[2], Jean-Yves Antoine[1]
University of Tours - LIFAT[1], Paris-Saclay University, CNRS - LISN[2],
lion.adam.otman@gmail.com
agata.savary@universite-paris-saclay.fr
jean-yves.antoine@univ-tours.fr

Abstract

Past research advocates that, in order to handle the unpredictable nature of multiword expressions (MWEs), their identification should be assisted with lexicons. The choice of the format for such lexicons, however, is far from obvious. We propose the first – to our knowledge – method to quantitatively evaluate some MWE lexicon formalisms based on the notion of observational adequacy. We apply it to derive a simple yet adequate MWE-lexicon formalism, dubbed λ-CSS, based on syntactic dependencies. It proves competitive with lexicons based on sequential representation of MWEs, and even comparable to a state-of-the art MWE identifier.

1 Introduction

Multiword expressions (MWEs), such as ***by and large***, ***carbon footprint*** or *to **pull** one's **leg*** 'to tease someone', exhibit irregularities which are challenging for text processing. Most notably, their meaning cannot be straightforwardly deduced from the meanings of their components, which is an obstacle for semantically-oriented applications. To help such applications process MWEs correctly, one solution is to pre-identify MWEs in text, so as to later apply dedicated procedures to them.

Recognizing MWEs occurrences in texts (henceforth referred to as MWE *identification*) is, according to Constant et al. (2017), one of the two main subtasks of MWE processing (the other being MWE *discovery*, the task of generating sets of MWEs) and still represents quite a challenge despite having been the focus of many works. Notably, PARSEME shared tasks on identification of verbal MWEs (Savary et al., 2017; Ramisch et al., 2018, 2020) have provided a controlled environment and focused challenges for MWE identification. Each edition of the task trying to put in focus those facets of the identification task which are the hardest.

One thing that PARSEME shared tasks definitely highlighted is that identification of MWEs unseen during training proves to be significantly harder than identification of seen MWEs. This can be seen in the results of editions 1.1 and 1.2 of the shared tasks when comparing the scores of various identifiers on seen vs unseen MWEs. The difficulty of identifying unseen MWE should not come as a surprise as this task can be seen as presenting the challenges of both identification and discovery.

Seeing this discrepancy between identification of seen and unseen MWEs, Savary et al. (2019b) argue that the use of MWE lexicons is key to high-quality MWE identification. Thus, shifting the burden of unseen MWEs on discovery and using lexicon as the interface between discovery and identification. This position is supported by experiments from Riedl and Biemann (2016) that show that MWEs lexical resources can be used in order to improve MWE identification.

In accordance with this argument, this paper investigates MWE-lexicon formalisms, how they can be compared and introduce one such MWE-lexicon formalisms.

2 Multiword Expression

We abide by PARSEME's definition of a MWE (Savary et al., 2018a), adapted from (Baldwin and Kim, 2010), as a (continuous or discontinuous) sequence of words, at least two of which are lexicalized (always realised by the same lexemes), which displays some degree of lexical, morphological, syntactic and/or semantic idiosyncrasy.

MWEs happen to present quite a few interesting properties. Of all the properties listed by (Savary et al., 2018a; Baldwin and Kim, 2010; Constant et al., 2017) we will only mention the following 3 for the impact they have on how MWEs can and should be represented and what MWE-lexicons need to accomplish.

Proceedings of the 19th Workshop on Multiword Expressions (MWE 2023), pages 121–130
May 6, 2023

Variability MWEs can appear under a variety of *forms* depending on the morphosyntactic context in which they occur (e.g. *I* ***pay*** *him a* ***visit*** */ The* ***visits*** *she* ***pays*** *me*), their components can be found in different orders, forms, or even differently syntactically related. This makes simple representations such as sequences of forms insufficiently descriptive and pushes us to more complex representations capturing all the forms under which a MWE could appear.

Discontinuity Discontinuity can be seen as a form of variability where component words of a MWE are not adjacent to one another but separated by a word or group of words named the *insertion*. We define two types of discontinuity: *linear discontinuity* where the component words of the MWE are not next to each other in the sentence (e.g. ***pay*** *someone a* ***visit***, where '*someone a*' is the insertion between '*pay*' and '*visit*') ; and *syntactic discontinuity* where a component of the MWE is not directly related by a syntactic dependency to any other component of the MWE (e.g. figure 1 where '*wanted*' is the insertion between '*visit*' and '*pay*'[1]).

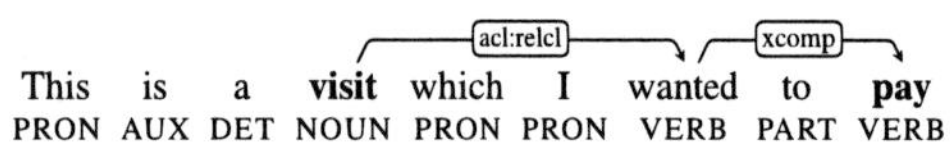

Figure 1: Syntactic discontinuity

Not all MWEs can be discontinued and anything cannot be inserted between MWE components. What can and cannot be inserted in a MWE depends on the MWE and should be described for a MWE representation to be complete.

Literal-idiomatic ambiguity While MWEs are defined as groups of words displaying some form of idiosyncrasy, sometimes the very group of words composing a given MWE can appear in a sentence without displaying any idiosyncrasy. In this case, we say that the occurrence is non-idiomatic (e.g. *I paid them a visit to the museum*) as opposed to idiomatic occurrences (e.g. *I* ***paid*** *them a* ***visit*** *at the hospital*). This very fact is the reason behind the need for MWE identification. Non-idiomatic occurrences can further be divided into literal and coincidental occurrence, (sec. 6.1), the former denoted by wavy underline, the latter by dashed underline.

[1]All syntactic analyses in this paper follow the Universal Dependencies formalism and are generated according to UDPipe 2.6 (english-ewt-ud-2.6-200830).

3 MWE-lexicon Formalisms

Numerous MWE-lexicons (MWE-Ls) have been put forward in the past. Each of them follows a MWE-L formalism, henceforth simply called *formalism*, which determines what kind of information can be stored and how. Unfortunately, formalisms are often only an afterthought, as a result, works on MWE-Ls often focus on MWE extraction and only touch upon how MWEs are represented in the MWE-L. Nevertheless, formalisms can be loosely categorized based on the kind of representation used to store their lexical entries.

Probably one of the biggest categories of MWE-L formalisms would be those based on phrase grammars. We further divide this category into two smaller: (i) formalisms based on list-like or regex-like structures (Breidt et al., 1996; Alegria et al., 2004; Oflazer et al., 2004; Sailer and Trawiński, 2006; Spina, 2010; Quochi et al., 2012; Al-Sabbagh et al., 2014; Al-Haj et al., 2014; Walsh et al., 2019), component words are listed in the order in which they can appear and discontinuities are most often denoted by special symbols imposing constraints on the types of insertions allowed (either by limiting the number of insertions or the words which can be inserted); (ii) formalisms based on more expressive phrase grammars (CFGs, TAGs, LFGs, HPSGs, ...) (Grégoire, 2010; Przepiórkowski et al., 2017; Savary et al., 2018b; Dyvik et al., 2019), here component words are usually terminals appearing in grammar rules, and discontinuities are denoted by non-terminals.

Less frequent are dependency-based formalisms, like PDT-Dep (Pecina, 2008), in which only bigrams of syntactically dependent words are considered.[2]

Other popular categories are driven by semantics (Villavicencio et al., 2004; Borin et al., 2013) or relational databases (Vondřička, 2019).

These categories do not cover all possibilities and whether a specific MWE-L belongs to one category over another could be disputed.

4 Evaluation of MWE-lexicon Formalisms

Seeing all these different MWE-Ls and formalisms, one might ask which one is best in order to assist MWE Identification. One part of

[2]Some other MWE-Ls encode syntactic dependencies as auxiliary data.

the answer comes us from Savary et al. (2019b) which recommend that MWE-Ls aiming to assist MWE identification should be distributed in extensional and standard format, and that the lemmas and POS of MWEs' component words, as well as the least syntactically marked dependency structure and some other morphosyntactic variants judged relevant should be accessible. The other part of the answer comes us from looking at how MWE-Ls have been compared up until now.

To our knowledge, there are only few studies comparing MWE-Ls. PARSEME's survey (Losnegaard et al., 2016) references more than fifty MWE lexicons and lists in dozens of languages, and compares their accessibility, languages represented, size, and capacity to encode discontinuous MWEs. Savary (2008) compares a few lexicons of continuous MWEs showing how their formalisms allow one to encode salient MWE properties.

Such comparisons are relevant to our work but are mostly qualitative in nature. Formalisms are compared on what they can and cannot express and quantitative comparisons are almost exclusively reserved to compare MWE-Ls' sizes. To our knowledge, MWE-L formalisms themselves have not yet been compared quantitatively. This brings us to the question of how MWE-L formalisms can be quantitatively compared.

5 Adequacy

In order to evaluate MWE-Ls, we borrow the notion of adequacy, first defined for grammars (Chomsky, 1965) then adapted to lexicons (Jackendoff, 1975). Adequacy can be divided into three levels, which, in the context of MWE-Ls, can be summarized as follows: (i) *observational adequacy*, which evaluates the coverage of MWE observations accounted for in a MWE-L; (ii) *descriptive adequacy*, which estimates whether a MWE-L accurately and exhaustively describes all the properties of the covered MWEs; (iii) *explanatory adequacy*, relating to how well a MWE-L explains the reasons behind MWE behavior. Note that these three levels of adequacy call for increasingly complex lexicon formalisms, e.g. explaining an MWE behavior needs more expressive power than just listing all correct forms of this MWE.

In this paper, we focus on observational adequacy (OA) since it is the easiest to quantify and is a measure of MWE identification.

This choice coincides with recommendations by Savary et al. (2019b), who advocate that MWE identification be assisted by MWE-Ls which use a relatively simple dependency-based formalism.

Perfect OA can more accurately be defined as the MWE-L accounting for all possible observations of MWEs and only those. In other words, all possible MWEs observations must be matched by at least one entry of the MWE-L. (here understood as surface forms). It follows that OA can be measured from the standpoint of generation or parsing. More precisely, MWE-Ls are evaluated on their capacity to either generate all possible MWE forms, or to recognize all MWE forms encountered in text.

OA can be measured in a multitude of ways. In this study we keep ourselves to precision and recall, which measure the proportion of actual MWE observations in those matched by the lexicon and in those existing in text, respectively. Note that the measure of precision from a generative standpoint causes issues, since MWE occurrences can be literal (cf. Sec. 6.1).

Finally, in order for OA to be applicable to formalisms, we propose that they should be evaluated in conjunction with an instantiation method and corpus. Thus, two formalisms can be compared provided that their respective MWE-Ls are instantiated on the same data, in similar fashion, and that OA is measured on the same corpus.

6 λ-CSS Lexicons

Now that we have suggested criteria for an optimal format of MWE-Ls, let us see how this format could look like.

6.1 Literal occurrences

Savary et al. (2019a) ask what exactly is a literal occurrence of a MWE and what distinguishes it from an idiomatic or coincidental occurrence. Roughly, when all the lexemes of a MWE appear in a sentence and they together display some form of idiosyncrasy, then we talk of an *idiomatic occurrence* of the MWE. Whereas when they display no idiosyncrasy, we talk of a *non-idiomatic occurrence* of the MWE. Non-idiomatic occurrences are furthermore divided into *literal occurrences* and *coincidental occurrences*. Savary et al. (2019a) define the former as an occurrence which appears in a syntactic configuration in which could have been idiomatic. The latter is then simply defined as a non-idiomatic occurrence which is not literal.

In the following: in **bold** in (1) an idiomatic

occurrence, in wavy underline in (2) a literal occurrence, and in dashed underline in (3) a coincidental occurrence :

(1) I **paid** them a **visit** at the hospital 'I visited them at the hospital'

(2) I paid them a visit to the museum

(3) I paid for a visit of the museum

In order to judge whether a non-idiomatic occurrence is in a syntactic configuration that could be idiomatic, it is compared to syntactic configurations of known idiomatic occurrences. To compare syntactic configurations, Savary et al. define the *Coarse Syntactic Structure* (*CSS*).

6.2 Coarse Syntactic Structure (CSS)

A CSS can be seen as a simplification of the dependency tree of a given MWE occurrence. More precisely, given a set of words σ and a sentence S, a CSS is the minimal connected dependency tree covering σ in S, where a word is either represented by a node containing its lemma and part of speech, if it is in σ, or by a dummy node otherwise. Nodes are connected by their relational dependencies.

For instance, for sentence (1), figure 2 shows its dependency tree, where word forms are replaced by their lemmas and parts of speech (POS). Then, figure 4a is the CSS of the MWE ***paid visit***, and figure 4b the CSS of the MWE with syntactic discontinuities from figure 3.

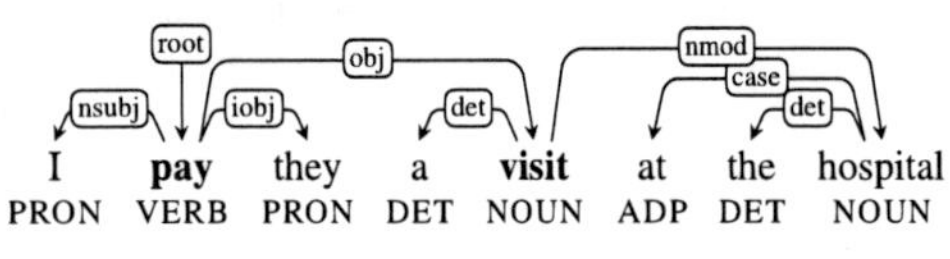

Figure 2: A dependency graph.

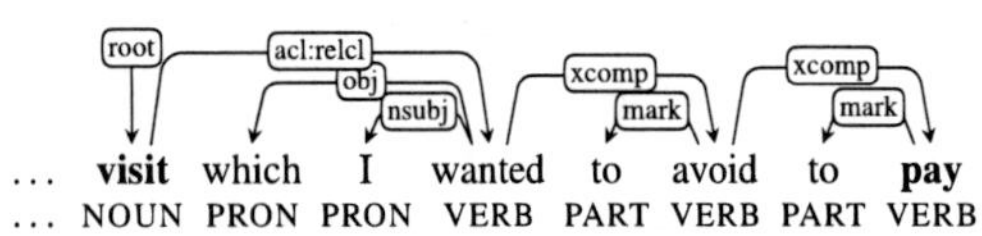

Figure 3: A dependency tree with syntactic discontinuities

CSSs were originally designed in order to put an applicable definition to the notion of a literal occurrence of a MWE. However, since literal occurrences of MWE are relatively infrequent (Savary et al., 2019a), we argue that CSSs could be used

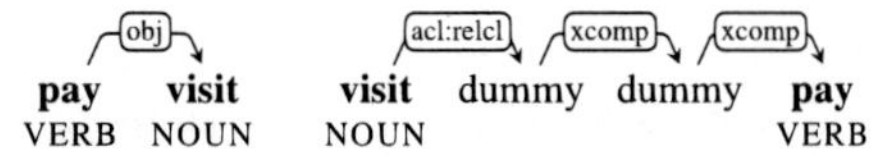

(a) (b)

Figure 4: Coarse syntactic structure Figures 2 and 3

as the basis of MWE-L formalisms with hopefully great observational adequacy.

MWE-Ls following such a formalism would simply consist in a set of CSSs of MWE occurrences. We will however first question the relevancy of component words being represented by their lemmas and POS and not some other features. Lemmas and POS do provide an approximation of lexemes, which lets CSSs do what they were designed to do (help approximate our intuitive notion of literal occurrence). We however would like for our lexicon to be as observationally adequate as possible, therefore we will wonder if representing MWEs by a different set of features would be beneficial.

For this reason, we propose a generalisation of CSSs, dubbed λ-CSS, where λ is the set of features used to describe MWEs.

6.3 λ-CSSs

We define a λ-CSS as the minimal connected dependency tree covering a given set of words σ in a given sentence S, where words in σ are represented not necessarily by their lemmas and POS, but by a set of properties λ. Words are still connected according to their syntactic dependencies, but these dependencies are only labeled if the corresponding feature (noted 'deprel') is in λ. Insertions (words necessary for the tree to be connected but not in σ) are represented by dummies. When a word in σ does not have a certain feature from λ (such as a noun not having a tense), the feature is marked as null for the word.

For instance, if figure 5 is the morphosyntactic analysis of sentence (1), then figure 6 is the $\{form, deprel, number\}$-CSS of the MWE component words. Similarly, figure 7 is the $\{lemma, pos, deprel\}$-CSS of the MWE in figure 3.

We will now ask which combination of features λ gives the best basis for a MWE-L formalism. We only consider formalisms where a unique set of features λ is used to describe all MWEs. While a formalism where each MWE is represented by its optimal set of features could be very interesting, we find that: (i) this would greatly increase the

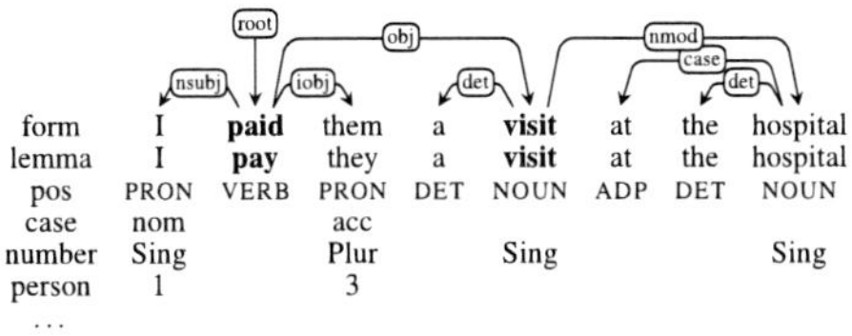

Figure 5: Dependency graph with all features of a sentence.

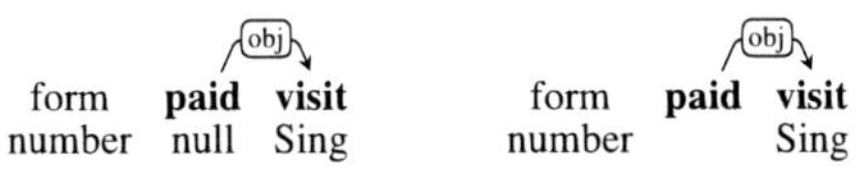

Figure 6: $\{form, deprel, number\}$-CSS of the MWE in 5, and its simplified representation (on the right).

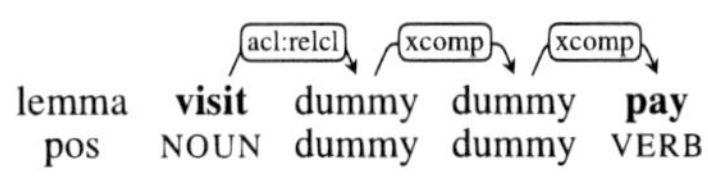

Figure 7: $\{\, lemma, pos, deprel \,\}$-CSS of the syntactically discontinuous subsequence in bold from figure 3

complexity of the experimental setup; (ii) results on less frequent MWEs would be dubious at best; (iii) it is still interesting to know which set of features is best on average.

7 Results

We use the German (DE), Greek (EL), French (FR), Hebrew (HE), Hindi (HI), Italian (IT), Polish (PL), Portuguese (PT), Swedish (SV), Turkish (TR) and Chinese (ZH) PARSEME shared task 1.2 corpus (Ramisch et al., 2020).[3]

Given a lexicon and a sentence, we define a *match* as a subsequence of the sentence which is accounted for (recognized by) the lexicon. A match can correspond to an idiomatic MWE occurrence or not. In the former case, it is called an *idiomatic match*. Then, given a lexicon and a corpus of sentences, we define: *precision* as the ratio of idiomatic matches to the total number of matches; and *recall* as the ratio of idiomatic matches to the number of idiomatic occurrences in the corpus. The aim is to maximise both measures.

As proposed earlier, formalisms will be evaluated in conjunction with a given instantiation method and instantiation corpus. To that end, during instantiation phase, we collect the λ-CSSs of all idiomatic occurrences annotated in the instantiation corpus. This method has the advantage of being very simple to implement and to introduce very little variation during the instantiation process. Its one downside (beside needing annotated data) is that some properties of MWEs cannot be deduced from single observations, i.e. the descriptive adequacy of the instantiated lexicon is limited.

7.1 Optimal set of features λ

In this section we aim to find the optimal set of features λ for MWE representation in MWE-Ls based on λ-CSS, or λ-CSS lexicons for short.

Since we have not one, but two evaluation criteria (precision and recall), and because we wish to avoid making a priori choices on how they should be combined (Hwang and Masud, 2012) (at least during the exploration of the solution space), we will for now only consider a solution A to be better than another solution B if A dominates B. That means that A is considered better than B on one criterion and better or equal on the other.

Depending on the language, from 17 to 40 features are considered. Some features such as $lemma$, $form$, $upos$ or $deprel$ are available in all languages and for all words, while others such as $Number$ or $Aspect$ only occur for some words and languages. Even with only 17 features the number of subsets of features that can be used for MWE representation is very high, a comprehensive exploration of the solution space is therefore out of the question.

Since our solution space is the powerset of the considered features, it can be seen as a lattice, i.e. a graph where each solution is represented by a node. Then, a solution A is connected to solutions with all features in A plus or minus one. Each solution therefore has a neighbourhood of similar solutions (with one feature of difference each). We then perform a greedy exploration of the solution space that considers non-dominated solutions as those to be explored. When two neighbouring solutions have equal precision and recall, we consider the simplest of the two neighbours to be the preferable solution. This criterion is not explicitly evaluated, but enforced by the exploration algorithm 1 (line 8), where $score(s)$ returns the position of a given solution in the objective space, and $pareto_front(S)$ returns the set of non-dominated solutions.

This algorithm was run 2-fold using TRAIN+DEV datasets, half of the dataset was used to generate MWE-Ls, and another half for OA evaluation. This was done twice per corpus,

[3]Basque, Irish and Romanian are skipped for technical reasons.

Algorithm 1: Bottom-up Greedy Pareto

Data:
$features$: the set of all considered features
s: starting subset of $features$

Initialization
  $res_{n-1} \leftarrow \{ s \}$
  $res \leftarrow \{ s \}$
while $res_{n-1} \neq \emptyset$ **do**
  $Q \leftarrow \emptyset$
  foreach $s_i \in res_{n-1}$ **do**
    foreach $f_i \in features \setminus s_i$ **do**
      if $score(s_i \cup \{ f_i \}) \neq score(s_i)$
        $Q \leftarrow Q \cup \{ s_i \cup \{ f_i \} \}$
  $res_{n-1} \leftarrow pareto\_front(res \cup Q) \cap Q$
  $res \leftarrow res \cup res_{n-1}$
Result: res

once with $\{ lemma \}$, and once with $\{ form \}$, as the starting set of features s.[4] All solutions generated in this way were then re-evaluated by instantiating the lexicon from TRAIN+DEV, and scoring it against the TEST dataset. In the end, 12, 142, 14, 36, 7, 20, 22, 22, 16, 22, 16 solutions were selected for DE, EL, FR, HE, HI, IT, PL, PT, SV, TR, ZH respectively.[5]

Table 1 presents the solutions provided by algorithm 1 on the French corpus. A clear distinction between solutions can be made depending on whether they use $form$ or $lemma$. The former have high precision and low recall, while the latter have more balanced precision and recall. Solutions using both act as the former.

As shown in table 2, the solutions with the highest precision always use $form$ and most of them use $deprel$. The solutions with the highest recall systematically use $lemma$. The most harmonious solutions (i.e. those with the highest F-scores) almost always use $deprel$, $lemma$ or both. However, Greek (EL), skipped in the table due to the large size of its optimal solution, Hebrew (HE), and Chinese (ZH) act in quite unique ways. On the Greek corpus, features such as the $case$ and the $voice$ are used in both the most precise and the most harmonious solutions. In Hebrew and Chinese, $form$ is used instead of $lemma$ in the most harmonious solutions. However, the solutions with the highest recall still use $\{ lemma \}$ with both languages.

P (%)	R (%)	solution features
71.78	75.06	lemma
73.18	74.91	lemma, upos
78.60	71.08	lemma, deprel
84.08	52.47	form
85.42	52.17	form, lemma
85.27	51.95	form, upos
85.54	51.80	form, lemma, upos
87.94	48.27	form, deprel
88.02	48.12	form, lemma, deprel
87.84	47.83	form, upos, deprel
87.94	47.76	form, lemma, upos, deprel
87.16	47.46	form, lemma, upos, deprel, Number
87.16	47.46	form, upos, deprel, Number
86.93	47.46	form, lemma, deprel, Number

Table 1: Precision(P) and Recall(R) for selected solution for French

	P	R	F
DE	lem+form+deprel	lem	lem+deprel
FR	lem+form+deprel	lem	lem+deprel
HE	form+upos+Voice	lem	form
HI	form+deprel	lem	lem+deprel
IT	form+deprel+upos	lem	lem+deprel
PL	form+deprel	lem	lem+deprel
PT	lem+form+deprel	lem	lem+deprel
SV	form,+deprel	lem	lem+deprel+upos
TR	lem+form+upos+ deprel	lem	lem+deprel
ZH	form+deprel+upos+lem	lem	form+deprel+upos

Table 2: Best performing solutions according to Precision (P) and Recall (R) and F-score (F); lem stand for $lemma$.

Table 3 presents the F-scores of the solutions $\{ lemma, deprel \}$, $\{ form, deprel \}$, $\{ lemma, deprel, upos \}$ and, when necessary, the solutions with the best F-score in order to: (i) get a better understanding of the impact of using $lemma$ over $form$ (used in conjunction with $deprel$ since this leads to more precise and more harmonious solutions), (ii) to compare the score of the original CSS ($\{ lemma, deprel, upos \}$) to what appears to be the most harmonious CSS for most languages: $\{ lemma, deprel \}$.

As expected, the scores of $form$ based solution in Hebrew and Chinese are well above those of $lemma$ based solution (This is most likely due to the poorer quality of the lemmatization in these corpora due to the difficulty to lemmatize those languages.) Conversely, for all other languages, $lemma$ based solution perform much better than $form$ based solutions. As for the differences between $\{ lemma, deprel \}$ and

[4] Solutions with neither of these features resulted in huge numbers of mostly non-idiomatic matches, not worthy of systematic exploration.

[5] Technical issues prevented algorithm 1 to be run in reasonable time on Greek with $\{ form \}$.

	DE	EL	FR	HE	HI	IT	PL	PT	SV	TR	ZH
form, deprel	57.66	51.12	62.33	**32.66**	47.21	47.85	61.41	49.54	56.77	38.66	**46.92**
lemma, deprel	**69.07**	59.71	**74.65**	7.49	**64.80**	**64.00**	**81.58**	**72.86**	**75.21**	**61.08**	14.81
lemma, deprel, upos	67.92	**59.80**	74.55	20.35	64.54	**64.00**	80.05	72.54	**75.21**	60.82	20.70
highest F		**60.93**		**37.65**							**47.44**

Table 3: F-score(%) of selected λ-CSS based lexicon

$\{\ lemma, deprel, upos\ \}$, we can see that in most languages adding $upos$ slightly deteriorates F-scores. This deterioration is however quite noticeable in German (DE) and Polish (PL). On the other side, in Greek (EL) and Swedish (SV), the results are only marginally better with $upos$. In short, apart from Hebrew (HE) and Chinese (ZH), the solution $\{\ lemma, deprel\ \}$ is either the one with best F-score or very close to be so, while it is also one of the simplest solutions.

7.2 Sequential discontinuity based lexicon and non-verbal MWE

We now compare our $\{\ lemma, deprel\ \}$-CSS lexicon format to various list-like formalisms analogous to those discussed in Sec. 3. The goal here is not a direct comparison to already existing lexicons, but a comparison between simple lexicon formalisms that can easily be instantiated in similar ways. In order to cover MWEs of all syntactic types, we use the French Sequoia corpus (Candito et al., 2021) annotated for both verbal and non-verbal MWEs, along with the French corpus of PARSEME shared task 1.2, annotated for verbal MWEs only.

As earlier, MWE-Ls are instantiated by looking at the MWEs annotated in the TRAIN+DEV corpora, then OA is evaluated on the TEST corpora.

All the list-like MWE-Ls considered here operate in similar fashion. Once an annotated MWE occurrence is encountered in the instantiation corpus, a lexical entry is created storing the $lemmas$ of the MWE components in the sequential order in which they appear. Discontinuities are handled with 4 different methods with varying details about the inserted elements, stored in between the components. Below, each method is explained and illustrated with the lexical entries instantiated from sentence (1):

1. contiguous: discontinuous MWEs are ignored, e.g. example (1) yields $\emptyset$
2. [$lemma$]: the list of $lemmas$ of the insertions is stored, here: **[pay**, [they, a], **visit]**
3. [$upos$]: the list of $upos$ of the insertions is stored, here: **[pay**, [PRON, DET], **visit]**
4. *: insertions are represented by the special character '*', meaning that any insertion (or none) can happen, here: **[pay**, *, **visit]**

A common practice is to limit the maximum size of discontinuities, in order both to reduce the computational cost of identification and to possibly improve precision. To mimic such a practice, we run our list-like MWE-Ls in 4 different configurations. With $n = [1, 2, 3, \infty]$, only insertions of n words or less are considered, occurrences with larger insertions are ignored during instantiation and identification. In the 4th configuration the size of insertions is ignored.

	FR Sequoia			FR PARSEME		
	P(%)	R(%)	F(%)	P(%)	R(%)	F(%)
λ-CSS	90.74	67.74	**77.57**	78.60	71.08	**74.65**
contiguous	91.76	56.45	69.90	71.63	48.49	57.83
[$lemma$]						
1	91.12	63.82	75.07	71.90	60.63	65.79
2	90.94	64.75	75.64	72.17	61.44	66.38
3	91.00	65.21	75.97	72.09	61.59	66.43
∞	91.00	65.21	75.97	72.08	61.74	66.51
[pos]						
1	90.85	64.06	75.14	72.10	63.50	67.53
2	90.68	64.98	75.70	72.52	65.05	68.58
3	90.73	65.44	76.04	72.47	65.27	68.68
∞	90.73	65.44	76.04	72.45	65.42	68.75
*						
1	86.42	64.52	73.88	67.26	66.37	66.81
2	79.56	66.36	72.36	63.13	71.82	67.19
3	74.23	67.05	70.46	58.20	73.66	65.02
∞	33.22	67.97	44.63	26.05	75.86	38.78

Table 4: Precision, Recall and F-score of λ-CSS MWE-L and list-like MWE-L on french corpora (with and without non verbal MWE respectively)

In table 4 we find the OA, measured by way of precision (P), recall (R) and F-score (F), of MWE-Ls based on $\{\ lemma, deprel\ \}$-CSS, and the 4 methods above. Results of the last three MWE-L formalisms are decomposed according to the maximal size of insertions.

	DE	EL	FR	HI	IT	PL	PT	SV	TR	HE	ZH
MTLB-STRUCT	76.17	**72.62**	**79.42**	**73.62**	63.76	81.02	73.34	71.58	69.46	**48.30**	**69.63**
union	**76.45**	71.12	78.87	73.29	62.92	81.41	**74.76**	73.74	**69.92**	44.29	58.43
$\{lemma, deprel\}$-lexicon	69.07	59.71	74.65	64.80	**64.00**	**81.58**	72.86	**75.21**	61.08	7.50	14.81

Table 5: F-score (%) of MTLB-STRUCT, our lexicon, and the union of their predictions.

We chose to ignore the MWE ***de le*** 'of the', annotated 34 times in the Sequoia's TRAIN+DEV and 2 times in the TEST. If not for this, the precision of the list-like MWE-Ls would go from around 90% to around only 45% since *de le* is an extremely frequent combination of words which is almost never idiomatic. This choice only barely affects the results of the $\{lemma, deprel\}$-CSS lexicon but allows for a much fairer comparison.

The first thing to notice is that precision is on the whole higher on Sequoia corpus than on the FR PARSEME corpus. This is somewhat expected since verbal MWEs are often harder to identify than non-verbal MWEs. Our takeaway, is that even though the $\{lemma, deprel\}$ was optimised for OA of verbal MWEs, $\{lemma, deprel\}$-CSS lexicon perform correctly (or even better) on MWEs not restricted to verbal MWEs. The second conclusion is that our MWE-L is more observationally adequate than any of the list-like MWE-Ls tested here. This seems especially true on verbal MWEs where the advantages of dependency representation are crucial.

7.3 Impact of lexicon on identification

In this section we compare $\{lemma, deprel\}$-CSS lexicons to a traditional MWE identifier. Not that we expect CSS-lexicon to outperform an identifier, but in order to gain a better appreciation of the OA to be expected of lexicons.

We profit of this comparison between $\{lemma, deprel\}$-CSS lexicons and a traditional MWE identifier to prod at the possibility of improving OA through the combined use of MWE identifier and $\{lemma, deprel\}$-CSS lexicons. To do so we use a naive a posteriori approach where we simply compare the MWE identifier scores to those of the union of the identifier and MWE-Ls annotations.

In table 5 we compare the F-scores of MTLB-STRUCT (Taslimipoor et al., 2020) – a BERT based MWE identifier fined tuned on identification on PARSEME TRAIN+DEV corpora, the winner of the PARSEME shared task 1.2 – to our $\{lemma, deprel\}$-CSS lexicon and the union of their predictions. Hewbrew (HE) and Chinese (ZH) aside (due to lemmatization issues), F-scores from our lexicons are higher than MTLB-STRUCT on 3 languages and within 10 points on the other languages, which shows that OA achieved by $\{lemma, deprel\}$-CSS lexicons can at the very least be high enough to be of interest. As for the unions of our lexicon and MTLB-STRUCT annotations, their F-scores are higher than MTLB-STRUCT's scores on 5 languages and are only within 2 points of MTLB-STRUCT's on 4 others. Given the highly naive nature of the combined use of MTLB-STRUCT and $\{lemma, deprel\}$-CSS lexicons those results are certainly encouraging. These show that $\{lemma, deprel\}$-CSS lexicons do match MWEs that traditional identifier would miss and therefore that they hold information that identifier could use.

8 Concluding Remarks

In this paper we proposed, to our knowledge, the first method of quantitatively evaluating some MWE-lexicon formalisms through observational adequacy. We also presented a MWE-lexicon formalism based on a generalisation of the concept of a Coarse Syntatic Structure, which we call $\{lemma, deprel\}$-CSS. We brought evidence that this specific set of features allows for higher observational adequacy than alternative sets of features on verbal MWEs in most of the 11 languages studied. Furthermore, we compared this formalism to MWE-lexicons based on sequential representation of MWEs. We showed that our formalism achieves higher observational adequacy on French regardless of the fact that only verbal or all types of MWEs are considered. Finally, we showed the observational adequacy of our formalism holds its own even when compared to annotations produced by a state-of-the-art MWE identifier. While this study focuses on MWE-lexicon formalisms instantiated on annotated corpora, our vision is that such lexicons should be instantiated through MWE discovery in large non-annotated corpora or through extraction from other MWE resources.

References

Hassan Al-Haj, Alon Itai, and Shuly Wintner. 2014. Lexical representation of multiword expressions in morphologically-complex languages. *International Journal of Lexicography*, 27(2):130–170.

Rania Al-Sabbagh, Roxana Girju, and Jana Diesner. 2014. Unsupervised construction of a lexicon and a repository of variation patterns for Arabic modal multiword expressions. In *Proceedings of the 10th Workshop on Multiword Expressions (MWE)*, pages 114–123, Gothenburg, Sweden. Association for Computational Linguistics.

Iñaki Alegria, Olatz Ansa, Xabier Artola, Nerea Ezeiza, Koldo Gojenola, and Ruben Urizar. 2004. Representation and treatment of multiword expressions in Basque. In *Proceedings of the Workshop on Multiword Expressions: Integrating Processing*, pages 48–55, Barcelona, Spain. Association for Computational Linguistics.

Timothy Baldwin and Su Nam Kim. 2010. Multiword expressions. In Nitin Indurkhya and Fred J. Damerau, editors, *Handbook of Natural Language Processing, Second edition*, pages 267–292. CRC Press, Boca Raton.

Lars Borin, Markus Forsberg, and Lennart Lönngren. 2013. Saldo: a touch of yin to wordnet's yang. *Language resources and evaluation*, 47(4):1191–1211.

Elisabeth Breidt, Frederique Segond, and Giuseppe Valetto. 1996. Formal description of multi-word lexemes with the finite-state formalism IDAREX. In *COLING 1996 Volume 2: The 16th International Conference on Computational Linguistics*.

Marie Candito, Mathieu Constant, Carlos Ramisch, Agata Savary, Bruno Guillaume, Yannick Parmentier, and Silvio Cordeiro. 2021. A french corpus annotated for multiword expressions and named entities. *Journal of Language Modelling*, 8(2).

Noam Chomsky. 1965. Aspects of the theory of syntax.

Mathieu Constant, Gülşen Eryiğit, Johanna Monti, Lonneke Van Der Plas, Carlos Ramisch, Michael Rosner, and Amalia Todirascu. 2017. Multiword expression processing: A survey. *Computational Linguistics*, 43(4):837–892.

Helge J Jakhelln Dyvik, Gyri Smørdal Losnegaard, and Victoria Rosén. 2019. Multiword expressions in an lfg grammar for norwegian.

Nicole Grégoire. 2010. Duelme: a dutch electronic lexicon of multiword expressions. *Language Resources and Evaluation*, 44(1):23–39.

C-L Hwang and Abu Syed Md Masud. 2012. *Multiple objective decision making—methods and applications: a state-of-the-art survey*, volume 164. Springer Science & Business Media.

Ray Jackendoff. 1975. Morphological and semantic regularities in the lexicon. *Language*, pages 639–671.

Gyri Smørdal Losnegaard, Federico Sangati, Carla Parra Escartín, Agata Savary, Sascha Bargmann, and Johanna Monti. 2016. Parseme survey on mwe resources. In *9th International Conference on Language Resources and Evaluation (LREC 2016)*, pages 2299–2306.

Kemal Oflazer, Özlem Çetinoğlu, and Bilge Say. 2004. Integrating morphology with multi-word expression processing in Turkish. In *Proceedings of the Workshop on Multiword Expressions: Integrating Processing*, pages 64–71, Barcelona, Spain. Association for Computational Linguistics.

Pavel Pecina. 2008. Reference data for czech collocation extraction. In *Proc. of the LREC Workshop Towards a Shared Task for MWEs (MWE 2008)*, pages 11–14.

Adam Przepiórkowski, Jan Hajič, Elżbieta Hajnicz, and Zdeňka Urešová. 2017. Phraseology in two Slavic valency dictionaries: Limitations and perspectives. *International Journal of Lexicography*, 30(1):1–38.

Valeria Quochi, Francesca Frontini, and Francesco Rubino. 2012. A MWE acquisition and lexicon builder web service. In *Proceedings of COLING 2012*, pages 2291–2306, Mumbai, India. The COLING 2012 Organizing Committee.

Carlos Ramisch, Silvio Ricardo Cordeiro, Agata Savary, Veronika Vincze, Verginica Barbu Mititelu, Archna Bhatia, Maja Buljan, Marie Candito, Polona Gantar, Voula Giouli, Tunga Güngör, Abdelati Hawwari, Uxoa Iñurrieta, Jolanta Kovalevskaitė, Simon Krek, Timm Lichte, Chaya Liebeskind, Johanna Monti, Carla Parra Escartín, Behrang QasemiZadeh, Renata Ramisch, Nathan Schneider, Ivelina Stoyanova, Ashwini Vaidya, and Abigail Walsh. 2018. Edition 1.1 of the PARSEME shared task on automatic identification of verbal multiword expressions. In *Proceedings of the Joint Workshop on Linguistic Annotation, Multiword Expressions and Constructions (LAW-MWE-CxG-2018)*, pages 222–240, Santa Fe, New Mexico, USA. Association for Computational Linguistics.

Carlos Ramisch, Agata Savary, Bruno Guillaume, Jakub Waszczuk, Marie Candito, Ashwini Vaidya, Verginica Barbu Mititelu, Archna Bhatia, Uxoa Iñurrieta, Voula Giouli, Tunga Güngör, Menghan Jiang, Timm Lichte, Chaya Liebeskind, Johanna Monti, Renata Ramisch, Sara Stymne, Abigail Walsh, and Hongzhi Xu. 2020. Edition 1.2 of the PARSEME shared task on semi-supervised identification of verbal multiword expressions. In *Proceedings of the Joint Workshop on Multiword Expressions and Electronic Lexicons*, pages 107–118, online. Association for Computational Linguistics.

Martin Riedl and Chris Biemann. 2016. Impact of MWE resources on multiword recognition. In *Pro-*

ceedings of the 12th Workshop on Multiword Expressions, pages 107–111, Berlin, Germany. Association for Computational Linguistics.

Manfred Sailer and Beata Trawiński. 2006. The collection of distributionally idiosyncratic items: A multilingual resource for linguistic research. In *Proceedings of the Fifth International Conference on Language Resources and Evaluation (LREC'06)*, Genoa, Italy. European Language Resources Association (ELRA).

Agata Savary. 2008. Computational inflection of multiword units. *Linguistic Issues in Language Technology*, 1.

Agata Savary, Marie Candito, Verginica Barbu Mititelu, Eduard Bejček, Fabienne Cap, Slavomír Čéplö, Silvio Ricardo Cordeiro, Gülşen Cebiroğlu Eryiğit, Voula Giouli, Maarten van Gompel, et al. 2018a. Parseme multilingual corpus of verbal multiword expressions. In *Multiword expressions at length and in depth: Extended papers from the MWE 2017 workshop*.

Agata Savary, Silvio Cordeiro, Timm Lichte, Carlos Ramisch, Uxoa Iñurrieta, and Voula Giouli. 2019a. Literal occurrences of multiword expressions: rare birds that cause a stir. *The Prague Bulletin of Mathematical Linguistics*.

Agata Savary, Silvio Cordeiro, and Carlos Ramisch. 2019b. Without lexicons, multiword expression identification will never fly: A position statement. In *Proceedings of the Joint Workshop on Multiword Expressions and WordNet (MWE-WN 2019)*.

Agata Savary, Simon Petitjean, Timm Lichte, Laura Kallmeyer, and Jakub Waszczuk. 2018b. Object-oriented lexical encoding of multiword expressions: Short and sweet. *arXiv preprint arXiv:1810.09947*.

Agata Savary, Carlos Ramisch, Silvio Cordeiro, Federico Sangati, Veronika Vincze, Behrang QasemiZadeh, Marie Candito, Fabienne Cap, Voula Giouli, Ivelina Stoyanova, and Antoine Doucet. 2017. The PARSEME shared task on automatic identification of verbal multiword expressions. In *Proceedings of the 13th Workshop on Multiword Expressions (MWE 2017)*, pages 31–47, Valencia, Spain. Association for Computational Linguistics.

Stefania Spina. 2010. The dictionary of Italian collocations: Design and integration in an online learning environment. In *Proceedings of the Seventh International Conference on Language Resources and Evaluation (LREC'10)*, Valletta, Malta. European Language Resources Association (ELRA).

Shiva Taslimipoor, Sara Bahaadini, and Ekaterina Kochmar. 2020. Mtlb-struct@ parseme 2020: Capturing unseen multiword expressions using multi-task learning and pre-trained masked language models. *arXiv preprint arXiv:2011.02541*.

Aline Villavicencio, Ann Copestake, Benjamin Waldron, and Fabre Lambeau. 2004. Lexical encoding of MWEs. In *Proceedings of the Workshop on Multiword Expressions: Integrating Processing*, pages 80–87, Barcelona, Spain. Association for Computational Linguistics.

Pavel Vondřička. 2019. Design of a multiword expressions database. *The Prague Bulletin of Mathematical Linguistics*, 112(1):83–101.

Abigail Walsh, Teresa Lynn, and Jennifer Foster. 2019. Ilfhocail: A lexicon of Irish MWEs. In *Proceedings of the Joint Workshop on Multiword Expressions and WordNet (MWE-WN 2019)*, pages 162–168, Florence, Italy. Association for Computational Linguistics.

Author Index